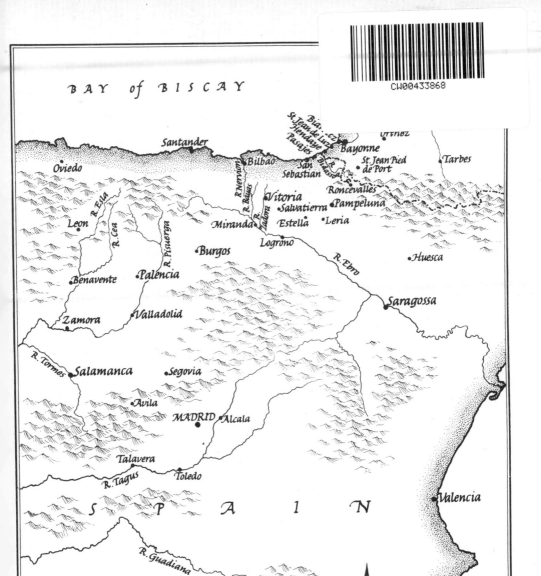

BAY of BISCAY

Santander

Oviedo

Leon

R. Esla

R. Cea

Benavente

Zamora

Palencia

R. Pisuerga

Valladolid

R. Tormes

Salamanca

Segovia

Avila

MADRID

Alcala

Talavera

R. Tagus

Toledo

Bilbao

R. Nervion

R. Bayas

R. Zadora

Vitoria

Salvatierra

Miranda

Estella

Logrono

Burgos

San Sebastian

Bidassoa

St. Jean de Luz

Hendaye

Pasajes

Bia...ez

Bayonne

Orthez

Tarbes

St. Jean Pied
de Port

Roncevalles

Pampeluna

Leria

R. Ebro

Huesca

Saragossa

S   P   A   I   N

Valencia

R. Guadiana

Beas

-N-

R. Guadalquivir

Miles 0   25   50   75   100   125   150   175   200

0   40   80   120   160   200   240   280   320 Kilometres

THE PORTRAIT OF
A GENERAL

General Colville's portrait by Raeburn, 1818

THE PORTRAIT OF
A GENERAL

A Chronicle of the Napoleonic Wars

JOHN COLVILLE

MICHAEL RUSSELL

First published in Great Britain 1980
by Michael Russell (Publishing) Ltd.,
The Chantry, Wilton,
Salisbury

© John Colville 1980
Maps drawn by Denys R. Baker
All rights reserved
ISBN 0 85955 076 1

Filmset in Monophoto Imprint
by Santype (International) Ltd.,
Salisbury, Wiltshire
Printed in Great Britain
by Biddles Ltd., Guildford, Surrey

Contents

Contents

Preface

I should not have written this story, but for the portrait of the General.

In February 1818 General the Hon. Sir Charles Colville, rising forty-eight years old and a veteran of many arduous campaigns, married Miss Jane Mure of Caldwell in the County of Ayrshire. To celebrate the event Miss Mure's parents commissioned Raeburn to paint their daughter and son-in-law. The two portraits remained in the Mure family until in 1912 an impoverished generation was obliged to sell them. Through the agency of Messrs Thomas Agnew, Lady Colville was bought for a large sum by the Sassoons and stayed in England; but the General crossed the Atlantic.

In 1940 Sir Charles was sold in New York for a mere $4,000, which was then less than £1,000. In homage to Mr J. J. Haverty, who was a constant benefactor of the High Museum of Art in Atlanta, Georgia, the portrait was presented to the Museum 'In Memory Lane'. In 1957 the Sassoons sold Lady Colville and I, her great-grandson, bought her for much less than she had fetched in 1912. Even so the cost was a strain on my bank account. Messrs Coutts & Co. had for some time been politely remonstrating about the size of my overdraft; but now, with an understanding and sympathy rare among bankers, they agreed to double it so that I could make the purchase. This showed acumen on their part, for I was so conscious of their civility that, far earlier than would otherwise have been the case, I took steps to reduce my overdraft to an acceptable figure.

Lady Colville was already established over the fireplace in my dining-room when, in the late autumn of 1957, I went to Chartwell to dine and stay the night with Sir Winston and Lady Churchill. This was quite a frequent excursion because Sir Winston liked to play bezique every evening after dinner and there were limits even to Lady Churchill's willingness to oblige him. An alternative opponent was periodically in demand.

vii

When dining with Sir Winston I knew from long experience that it was not only futile, but positively ill-received to make conversation with the soup. When the fish arrived, it was permissible to speak. At that stage, being temporarily short of any political or financial gossip, I told Sir Winston about the two Raeburn portraits and my purchase of Lady Colville.

'And what', he asked, 'of the General?'

I explained that he was irretrievably incarcerated 'In Memory Lane' at Atlanta, Georgia.

'Raeburn', said Sir Winston, 'was a great artist.'

The fish was replaced by cutlets. Sir Winston brooded. Then he spoke to this effect: 'I, of course, make no pretence to be a great artist. But I love painting, and it seems that my pictures have a curiosity value. It may perhaps be that the citizens of Atlanta would find one of my pictures, unworthy though they be, of greater interest than the portrait of a Scottish general who had nothing to do with Georgia and never set foot in the United States. I do, after all, have American connections. I hate to think of the General being parted from his wife for all these years, and so, my dear boy, you may take one of my pictures off the wall here and offer it in exchange.'

I did so. The High Museum of Art said no: for Sir Charles had been given to them 'In Memory Lane'.

Seven years later Sir Winston died, but Lady Churchill, remembering her husband's offer, said that if the High Museum should change its mind, she would gladly give me one of his best pictures for the transaction. I tried once more and, for the same reason, the answer was again no.

Twenty years after Sir Winston's initiative on Sir Charles's behalf, Lady Churchill died. A few months before her death she gave me one of Sir Winston's early and delightful pictures, *Green Trees and Poppies at Lullenden*, to be available for the exchange if it should ever become possible. Meanwhile, several eminent Americans, including Alfred Frankfurter, well known in the New York art world, Armand Hammer, Chairman of Occidental Oil, Nancy Hanks, Chairman of the National Endowment for the Arts and trusted adviser to the President on such matters, and finally Mr Vic Prall, Senior Vice-President of Citibank, all brought powerful guns to bear. Mr Prall even enlisted the support of the Coca-Cola company which has immense power and influence in Atlanta, Georgia. But the ramparts of the High Museum were apparently impregnable.

However, in April 1978 the fortress, so long beleaguered, fell and on the basis of a semi-permanent loan Sir Charles came back to England to be reunited with Jane, his wife. Churchill's *Green Trees and Poppies at Lullenden* hangs cheerfully on the walls of the High Museum at Atlanta, by no means ashamed to share those walls with Monet and Turner even if its artistic merit is at least equalled by its 'curiosity value'. I think Sir Winston would have been pleased, and I am told that the Museum and the citizens of Atlanta are too.

When the General came home, with much family rejoicing, I thought the time had also come to tell his story. He was not a famous general; his name appears briefly in the text or the foot-notes of the military histories of his time. All the same he took part in some of the most fateful campaigns in English history, he acquitted himself with courage and distinction and he was a prolific, if sometimes almost illegible, letter writer.

Fortunately my late cousin, Jack Colville, spent years deciphering the letters. Had it not been for his painstaking labours, I could not have written this book. Jack himself deserves words of recog-nition, for he was a good, intelligent and unselfish man, devoid of all pretensions, who like my own father was educated at Winchester College in days, long past, when that august and scholarly institu-tion contrived to instil sound learning, good manners and the highest moral principles while at the same time destroying any native ambition. It did not, however, destroy either courage or quiet initiative. Side by side with his elder brother, Jack fought at the Battle of Jutland in H.M.S. *Barham*. He was subsequently re-christened Mark because after that great, if indecisive, engage-ment of the British and German fleets, Admiral Evan Thomas, whose flag flew on *Barham*, presented his dog to the two brothers. This praiseworthy animal had, like the two brothers, been present at the battle, sitting patiently in the Admiral's cabin unperturbed by the noise of the fifteen-inch salvos. As it was also called Jack, it seemed important to distinguish the two. Jack's grave, with a head-stone commemorating his canine battle honours, is half buried in the undergrowth of a wooded garden on Vancouver Island where the two brothers settled for some years after the First World War; and the other Jack (or Mark) devoted himself to assembling, arranging and deciphering the mass of letters on which the story in this book is based.

JOHN COLVILLE

ix

1

The Early Years

Charles Colville was born in August 1770, almost exactly one year after Napoleon Bonaparte and fifteen months after the Duke of Wellington, the two men who were to exert the main influence on his career. He was the third son (and ultimately the heir) of John, eighth Lord Colville of Culross in the peerage of Scotland, who a few months before Charles was born had succeeded his brother Alexander, an admiral of doubtful amiability but also of inadequately recorded distinction. That distinction lies in the possibility, seldom if ever mentioned in the history books, that had it not been for Alexander, Canada might have remained a French dominion.

It happened thus. After Wolfe died capturing Quebec in the great Year of Victories, the *Annus Mirabilis* of 1759, the triumphant British army garrisoned the city with a force of 6,000 men under Governor Murray. They had little food and no winter clothing, so that by the spring of 1760 half of them were either dead or unfit for combat. The French under General de Lévis advanced from Montreal with 10,000 men and a motley host of Red Indian allies. It seemed that Quebec must be recaptured for France, especially when Governor Murray sallied forth from the citadel to challenge de Lévis and lost 1,000 out of his 3,000 surviving soldiers in the ensuing battle. Admiral Lord Colville, Commander-in-Chief of the Fleet in Canadian waters, sent two frigates up the St. Lawrence through the melting ice-floes and followed hard behind in his flagship, *Northumberland*. Quebec was relieved and three years later the whole of Canada passed to the British Crown. It is hard for a generation that takes mechanical propulsion for granted to visualise the skill required to sail a seventy-four-gun ship of the line forty or fifty miles up a river in full flood and to avoid huge blocks of ice, racing down stream, which would have sufficed to damage or even sink a wooden man-of-war.

I

Alexander was promoted to be Vice-Admiral of the White, there being three naval commands, the Red, the White and the Blue, of which the ensigns flown by British ships today are a relic. He had no legitimate children, though he sired two bastards whose reprehensible behaviour was a source of considerable irritation and embarrassment to his nephews in later years. When he died, his brother John succeeded to the peerage. John had been a soldier all his active life, serving at Fontenoy, that bloody but indecisive battle in which the English courteously invited the French to fire first (although some maintain that it was the other way round). In the same year, 1745, John fought under the Duke of Cumberland at Culloden. Being, as his letters show, a kindly man, he can probably be absolved from any personal participation in the subsequent horrors. The Colvilles, like most Lowlanders, were strong supporters of the Hanoverian dynasty against the wild and woolly Jacobites, who appear more romantic and appealing to later generations than they did to the sensible majority of their contemporaries.

Disliking cold climates and being a sufferer from rheumatism, John decided, when Charles was ten years old, to leave his home in Edinburgh and move to the more salubrious neighbourhood of Bath. While stationed at Gibraltar he had married a lady called Amelia Webber, aunt of that poor Mr Huskisson who was a Minister in Lord Liverpool's Government and was run over by one of the first railway trains. By her he had four sons and three daughters. The eldest, James, Master of Colville, went into the Navy and died at the age of twenty-three. The second, John, also became a sailor. He was close in age and friendship to Charles and ended his naval career by becoming Admiral of the White and a Scottish representative peer. No doubt in order to ring the changes, Charles and the youngest son, George, were destined for the Army, and when Charles was eleven his father persuaded an old friend, the Colonel of the 28th Foot, to give him a commission as ensign in his regiment. Boys of that age sometimes went to sea as midshipmen, but even in 1781 eleven was thought rather young for active service in the Army. So Charles was given leave of absence to finish his studies.

French was an important part of those studies and in 1784, aged fourteen, he was sent to France to stay with the Marquis de Bombelles, a cavalry officer who had been attached to the French Embassy in London. In a series of letters to his father he gives an account of his journey across the Channel that Christmas, and of the life he was expected to lead in the anthill of parasitic courtiers which Louis XIV and his successors had established at Versailles:

Calais, 24th Decr. 1784

While they are examining our baggage at the Customs, I sit down to give you, my dear Father, news of my journey since I had the pleasure of writing to you from London.

After having drunk chocolate with Mrs Blair, we left Portland Place on the 21st, at 8 o'clock in the morning, in a four horse carriage, the two best seats being filled by M. de Bombelles and the Comte d'Ermenonville, who was also returning to Paris, and the other two by myself and Thevening, whom, if you will remember, you used to know at Clent! Having much of the town to pass through, we went at a slow pace for some time, the road being so slippery that the horses were continually stumbling. The outskirts of London were simply a sheet of ice. In going up the hill by Blackheath we were obliged to use six horses, and leaving the carriage behind we crossed the plain on foot, taking the carriage again before arrival at our first stage, Dartford. The town is well enough, but the inn execrable.

The snow was everywhere very deep, but the road fairly clear and the surface splendid. As we invariably sent the post-chaise with the servants on ahead, we found the horses ready on our arrival at the stage, and having reserved a carriage as far as Versailles, we were put to very little trouble. Rochester was the next stage, and there, three towns adjoining each other, namely, Stroud, Rochester and Chatham, the road through them is three miles long as far as Chatham, which is situated on the river Medway and is a royal arsenal. There were several vessels of war there.

We found M. d'Ermenonville to be a very pleasant companion, and his speaking English so very well was most agreeable to me. From Rochester we went to Sittingbourne, and thence to Canterbury where we dined. It being now dark we could not see the country. We reached Dover about 10 o'clock, and having arranged with a captain to take us over to France, went straight to bed, counting on leaving early in the morning the following day, but in this hope we deceived ourselves as did the servants who had put the carriage on board; for at 5 o'clock we learnt that the captain would not leave the harbour on account of

3

the strength of the wind as well as its being contrary. This was not comforting news, for seemingly we could hardly amuse ourselves in a place like Dover.

After luncheon, M. de Bombelles and M. d'Ermenonville called on the Duc de Scaubres, who spends much time in England, I think rather of necessity than by choice. Though perhaps hardly forty years old, he has already got through a large part of his fortune, which was immense, without any credit or glory, squandering it in low society which he enjoys to such a degree that he is never seen in any other company. He has at present got with him a mistress from the streets of London, with whom he is madly in love. He is also en route for Paris, but has stopped here to view the departure of M. Blanchard's balloon, which is at the castle awaiting a favourable wind to cross over to Calais. As it has never ceased to pour with rain, we have been unable to see it or the town today.

Before dinner we were joined by M. d'Aborde, another Frenchman, son of a Paris banker, who starting with nothing has by his business ability amassed a fortune of half a million. Having spent the whole summer in England hunting, he is returning to Paris in order to receive from the King a position which is practically a sinecure, and worth £16,000. Being alone, he asked us to let him take Thevening's place in the carriage, and to put the latter in the chaise with his own servant.

When in our rooms, we were startled by a terrible noise which came from below. Running to the door, I found the Duc's mistress on her knees in a room full of people, praying her audience to save her from the fury of the Duc, who after some petty quarrel in which she had threatened to leave him, appears to have followed her as far as this room with a pistol in his hand, saying he would kill her. Throwing herself against the glass door, she made the noise which had brought us downstairs, and implored the help of the spectators in the name of God. Some Englishmen who were staying in the inn took her to their room, where presently the Duc followed her, and after his begging her pardon, they were immediately reconciled and as good friends as ever before. Such a rapid reconciliation will not astonish you, when you consider that they have lived together in this way for upwards of two years.

The wind still being contrary in the evening, we went to bed without expecting to be called upon to sail on the next day. On the 23rd the wind was still contrary, but the weather very fine. After luncheon M. d'Ermenonville and I went out to see the town and harbour. The former is very small but pretty enough and well kept; the latter is a fairly good one, but there is very little trade, as it is full of *paquebots* of which there are very many, and which sail to Ostend and Calais whenever the wind is favourable.

On one side of the town is the Castle, which is said to have been built by Julius Caesar at the time of his invasion of England. Not altogether a ruin, it is very nearly so. The building is in general very interesting, the walls being very thick and the mortar used being of that nature always employed by the Romans in every building erected by them in England. There are quarters for a fairly large number of soldiers, but at this moment only a small part of the 69th Regiment are stationed there. On the hill where the Castle stands we saw the preparations being made for the departure of M. Blanchard's balloon! We also saw a cannon 22 ft. long, which goes by the name of 'the pocket pistol of Queen Elizabeth' and was presented to her by the United Provinces. Its range is seven miles. From the Castle the town is almost hidden from view by the chalk cliffs. The sea dotted with little fishing boats plying to and fro, and the hills of the French coast near Boulogne, make a pretty picture.

This morning the Duc and his Mistress had another quarrel in which she decided to leave him. This he consented to, and allowed her to go off alone in a post-chaise, but changing his mind, followed her in another.

In the evening M. d'E. and I went to a little theatre where a second rate troupe of comedians tried to act 'The Angry Husband', but it was indeed massacred. Before the end of the play we were told that the wind had changed, and the vessels were due to sail without delay. In half an hour we were on board, and setting sail at once were in a very short time outside the harbour.

M. d'Aborde hired a ship for himself, but the rest of us were crowded up with a dozen other passengers in a little cabin, where some went to sleep at once and those who could not do so began to vomit; scarcely pleasant music to the ears of those whose powers of being able to lapse into sweet oblivion were not as great as mine. As for me, in half an hour's time I was in the breach of some besieged town, and suppose that the cries and groans of these poor people, who with disgust disgorged the roast beef and mutton they had eaten with zest at Dover, sounded in my ears like the pitiful wailing of mothers who had lost their husbands, or of children bewailing the fathers who had been killed. So I dreamed, until eight o'clock in the morning when we were in sight of Calais, a very pleasing spectacle to all the French on board, and at 9.30 we entered the harbour by a long quay. In an instant the deck was alive with people of a most villainous appearance, who I took for customs officials but I was told afterwards that they were only inn-keepers, who came to solicit the patronage of the passengers. I take this as an example of French civility: they came to save us the trouble of going to find them.

Taking me with him, M. de Bombelles left the servants on board with our belongings and went at once to show his passport. One could only enter the town by one gate, where they questioned our passports, but on showing a packet full of letters from the ambassador, they let us pass.

Leaving me at the inn he went off to show his papers and to see his effects examined by the Customs Officials. I have seized the opportunity afforded by his absence to write you this letter, and I hope to have the equal pleasure of doing so on arrival at Versailles, whither we depart after dinner. I hope that the length of my letters does not displease you, for my idea is not to bore you, but to amuse insofar as my poor talents admit.

With all respect
I remain yours
C. COLVILL

Versailles, 27th Decr. 1784

Perhaps you will not believe me, my dear Father, but I am already surfeited with honour and joy, as you shall see from the following. In my last letter I left you in the inn at Calais, from which place I wrote to you. As I was closing my letter, I saw the door open and a figure entered which at first I could only look upon as something supernatural. He advanced and, handing me a paper on which there was English writing, informed me that he belonged to an Order of Monks called Capuchins who having no money for their subsistence were obliged to beg charity from foreigners so as not to die of starvation. Signifying that I could not express myself in French, we talked Latin, and I told him in this tongue that I had nothing to give him, but that if he came back later he would find a person of his own Faith who would perhaps have pity on him. I will not at this moment give you a description of his dress, reserving such a pleasure until such time as I have more knowledge of their rules, as of those of other monks, because one may say it will be a source of much amusement. The Capuchin and I parted very good friends, and he left me making the Sign of the Cross.

At 1 o'clock the Marquis and the other gentlemen returned after having had all their effects opened and examined by the Customs. It was amusing to watch with what avidity the French themselves tried to decrease the revenue of their own country by smuggling English goods. These three gentlemen had employed the whole crew of the ship in concealing their merchandise, and the room was full of such people producing articles of cotton, works in steel, etc. from pockets inside their coats, and even inside their trousers, but I don't think the owners made much out of their smuggling, as they had to pay their agents well. When all this was over, we sat down to a very good dinner, but before we had finished the monk reappeared, and after many prayers (at which I roared with laughter) M. de Bombelles gave him 12 sous, for which he received in return at least as many blessings. M. de B. reproved me a little for my mirth, but as a matter of fact, himself excepted, there was no-one in the company who did not laugh, and since France is the country of civility, I shall evidently acquire better manners than I now possess.

After dinner we left for Boulogne, where we arranged to pass the night on our way to Versailles. I will not give you a description of the road, or recount the distances between the towns through which we passed, leaving all that for when I return, and I shall only mention those things which appear to me to be of most interest. The country through which we passed was flat, and seemed dull to an eye accustomed to the pleasant variety of scene which is England's charm. We came across many little canals, six and seven feet in width, which extended from town to town in this flat country, and which are used for transport of firewood etc. The snow appeared to be of much the same depth as in England. We slept at Boulogne, and the next day being Christmas, we continued our journey. As it was a holiday, the only people we saw on the road were pedestrians, the men in cloaks with swords at their sides and hats under their arms, the women in simple bonnets, and all, both men and women, having big muffs which suggested the opposite of heat, which one would have thought they felt from the way they kept their heads uncovered. Judging by their dress, I took them to be of a class at any rate superior to the common

7

people, and had got it into my head that the French upper classes were very fond of walking, but I stood corrected when I was told that they were probably only common people.

During the journey we passed through many towns, amongst others Montreuil where we had luncheon, and then Abbeville which is of quite a size. Travelling in this country is far from being as convenient as in England. Unlike the latter one does not find a carriage at each stage, but is obliged to buy one before starting on a journey. The number of horses one has to take is in proportion to the passengers: we have six. The horses are wretched and the harness is of rope. The postillions are even worse, and drive as they please: if you complain they dismount and tell you to drive yourself. I can imagine no picture more comical, or likely to make people laugh, than one of these carriages and its crew in the streets of London. To begin with the carriages are in particular post-chaises, and horribly ugly. Six horses, such as one would not harness to a plough, draw them, and these are ridden by a couple of postillions in boots big enough to put a sheep inside, leather trousers, blue coats with a little silver border, cotton night caps, and finally queus, which reach their saddles. When it is cold, instead of caps they wear large fur bonnets and gloves. Each stage afforded me a fresh excuse for laughter, which annoyed the Marquis de Bombelles, who said one ought never to visit a country in order to make fun of its inhabitants.

During the whole journey we stopped only at Amiens to eat. This is another big town. As it was night on our arrival there, we supped, and as we were going to travel all night, we had an extra glass or two to make us sleep better in the carriage. This had a very good effect, as I slept the night through except for the noise M. de B. made at the stage in trying to hurry the people there, who would have left us out in the cold for an hour at least, had we allowed them to make all the preparations they wished for our departure.

The French hardly ever have any breakfast for which I was very sorry, because it was not till about noon on the following day that I broke my fast with a piece of cake which I ate or rather devoured at Chantilly. Here M. d'Ermenonville left us to see his father, who lives a league or two away in one of the prettiest parts of France. M. d'Aborde was still with us, but he also got out at St. Denis to go to Paris, and we headed for Versailles which was only two or three leagues further on. M. de Bombelles tried to recall to me the gaiety which he saw I had abandoned at the thought of the new kind of life I was about to take up, and assured me that he would do his utmost to make me spend my time happily, and that it would be my own fault if I had reason to regret anything that was likely to happen to me in his house.

After having passed through a forest, which is called the Bois de Boulogne, we reached the main road between Paris and Versailles. There were lights all along it, which gave a good impression. The Marquis took great trouble to tell me the names of the owners of the many carriages which were going at such a pace to Versailles, and who were going to pay their court to the King, as is the custom amongst courtiers in this country on Sundays. Being as dark as the infernal regions, we could only see the lanterns carried by five or six footmen behind the carriages. The Château of Versailles soon made itself known by the abundance of lights which we saw at a great distance, and which I knew must be the residence of a great Monarch before being told so. We entered the town through a place which did not leave such a good impression, and, in great fear lest the carriage should upset on the ice, the Marquis and I got out and went on foot as far as the door of a large house which he said was his home. This news astonished me and I began to be afraid (if you could have seen the horrible appearance of the house, you would excuse this expression) that instead of that of a great gentleman, I had been placed in the care of someone concerning whom I cannot give expression to my fears. We entered by a door which had been glazed, but which instead of broken panes had pieces of wood which had been fixed in it to keep out the cold.

Thence through a passage, which led us to a large room without our seeing a soul, and from there to a small room, prettily furnished, where we saw a servant putting wood on the fire, and who pleased me by the respectful way in which he spoke to the Marquis. His wife and children were out, so he summoned a servant and we went upstairs by a ladder rather than a staircase to a little hole which was destined to be my room. He began, as he might well do, by asking me to forgive him for putting me in a room which he saw I did not like, giving as reason the situation he was now in, of having to rent a house where there was not enough room, but as he promised that everything would be well looked after, I was content.

Madame la Marquise and her children came in soon after:

the former seemed very pleased to see her husband, and the latter their father. Madame la Marquise welcomed me very nicely, or so it seemed to me, for she did not speak English, and I did not hear what she said. It was now time to think of a meal, and supper was soon announced, much to my joy. When we had finished, the Marquis and his wife went to see their relations and left me with the children who I left very soon to go to bed.

The next morning I got up about 8 o'clock, and when I went downstairs found Mons. de B. with two gentlemen one of whom was M. de Langrais, a fat little man, who was the Marquis' secretary. Mdme. la Marquise came down very soon afterwards, and pleased me very much by the kind way in which she greeted me. As we came from England, we were given tea for breakfast, a rare occurrence in France. After breakfast they discussed what was to be done with me, and as a result they decided on taking me to see the King at Chapelle, whither M. Longrais accompanied me as also M. de B. in order to pay his respects to the King.

We went by way of the Rue de la Chancellerie in which we lived, and passed through a guard of soldiers who conducted us to a great courtyard which was part of the Château, and which we had to cross to reach the Chapelle. One of the guards stopped me at the gate because I had not got 'mes cheveux en bourse' or my sword at my side, but when M. de Langrais told him that I was the son of an English nobleman, who had only just arrived from that country, they let us enter the gallery from which place I had a good view of the King and Royal Family. After the service we passed through a gallery into a large room in the Château, where the people of the Court meet every day to discuss events and each other. We saw there the King's brothers pass by on their way from the Chapelle to their own apartments. We then went home for luncheon. In the evening M. de B. took me to see those of his family who were about Court. First we went to the house of Mdme. la Baronne de Mackau, Mdme. de B.'s mother, a good looking woman for her age, who held herself very erect, and showed perhaps in addition a little haughtiness. The Comtesse de Souci, aunt of Mdme. de B. was also there. We then went to the house of the Marquise de Souci, sister of Mdme. de B. Her husband and the Marquis received us at the door, and took us to a room full of people who were playing music. Amongst others la Marquise sang and the Marquis played the piano, both performances winning much applause. Among others to whom I was introduced was the young Madame de Mackau, sister-in-law of Mdme. de B. She is quite young and by far the prettiest woman in the room. There were several gentlemen who could speak a little English, and you may be sure they did not lose such a good opportunity of addressing me in that language. As soon as the concert had finished, I accompanied the Marquis, his wife and the young Baronne to a large room in the Chateau in which the King allowed the manufacturers of the porcelain made at Sèvres (a village near Paris) to exhibit their wares, as much to give them an opportunity of selling them as to show strangers visiting France the beauty of a craft which doubtless has no parallel in other countries.

We found the King and his brother there. The latter had dined with the Minister, M. de Vergennes, and had met M. de Bombelles there. In the course of conversation Monsieur [the Comte de Provence, afterwards Louis XVIII] remarked that he had noticed in the Chapelle and later in the Chateau a young man with hair falling down on to his shoulders, and giving an exact description of my clothes, concluded by saying that he took him to be a jockey, and was surprised that such people should be allowed inside. The Marquis told him that he was mistaken, and that it was the son of a Scotch Peer of noble descent whom he had taken for a jockey, and that my dress was that of my country, very different to be sure from that of the French. The moment he saw me in the salon he came up to speak to the Marquis, and addressed some remark to me which I did not understand. As he was going away, he said that he was going to bring the King to see me, but the moment I learnt his intention I started to run away, and had already got through the door when M. de Bombelles stopped me and begged me to return as the King was waiting in the salon. So I went back into the salon where I found the King, who looked at me very intently, and the Marquis said he was sure he would have come up and spoken to me had he not thought he would frighten me. Turning to the gentlemen in attendance, he remarked that he was astonished that English noblemen should dress their children like stable boys, but added at the same time that I had 'la physionmy bien spirituelle'. Do not forget to tell my dear Mother and all my young friends at Bath that before I had been 24 hours at Versailles, the two greatest men in the Kingdom had taken such notice of me, and that above all the King thought that I had 'un physionmie d'esprit', and they will agree with me that I had good reason to say that I am surfeited with honour. (See the beginning of this letter.)

When we had been round the salon several times, and all the great people of the Court had been pointed out to me, we went back to Mdme. de Mackaus' for supper. She is a widow, and her three children are the Baron, husband of the young Baronne, the Marquise de Souci, and Mdme. de Bombelles. The evening passed very pleasantly, and I was very gratified to notice that of my suggestions, there were few which did not excite the company. Vanity makes me hope that this was due to the originality of my ideas, but my natural modesty makes me fear that it was but my gauche way of expressing myself which brought it about.

Now I think I have troubled you enough for this time, but conclude with a promise that I will write again very soon.

I have the honour etc.

CHARLES COLVILL

Versailles, Jany. 14th 1785

I have just received the letter from my brother George which tells me of the death of my Aunt. Although I have been expecting this for a long time, I cannot tell you how much pain it has caused me. Yes, my dear father, I shall always regret. The memory of her will be ever dear to me, and will be always that of the loving Aunt she has proved to be. I am sure that your sorrow must be very great, if one may judge by the way you behaved to her during her life time.

At present I am happy; the only complaint I make is that of having nothing to do, a state of affairs which I begin to see is much more disagreeable than I should have thought possible. I spent the first few days after my last letter pleasantly enough. I got up late in the morning and went for a walk with Thevening or M. de Langrais. The evenings were spent in listening to the music at M. de Souci's or in going to little parties at Mdme. de Mackau's. The latter were by far the most pleasant, as there was no one there but friends of the family, but their success was principally due to the efforts of Mdme. de Bombelles and her 'petite belle soeur', for so she calls the little Baronne de Mackau, who, both of them pretty as a couple of angels, made everything so agreeable by their charm.

During this time it was decided to make me look still more like a monkey by dressing me in French clothes. So to achieve this great object they started by curling my hair. This took place on the 28th of last month, when they pulled my hair about to such a degree that I had a bad head ache for the whole of that day, and they then applied powder and pomade in such quantities as to entirely alter my appearance. At the same time the tailor measured me for the sort of clothes that are worn in this country.

I often go to see the people in the *salon de porcelaine*, and I cannot marvel sufficiently at the beauty of this manufacture. The porcelain is good, perhaps even better than that of China, but the colours and the way in which they are painted are wonderful. I take great pleasure in walking round the tables and asking the price of all the pretty things I see, and my astonishment and admiration are by this means aroused, for I see often there tea and coffee cups priced at eight or ten louis apiece. It is also in this place that I have started to recognise the people of quality by sight. The men lose much if you compare them with the English; as a rule they are very small, of a poor build and darkish complexion. Their clothes are quite different from ours excepting in the morning, when the young fops pride themselves in dressing like the English: otherwise they always wear coats with rich lace manchettes and hats which are only meant to be carried under the arm: so much is this the case, that I have often seen very fine gentlemen walking in the streets bare headed even when it was snowing.

New Year's Day, besides being a holiday in this country, is also kept as the anniversary of the Order du Saint Esprit, the most noble in France, and of which the King is Master. As a great favour the Marquis got me a place in the Chapelle to witness the ceremonies in connection with this. The proceedings started by the procession of the Knights in the robes of their Order, which are of a wonderful richness, headed by the King and Princes of the royal blood, who entered the Chapelle to the accompaniment of the big drums played by the Hundred Swiss (a body guard akin to our Yeomen) and who made enough noise to be heard a league away. The Knights, being all in their places, fell on their knees making the Sign of the Cross and listened to the long prayers which the Bishops of the Order intoned at the great altar. After the first prayers and while the men who sang the Psalms in Latin were accompanied by music, one of the Court ladies, magnificently dressed and carrying a 'quête' (a kind of purse, such as those the begging Orders make use of) bowed very low to each of the Knights, who dropped in it money for the poor. The music ever sounding, the King advanced and prostrated himself before the altar. The Archbishop blessed him and he then ascended a temporary throne of gold tapestry, magnificently adorned with feathers etc. Having sat there for some moments, he returned to his seat at the end of the Chapelle, where he listened to some more prayers. The Archbishop elevated the Host, and the ceremony finished as it began with the procession.

Charles remained at Versailles till the end of 1785. His subsequent letters from the Bombelles' house are lost; but his appearance evidently continued to attract attention, for many years later he told his son, who passed the story on to his own children, of a further episode. It seems that the Bombelles family took him to a ball in the Palace. No doubt his hair was specially curled for the occasion and he wore his new French-tailored suit; but he did not wear a wig, and he found himself to be the only male in the entire Salle des Glaces without that indispensable article of court dress. The Queen noticed this solecism and sent for him. She was amused by his embarrassed explanation, in halting French, and she invited him to join her in a quadrille. Many curious links with the past can be cited, but certainly my father, who died in 1943, provided a striking example when he said that his grandfather had danced with Marie Antoinette.

At sixteen Charles joined his regiment and in 1787 he was posted to Dublin, where he purchased his lieutenancy. By 1791 he was a captain and, seeking active employment, he transferred to the 13th Regiment of Foot which was stationed in Jamaica. It was the regiment of his own county, later to be renamed the Somersetshire Light Infantry. Two years later, the French Revolution having degenerated into the Terror and become a menace to European stability, Great Britain went to war with France. Charles set off from Jamaica with an expeditionary force to capture San Domingo, but not before, in a matter where he felt his honour involved, he had fought a duel with a major in his regiment named Scott. Neither contestant was damaged and honour was, it seems, reasonably satisfied. However, San Domingo proved more dangerous than Major Scott. Charles was wounded in the leg by a musket ball and stricken by one of the many fevers rampant in the West Indies. He saw his brother, George, a lieutenant in the 41st Regiment, newly arrived in San Domingo from Guadeloupe and Martinique, die of yellow fever. Between 1794 and 1796 40,000 British soldiers died or were killed in the West Indies.

14

Fever claimed more lives than musket balls, but Charles recovered from both and was shipped home on sick-leave. In 1795 he was sufficiently restored to resume his service, to be gazetted a major and, with a little financial support from his by no means affluent father, to buy the junior lieutenant-colonelcy in his regiment which opportunely fell vacant.

Already at twenty-six high in military rank, to some extent by fortune and favour but also by merit, he set off again for Ireland in 1798 to help suppress the rebellion. This uprising of the extremist 'United Irishmen' movement was assisted in its endeavours by the arrival in Killala Bay of a small French army under General Humbert. The majority of the Irish peasantry remained loyal to the Crown, or at least passive, and the French were ignominiously defeated by Lord Gort at the Battle of Coloony without substantial help from the British regular forces. However, Ireland had to be garrisoned and the 13th stayed there for two years. Charles, according to his son, fell in love while in Dublin with the pretty but exasperating Kitty Pakenham. He was spared progress with his suit by the fact that she was betrothed to Arthur Wellesley, who was away winning battles in India. The victorious Wellesley found on his return that, seen through more experienced eyes, the lady's charms had much diminished, but he felt it his duty to go through with the marriage.

By then Charles was abroad again. In August 1800 he was included in an expedition under Sir James Pulteney which sailed from Portsmouth to capture Ferrol in Spain. British Intelligence was at fault, for Ferrol was much too strongly defended to be captured by a small force. After a temporary occupation of the heights above the city, Pulteney abandoned the project and transported his men to Gibraltar. There he joined Sir Ralph Abercromby whose orders were to drive the French out of Egypt.

Accordingly the 13th Regiment was incorporated in Abercromby's 2nd Division. It landed at Aboukir on 2 March 1801, against formidable opposition, and fought two successful engagements. Napoleon, thwarted of his ambition to occupy the Middle East and capture Constantinople, had already returned to France, leaving nearly 30,000 men behind in Egypt. There were some 10,000 French troops in Cairo and still more in Alexandria. Abercromby himself was killed in the opening battle at Aboukir, but under his successor, Hutchinson, the British forced Cairo to capitulate and in August 1801 captured Alexandria.

The Egyptian Khedive marked his recognition of Abercromby's victory by the gift of an ancient obelisk known as Cleopatra's

Needle, though it was carved and decorated some fifteen hundred years before Cleopatra was born. The British ungraciously left it lying in the sand near Alexandria for seventy-five years. It was then retrieved, towed to London in a metal container and erected on the Thames Embankment.

Charles fought valiantly in the two opening battles and when the senior lieutenant-colonel fell sick commanded the 13th for the remainder of the campaign. In March 1802, two years after the Aboukir landing, the regiment left Egypt for Malta and he made use of the short truce provided by the Peace of Amiens to take a few months' leave. Returning to England, he was appointed senior lieutenant-colonel of his regiment, with a junior lieutenant-colonel of only twenty-two, John Keane, as his second-in-command.

The truce soon ended, whereupon he sailed to rejoin his men in Gibraltar and remained there till the end of 1805. He was gazetted a full colonel shortly after his thirty-fourth birthday, but had the unhappiness of seeing his men die of fever in great numbers. In those days Gibraltar was almost as pestilential a place as the West Indies. The 13th returned home much reduced in strength and went to Ireland to make up their numbers from the Irish militia, a useful source of recruits for the British Army.

In 1808 they were sent to Bermuda and thence to Barbados to prepare for an assault on the French colony of Martinique. Charles was promoted brigadier-general and given command of the brigade in which his old regiment was incorporated.

Gathering forces from St. Lucia and St. Vincent, the expedition sailed from Barbados at the end of January 1809, and surprised the French by landing on the windward side of Martinique in the small shallow Baie de Robert. They captured Fort Edouard, turning its guns on the more powerful Fort Bourbon. Though it never stopped raining and the movement of artillery over slippery, uneven tracks was exceedingly difficult, they forced the French to surrender within a month of the landing. Guadeloupe was the next target for assault and when that island was taken, France had lost the last of her colonies. Napoleon's Empire was confined to Europe.

Before the attack on Guadeloupe, Charles was ordered to abandon his brigade and take temporary command of the island of Grenada. He found this honour a mixed blessing. His baggage was lost and his best horse injured during embarkation. The President of the Grenada Council declined to let him use Government House, despite the absent Governor's invitation to do so, and with the roads impassable from the unprecedented and continuing rainfall, he could not reach the outposts of his command. There were also unavoidable invitations to what he called 'overgrown dinners that disgust by their heat and duration'. Life was very expensive and, as he wrote to his father, 'the trouble of housekeeping with any attention to economy is indeed most fatiguing'. Then there was the garden: 'I found it advisable to buy a flock of fifteen sheep and lambs to keep down the too rapid vegetation of the season, but I have already lost two of the latter, one by theft and the other by death, so that if not more fortunate in future I shall find my farming a bad speculation.'

Meanwhile his brother John had asked him not to plague himself by sending things home from Grenada, 'but I must except castor oil, of which considerable use is made by the dear Colville family, and Cayenne pepper.' Charles replied that Grenada was not famous for castor oil, but he nevertheless contrived to procure, and to send home, 'six quarts of castor oil, about 14 lbs of arrow-root, 27 lbs of chocolate and eight stuffed humming-birds', adding the up-to-date medical advice that 'with Europeans in this Island the use of castor oil has latterly much given way to calomel'.

After a year's struggle with housekeeping, inaccessible outposts, disobliging civilian councillors, overgrown gardens and maimed horses, Charles was summoned back to England in June 1810 and was promoted major-general shortly before his fortieth birthday. This was commendable, but for an officer who was thought promising it was not an unusually early age for promotion to high military rank. Arthur Wellesley, for instance, with his scintillating Indian victories and a politically important elder brother behind him, had become a lieutenant-general at thirty-five and Sir Rowland Hill was a major-general at thirty-three.

Nonetheless Charles had behind him a considerable and varied experience of active service and his rise up the military ladder had been quite acceptably brisk. Now, some six weeks after his return home, he set off abroad again to take part in one of the hardest fought and most successful campaigns in British history, the Peninsular War.

2

Stalemate in Portugal

The officers of Wellington's army and also, as Private Wheeler's letters show, the literate other ranks had no inhibitions at all about sending home detailed accounts of their movements. Their proud relations often retailed this information to the newspapers, and the French Government were thus provided with ready made sources of intelligence. Charles Colville was no exception to the rule, but his family seem to have been more discreet in their use of the information he sent them than were some others. Censorship, apart from the organisation required and the shortage of staff available, would doubtless have been considered an infringement of freedom of speech. In days when it was generally thought permissible to give a soldier a thousand lashes, it was intolerable to deny any man's right to say what he wanted provided his words were neither blasphemous, treasonable nor libellous. Periodic appeals for caution were, for the most part, unheeded.

It is not the object of this book to provide a potted history of events in the Iberian peninsula between 1808 and 1814, but some account of the military situation must be given as the frame within which Charles Colville's letters are set. War was waged in Catalonia and Andalusia, and the Spanish irregular forces kept the French constantly on the alert in Galicia, Asturias and Vizcaya; but the vital area was that in which Wellington fought and defeated a succession of Napoleon's most illustrious Marshals. It was in that area alone that Charles Colville served.

In October 1810, when Charles landed from a frigate in Lisbon, a fortnight after sailing from the anchorage off Deal known as the Downs, Napoleon had over 300,000 men endeavouring to hold down Spain and Portugal against active popular revolt and to confirm his brother Joseph on the usurped throne of the Spanish Bourbons. The first British intervention had failed. In January 1809, Sir John Moore's small army, faced by Marshal Soult and by Napoleon himself, was forced to retreat through Galicia in conditions of severe hardship and to embark from Corunna. It was a small nineteenth-century Dunkirk, with the same inadvertent reward of dislocating the Dictator's plans. Shortly before this disaster, Sir Arthur Wellesley had decisively defeated Marshal Junot at Vimeiro in Portugal, but he had been thwarted by his own senior officers who signed a Convention at Cintra allowing the beaten French army to return to France by sea and live to fight on other fields. Wellesley himself went home in disgust.

The Spanish armies were as futile as their guerillas were magnificent. They were defeated again and again. By the spring of 1809 Soult was occupying northern Portugal and holding court at Oporto while his subordinate, Marshal Ney, was trying to subjugate Galicia. In April that year, Wellesley, with the powerful support of Castlereagh (one of the most maligned men in English history), returned to Portugal. He had 26,000 British soldiers and at his request General Beresford, appointed a Marshal in the Army of Portugal, was training thousands of enthusiastic Portuguese levies with imagination and success.

With his own men and 15,000 of Beresford's local recruits, Wellesley drove Soult out of Oporto. The Marshal lost 6,000 French soldiers and all his artillery. Already, in July 1808, Charles's elder brother, John, captain of H.M.S. *Hercule*, then stationed off the coast of Portugal, had written of affairs in Oporto: 'There the population in arms is already great, headed by their gallant Bishop, whom Colonel Brown of the Duke of York's staff has seen reviewing his forces, in a great measure composed of priests.' The Portuguese, priests and all, now rose to the occasion and made an invaluable contribution. A few months after Soult fled from Oporto, Wellesley entered Spain and beat Marshal Victor at Talavera on the Tagus; but he himself lost 5,000 men in a singularly bloody battle and felt obliged to fall back into Portugal. During the winter of 1809–10 Viscount Wellington (as Wellesley now became) constructed the three concentric lines of Torres Vedras round Lisbon with a secrecy as surprising as it was unusual, for the French learned nothing of these new defences and for once the British army must have accepted some kind of self-imposed censorship.

Napoleon had given Marshal Masséna command of the Army of Portugal with 65,000 men. It was these whom Wellington fought and defeated at the Battle of Busaco in September 1810, killing nearly 5,000 Frenchmen and losing only a little over a thousand of his own troops. The Portuguese, with much self-sacrifice, agreed

to a 'scorched earth' policy, so that when Wellington deliberately
fell back from Busaco towards Lisbon, the French, who made
a practice of living off the country, found less means of sustenance
than they expected. They gave expression to their wrath and disappointment by wanton destruction, notably in Coimbra and, as
can be seen to this day, in the beautiful abbey at Alcobaça. They
were greatly superior in men and artillery and, despite Busaco,
they still believed they could drive the British from Portugal.
So they advanced towards Lisbon.

Wellington's army was safe within the lines of Torres Vedras
by 10 October 1810. It was not until four days later that Masséna
himself even heard of the existence of those formidable redoubts.
Meanwhile, on 7 October, Charles Colville landed at Lisbon 'just
in time' he wrote to his father a few days later, 'as it immediately
after began to blow strong from the south-west with torrents of
rain which have scarcely intermitted for an hour at a time ever
since, nor will they, I am told, till the change of the moon.'
On arrival he was appointed to command a brigade in General
Picton's 3rd Division, with a total strength of 1,900 other ranks.
These were contained in the 2nd Battalion of the 'Fighting 5th',
the 83rd and the 94th Regiments. It soon became one of the
best-trained and most courageous formations in the army. By this
time the total strength of Wellington's command was 34,000 British,
24,000 Portuguese and 8,000 Spaniards.

The 3rd Division was at first responsible for the line from
Torres Vedras to the sea, but the French massed their forces
at Sobral, halfway between Torres Vedras and the Tagus. There
was a skirmish and a frontal attack was expected. So Wellington
moved his 3rd Division to the right in support of the troops
facing Sobral, and its headquarters were established in the village
of Cadacocira. There, on 20 October, Charles wrote to his father:

In half an hour after closing my letter to your Lordship
of the 13th, and having previously despatched my two servants
and three loaded mules, I set out from Lisbon intending to
make the best of my way for Torres Vedras where I had reason
to suppose my Brigade was, but to which I was recommended
to go by the circuitous route of Mafra to avoid the confusion
of the principal road. Without a guide or the assistance of a
direction post the whole way, and ignorant of the language
of the country, there was no wonder I should lose my road,
and accordingly I did not get into Bellas, distant in a straight
line but eight or nine miles from Lisbon, till after dark, but

fortunately found my baggage arrived before me and accommodation, such as it was, prepared at a tavern. Whence having
stocked myself with such an army of fleas etc. as has taken
me half the time since to rid myself of, I again set off at
half past four in the morning and reached Mafra in time to
breakfast with General Anson who is stationed there recruiting
his Brigade of cavalry.

This place is remarkable for an enormous royal palace and
convent in one, the Escurial of Portugal, which I visited and
heard High Mass while my horses baited, seeing also its fine
library. Troops are quartered in part of the palace. I here learnt
from some sick of my Brigade going to Lisbon that it had
fallen back from Torres Vedras, but to what point they were
uncertain. Taking the direction of the park wall of Mafra I
soon fell in with the redoubts forming the second defensive
line for our army to retire to in case of being pressed, and
which with the natural features of the country make it very
strong. The country I had passed hitherto was far from pleasing,
a great deal of heath, little wood, and the soil whence the corn
crop had been taken off of a perfectly arid appearance after
the long summer drought, and not having had time to revive
after the late rains. At Gradil I came into a very picturesque
vine country, studded with numerous Quintas (country seats).
I was overtaken with a torrent of rain with violent wind by
which I was completely drenched through my Portugal cloak,
but luckily I found some British artillery there.

Got a comfortable dinner and should have been glad to stay
the night there, but hearing that Sir B. Spencer, having retired
out of the town of Sobral, which was immediately after occupied
in great force by the French, had had his picquets attacked
that afternoon and that every thing betokened an early general
advance of the enemy, I proceeded, tho' now dark, in quest
of my Brigade now said to be at St. Sebastian's, perhaps two
miles off. I soon however perceived that the guide sent with
me knew no more of the country than myself, and after wandering
over most diabolical roads with this fellow alone, my servants
and baggage being behind, and frequently being tempted to
take up my abode under a tree for the night, so tired were
both myself and horse, I got in at half past nine to Runa,
a town three or four miles in front of that I was looking for.
I thought myself very lucky in finding a Portuguese corps there,
commanded by Baron Eben, whose name I think I have read
of as of the Prince of Wales's parties, and who gave his stabling

for my horse and a paillasse for myself, being the best accommodation to be expected in a town totally abandoned by its inhabitants, as is unfortunately the case with most of them in this part of the country.

Here I cannot pass unnoticed the pitiable state of these poor people. Being recommended by us to quit their habitations, they have mostly complied, and Lisbon and the roads leading to it are filled with them. Those on the latter are carrying what they can with them, but that of course is very little, and as every thing left behind becomes a prey to either friend or foe, it is impossible to look forward to their future condition without apprehension and regret; but they themselves seem to bear their present state with wonderful fortitude and great show of attachment to the general cause and antipathy of the French. I asked in Lisbon what had been done for their assistance, and was told that for the poorer classes eating houses had been established, perhaps as efficient a charity as could have been thought of.

The night, contrary to expectation, passed quiet and without alarm of any kind, so retracing in part my steps in the morning and passing through the two left Divisions of our line, I found my own, Genl. Picton's the 3rd, here and at an adjoining village where they had been brought under cover from the rains. Genl. Picton, having more calls upon him than me, resides in a house in the village hardly fit to put pigs in. I am at a Quinta a little way off, where with the assistance of a small tooth comb and plenty of water I am able to keep myself tolerably clean, have refreshed my cattle which they much wanted, and see a party of three or four every day to dinner.

My Brigade is a weak one as I cannot at present depend upon more than 1,130 bayonets, having many sick absent, but what there is of them are effective and seasoned troops. It will be enough for me to say that every one here is in the best spirits, the sick in the field not increasing, and those at Lisbon returning to us fast. That the French are so long of attacking is subject of much conversation. Cannon shot were heard yesterday, and at Villa Franca the French General, La Croix, commanding their cavalry, lost his head a few days since by a shot from our gun boats, which will we trust be found very serviceable in that low swampy part.

Masséna, smarting from his painful experience of frontal attack on the British at Busaco, decided not to assault the lines of Torres

Vedras. He was in a difficult position, for not only had the Portuguese, vacating their villages as the French advanced, carried most
of their provisions away with them, but his communications were
constantly attacked by guerilla detachments operating under British
officers. For a month he sat in front of the lines of Torres Vedras
sending urgent demands for reinforcements. None came.

Wellington later described Masséna as the most dangerous and
difficult antagonist he ever fought. But now the victor of the
Battle of Rivoli, christened by Napoleon 'enfant chéri de la victoire',
had met his match. He could not cross either the Tagus or the
Zezere rivers, for all the boats had been destroyed; and so while
his three army corps sat, with scarcely any shelter, before Wellington's snug redoubts, he collected all the artificers in his army
and built a bridge at Santarem. Thus there was no active service
for Charles to describe during October and November, but he
continued dutifully to write to his father. These are some of the
extracts from his letters. It may be noted that movement was
restricted by the shortage of horse-shoes which, as far as the
cavalry, artillery and supply trains were concerned, were comparable
in importance with tank-tracks in the Second World War.

The apparent inactivity of the *ci-devant* darling of victory
left me nothing very particular to say by the mail of last week,
which is generally made up on Saturday at Head Quarters,
so that having despatched a letter to your Lordship on the
20th I gave my eyes a holiday at that moment, which they
much required, as I fear they always will after much use or
exposure to severe weather, either of heat, cold, or wind, and
we had a good sample of each in the short period in question,
transitions which little lead me to think this the healthy climate
generally represented. Our troops being all under cover of some
kind or another, the defences of our position completed, and
supplies well at hand, will have the least to suffer, whereas
the enemy have much to apprehend and will probably be com-
pelled to hasten a decision they seem not very anxious to make.
I yesterday dined with an acquaintance, Lt. Col. Campbell
of the 31st, a Brigadier in the Portuguese service, and previously
saw his Brigade consisting of two Regts. of between eleven
and twelve hundred each, near effective in that number in the
field, a great change in their mode of going on since first our
officers took them in hand. They were fine young men to outward
appearances and steady under arms, and it is at present much
the fashion to speak well of their conduct in face of the enemy.

The encouragement they have indeed met with from us in good food and clothing, and protection from the mean exactions of their own officers, ought well to call for such an improvement in both their appearance and behaviour.

The state of inactivity I have mentioned proceeds from three causes:— *in primo*: that of Mr. Masséna. Secondly: the position of my cantonment, which is so much at present retired from what is intended as our fighting arc; and thirdly: the activity and stirring disposition of my Chief of Dvn. (Picton) which leaves little for others to do. I think him however a fine manly character, consistent with his mode of carrying on duty, which by some however (not myself) may be thought rather severe, and cheerful and gentlemanlike in his conversation, so that I am altogether very well satisfied in being with him. He and his family,* consisting of three more, and my old friend Burton, making a party of eight, dine with me today, being however two more than I generally attempt to provide for. Six I have most days, getting that way acquainted with my Brigade. The King provides good soup and *bouillé*, and poultry has not yet failed, and at reasonable prices at least to what I have been used to; well fed geese at a dollar, and turkeys something under that. In addition, wine of a very tolerable quality at not perhaps above a shilling a bottle.

November 10th, 1810

My last which mentioned my not having yet been introduced to the Commander of the Forces had hardly left the house when I received an invitation to dine with him that day at 6 o'clock eight miles off, which it took me three hours to accomplish, nearly wet through, losing my way and arriving when dinner was half over with the comfort of returning the same distance after it to my quarters. However, it was gratifying to make the acquaintance I then did, among the rest the Marquis de la Romana, Carriera and the younger O'Donnell, the three Spanish Generals who have joined us with about 5,000 troops in, I understand, a very bad condition as to officers and equipment. It is said, I think, in Spain that their cooperation was necessary for our salvation from the French, but I believe their real motive is to keep out of the way of mischief, being in our rear much safer than when depending entirely upon themselves, and where they will be no longer liable to attacks which

---

* In the eighteenth and early nineteenth centuries a general's personal staff was colloquially called his 'family'.

hitherto they have thought only how to run away from. From this you will understand that my gratification in meeting this chieftain was entirely that of curiosity. His character, appearance, manners and conversation are uninteresting. Indeed his looks would be called even mean were it not for an evident wish to please and be affable, speaking English and entering into our ways as well as he can.

I must mention an anecdote of my science in painting. I asked Lord Wellington if a picture hanging in his eating room was not a portrait of our Queen Anne; he allowed that it seemed to be so, but we were corrected by a Portuguese officer present who declared it to be the Empress Queen of Hungary, as the name written in the corner would prove. I then asked leave to rise from table for nearer inspection, and behold I found the 'George' pendant to the blue ribbon that I had before observed about the neck. Thus were all the other portraits equally misnomered. I remember a beautiful original of this picture at Windsor.

The papers will no doubt give a detailed account of the entertainment given by Lord Wellington at the united palace and convent of Mafra upon the investiture of Marshal Beresford with the Red Ribbon. The ceremony itself was far from grand or imposing, consisting of nothing more than the reading (inarticulate enough) of two short papers by his Lordship, and his laying his sword on the new Knight's shoulder, when indeed the difficulty he found in returning it to the scabbard struck myself (if it did no others) with a kind of characteristic reference to his imputed love of war, which however I hope he no further possesses than under the conviction that, in its perfection of science and of valour, it is the firmest supporter of peace and tranquillity.

The best performed part of the ceremony was the graceful introduction and subsequent salutation of the new Knight by Sir Brent Spencer. I always thought his manner as good and modest in the drawing room as energetic in the field, and his intercourse with courts and camps since I have seen much of him have not caused him to fall off in either. This took place in the grand audience chamber where, and in an adjoining drawing room, a downright crowd were jammed in from five o'clock (the hour appointed for dinner) till near eight, when numbers composed of juniors of the Allied Army, who had only been invited for the evening party, thought they might as well also partake of what was going on, and a general rush took place into the dining rooms where very elegant and plentiful provision had been made for 200, but which stood no chance with double that number, so that in fact our noble host was stopt short in a round of appropriate toasts that he had commenced by a message from his aide de camp that there was not another drop of wine to be had. He got rid of that awkward circumstance by an admirable ruse de guerre, which both concealed the deficiency and punished the intruders: for calling all his aides de camp suddenly and rather ostentatiously, he instructed them to go round and to order all the officers to their post as the enemy were indicating an attack. The seniors, however, were directed to remain till they received their orders which, when the young ones were clearly off, was understood to be only to remain to supper. This droll circumstance caused much merriment during the rest of the evening. The squeeze indeed had been very unmannerly; I thought I should have lost my hat, but came off only minus a sword knot. My aide de camp lost his spur. I was glad to get a chair, civilly enough offered, between a Portuguese and a Surgeon's mate who, almost sitting upon my knee, observed as he shoved himself in that 'there was lots of room'. With due patience I got a plate of pigs' head stewed and some half raw ham which, with some sweet biscuits, made my dinner. I drank the King's health in wine and water that I had mixed in my tumbler. However there was perhaps more fun in this than would have attended a better bred but more formal party. A few couples stood up to dance in the evening, the ladies, of course, from Lisbon, including Lady G. Berkeley and a few very tolerable looking Portuguese, and I understand there was another grand 'rhow' at supper; but having a three hours ride to perform I left them at eleven, the whole party being of course at their posts by daybreak, not knowing what other amusement Masséna, hearing of the fête, might have in store for us. Everything however passed off very quietly, and except at the outposts one would hardly suppose there was a Frenchman within fifty miles of us.

On the day Charles described the party at Mafra, Masséna, hoping to find more food further eastwards, gave the order for a retreat to Santarem. The movement took a week and was much aided by a fog, so that it was not until 15 November that Wellington discovered the French army had started to retire. He moved his divisions out of the lines in pursuit. However, the 3rd Division stayed behind at Torres Vedras itself, for it was believed that a force of 15,000 Frenchmen had moved to the northwards and a surprise attack could not be excluded. Charles reported the continued inactivity in letters to his father and brother throughout November and December. He was distressed to hear that King George III had now succumbed to another and, as it proved, ultimate attack of insanity.

Torres Vedras, Novr. 17th, 1810

The day before yesterday, just as I was mounting my horse to ride some miles distance to overlook the removal of a glazed sash or two from the unfinished royal palace of Runa to place in the house I was then inhabiting, where I had only the choice, in bad weather and when necessary to shut doors and wooden windows, of sitting by lamp light or almost in darkness, I learnt that the French had moved off from their position in front of our lines early the preceding night. An hour and a half after I was in march for this place, about four miles from my former cantonments. Since then the troops collected here under Genl. Picton, consisting of his own British Divn. and Portuguese regulars to the amount of about ten thousand men, have not made any movements, but all the cavalry have advanced, tho' I fear there will be occasion to regret that this measure did not take place with all the promptitude it might.

Lord Wellington's Head Quarters were yesterday, I learn, at Alenquer which had been the principal position of Masséna. The Light Divn., which was on the right of our centre, I hear had moved on rapidly. Of the rest of the Army I don't know enough to hazard an account. Reports are, as hitherto, numerous and fluctuating, but I don't believe that my General of Divn. knows more of the real situation of the enemy at this moment or our Cmmdr. in Chief's arrangements. We are in readiness to march at half an hour's notice, but unless with a certainty of meeting the enemy I suppose the move will be rather backwards than forward as the scarcities must increase with our advance.

I have heard of stoves being had up from Lisbon by some of the General Staff, and among other measures General Picton had removed to my Quinta. He had certainly endured a great deal of inconvenience for the month he had inhabited his miserable dwelling, and the ruined one to which I removed was better adapted to my family than his more numerous one. With what I had done by force of manual labour, and was still employed in doing for it, I amused myself. My aide de camp took a pride in making the removal appear as little to be considered as the lot of the junior General as possible. When we had stopt up a few more air holes, I don't know that I should have much regretted the exchange. It showed some ingenuity to employ masons and carpenters with hardly any other tools than their fingers, but one of the greatest difficulties was to persuade my Portuguese landlord that in removing out of his house and stable waggon loads of dirt, or in the repairs I had made, I was doing him a service.

Torres Vedras, Novr. 28th, 1810

We have greatly the advantage of most of our brethren in arms, being all well housed and regularly victualled, when at least in the first particular the others must be badly off in this weather, it having rained every day since that on which the French moved off, at times very heavily so that the country has been in many parts as much flooded as it ever is; but some of the streams fall as quickly as they rise. We had a fortnight ago pear and other fruit trees in blow, as are yet different heaths, furze and other wild shrubs, but there is at this moment a villainous cold north-wester blowing enough to repel anything of a delicate kind. Such a day with rain is severely felt here, as it is only on horseback that one can take exercise enough to warm oneself. The Portuguese in making their streets or roads have never considered foot passengers, and even the fields, saturated as they are with wet, are with difficulty passed over on foot or horseback. Fireplaces, except in the kitchen, I have not seen since I came into Portugal. In this servants have an advantage compensating for others which we may enjoy over them, and which I hope they have reason and gratitude enough to remark upon to their own real solace and comfort.

I consider myself very fortunate in having as yet kept off my old enemy, the rheumatism, and which I endeavour to do by giving myself as copious a cold bath as I conveniently can manage the instant I get out of bed every morning.

We have not much to amuse ourselves with here, but the young men made out a small race course, and I should like more to vary the scene and go over greater range of country.

Torres Vedras, Decr. 11th & 12th, 1810

I noticed in my letter to my brother from Lisbon the curious costume into which the officers of this army had thrown themselves. Their precautions for keeping out the wet are more sensible and equally various in hat covers, shoe stirrups, pantaloons,

clogs, great-coats and cloaks of oiled silk, cloth—plain and pat-
terned—so that the only invention for the purpose which I have
not yet seen adopted by our officers is the thatched coat and
cap worn by the bullock drivers, an excellent covering, at least
for people on foot, but which has the appearance of so many
moving corn ricks.

The reinforcements Masséna has as yet received are conceived
of little consequence either in number or composition. In the
meantime Lord Wellington has commenced fortifying the heights
of Almada opposite to Lisbon. We have occasionally the mortification to hear of the success of the French on their marauding
parties owing to the superficial way, whatever was at first said
to the contrary, in which the country abandoned by the inhabitants had been previously driven. Near to Alcobaça, a few nights
since, they drove off 10,000 sheep and goats and an hundred
and fifty head of cattle. In like manner they, I believe, have
hitherto suffered little for want of grain; the poor villagers had
secreted it, no wonder, in holes cut in their mud floors, but
the French are too much used to this kind of thing and were
not to be impeded in their research by the monticules of dung
and filth of all sorts which cover not only the avenues but
the floor itself of a Portuguese cottage or farm house.

It would ill become me writing to one whose sentiments of
loyalty and respectful attachment to our venerable Monarch I
am so well acquainted with, were I not to offer my condolence
with your Lordship in the misfortunes which have unhappily
of late accumulated on His Majesty. The duration of his former
illness of similar nature exceeding what we yet here know of
his present one, leaves me yet to hope that while God grants
him life he may again be in possession of that without which
it cannot be desirable, either on his own account or for the
welfare of his own subjects or of those of foreign nations who
still look forward to Great Britain for their redemption from
disgrace and persecution.

The 3rd Division was in excellent health; but the 5th, stationed
at Alcoentre (some forty miles north of Lisbon) was not. Several
of its regiments had taken part in the ill-conducted expedition
to Walcheren in Holland and 'I am sorry to say they still retain
a tendency to the disease of that country'. So in December the
3rd exchanged places with the 5th. The march to Alcoentre, which
is in hilly country near the main Lisbon-Oporto road, lasted
two days over tracks 'in the worst state possible, so that those

29

who had travelled the most in Spain and Portugal declared that nothing for the short distance had equalled this in difficulty for man and beast'.

Our troubles were increased by our assistant Q.M.G. a very young gentleman, who it would seem had not made himself sufficiently acquainted with the route, and brought us by a would-be short cut instead of by the regular paved road. Disasters were numerous, some ridiculous enough to those who had only to look on at them, but not to those who lost their dinners or their bedding for the night by their mules upsetting or sticking fast in the mud, and not rejoining until a day or two after. I myself got off with the loss of nine out of a dozen fowls crushed to death, and was lucky enough, out of what I had managed to bring from that comparatively plentiful country, to save a couple of turkeys to grace the two great festivals of the Season.

Charles's Christmas festivities were interrupted by his having to participate in a court martial at Azambuja, a twelve-mile ride from his new headquarters. It assembled on 21st December and continued sitting on Christmas Day. It paid little attention to the Christmas spirit, for three men in British regiments and three belonging to the King's German Legion were convicted of desertion and all six were sentenced to receive a thousand lashes. Deserters were, for both sides, suppliers of useful military intelligence, and since the French, unlike the British, could count on no willing help from the local inhabitants, the deserters reaching them from the British lines were an invaluable asset. Thus no deterrent was deemed to be too harsh. The sentences were confirmed by Wellington and carried out.

Also before the court martial was a regimental surgeon who was tried on a charge of confining in the guard-room a Portuguese whom he accused of stealing a horse. He was found guilty and sentenced to be reprimanded, but was acquitted on a charge of conduct prejudicial to discipline and good order. Wellington, who had thought the sentences on the six deserters entirely proper, objected to the insufficiency of the sentence on the surgeon. He wrote to Charles to complain and then proceeded to issue an army order which included this sentence: 'The officers and soldiers of the army are again warned that they have no more right to confine in a Military Guard an inhabitant of Portugal than they would have the right to confine one of His Majesty's subjects in Great Britain, and he forbids the practice.'

As the new year, 1811, opened, the future course of military events was unpredictable. Masséna was under orders from Napoleon to drive the British out of Portugal, and he still had a superiority of men, munitions and material adequate to do so. The British faced the possibility of being obliged to fall back on the three formidable lines of Torres Vedras and of confining themselves, at least for some months, to defending Lisbon and their access to the sea.

If Masséna could keep his army supplied with food and shelter till the spring came, he might yet add a few more laurels to his well-adorned victor's crown. What he could not, in the event, surmount was the unrelenting hostility of the Portuguese people, a hostility which deprived his army of both security and supplies.

3

Portugal Liberated

On 4 January 1811 Charles wrote to his father of Masséna's uneasy situation and rapidly diminishing supplies.

At present, however, he makes a show of plenty, grazing about 500 head of cattle in the plain, this side of Santarem, and an impudent fellow, supposed to be an American, the occasional bearer of a flag of truce, said the other day that they were baking just enough bread to take them to Lisbon, to which the officer receiving him very properly replied that he apprehended a good many of them would lose their appetites before they arrived there. In case of their advance, everything denotes it to be Lord Wellington's intention to receive them in the position we occupied before our recent move.

Our army (as is also that of the enemy) are all well housed at present with the exception of our side of Santarem. Of doors, windows and everything else of wood, the French in their wantonness and the Allies, I am sorry to say, very frequently in their idleness, have made a most destructive havoc rather than take the trouble of cutting the pine of which there is plenty in these parts. We have consequently plenty of firing, a happy precaution against the damp of this and many other of our cantonments. At Azambugia in particular the proprietors (if they ever return) will hardly know their houses again from the comfortable fireplaces the English officers have contrived to make in them. In the house I now inhabit, I was fortunate to find one ready to my hand.

Beyond the Portuguese frontier, there was more activity than at Santarem. On 8 January the Spaniards failed to destroy the bridge over the River Guadiana at Merida, near Badajos, and the French were able to cross the flooded river. Charles expressed

the disillusionment with the Spanish army felt throughout Wellington's command, a sentiment matched by approval of the Portuguese
whose good performance was ascribed, with native British smugness
(and doubtless some justification), to their being led by British
officers.

The neglect by the Spaniards of the bridge of Merida, to
which his Lordship had particularly directed their attention, is
another instance of the great cause of complaint he has against
them, and of his great patience in being able to keep on any
terms with them. The corps of that nation now at Villa Franca
in our rear is a perfect nuisance, and tho' for policy's sake
Lord Wellington bedaubs them with praise in his Despatches,
he cannot but wish he was without them. His Lordship having
lately mentioned to O'Donnell, the Commander of their Infantry,
the frequent complaints of plunder and other misconduct by
his people, receives the answer (whatever the fool could have
meant by it) 'That the brave Spaniards knew not recrimination'.
Upon being requested by the Assistant Quarter Master General
to follow the example of the British and clean the place out,
if only for the prevention of disease, O'Donnell said that the
Spanish patriots were not made to become scavengers to the
filthy Portuguese. It can only be from civility to the British
that these last suffer them at all in the country. The bombastical
accounts of their opposition to the French, which have been
far too readily credited, made even me forget the days when
I was at Gibraltar during the war with Spain. Riding along
the sands, I used to come upon their sentries lying asleep on
the sandhills rolled up in their cloaks, and if I wanted to prolong
my gallop, I used to throw them half a dollar so soon as the
sound of my horses feet roused them from their recumbent
positions. I find them not improved either in conduct or appearance since then.

Their former history, as well as the recent improvements
in the Portuguese army, would make an improvement in their
army also appear probable. Unfortunately the officers are drawn
from a class of the population which must have miserably
degenerated since the bright days of Spanish history; besides
which in those days the military provinces of Italy contributed
greatly (in officers especially) to the splendour of the Spanish
name. In Spain the lower classes are less tractable than in Portugal
and the ill judging pride of their nation at large will not admit
of their being so exclusively under British discipline as is indis-

33

pensable if they are to be of any use when acting near us; so much for the Dons.

Since my last there has not been any movement of consequence in our army. Sir William Beresford has the command in Alentejo in the room of General Hill who, as well as several other Generals, have left or are leaving this country from ill-health or to attend to their Parliamentary interests. [In the years before the Reform Bill of 1832 it is notable how many professional soldiers contrived to combine military service with membership of the House of Commons, as a cursory glance at the biographical notes at the end of this book will amply demonstrate.] General Hill will be both missed and regretted.

On 25 January Charles wrote commenting on the death of the general commanding the Spanish troops:

The Marquis de Romana died two days ago at Cortaxo. He had a little illness before, but at the last went off so suddenly from a spasm that I understand that Lord Wellington was in his room at the time. The regard His Lordship entertained for him is the best proof of the Marquis's merits. Without being a man of talent, he was strictly honourable and patriotic, and was much looked up to by the loyal of his own nation. If the opinions he gave were not always good, at least the information he contributed was the best to be procured. His corps, to the great satisfaction of the British and Portuguese, had been sent a few days before across the Tagus to the frontier upon the advance of Mortier, who intends according to report to besiege Badajos. The French, so we heard yesterday, have lost their celebrated Junot; at all events we know him to have been wounded in the face by a carbine ball shot by one of our Hanoverian Hussars.

On the 19th inst. I received an express from the Commanding Officer of two squadrons of Cavalry posted at Rio Maior, ten miles or so in front of this, that the French were advancing with columns of Cavalry and Infantry, and that he expected they would be in half an hour in occupation of the town. This took place and part of their Cavalry even forded the river, which was low after several days of dry weather, and rode a couple of miles along it. They then retired and were followed by our dragoons who took such opportunities as offered of firing at them, and among others it is said that the promise by an Hanoverian Sergeant, who will, I hope, reap the reward of his zeal,

34

of a dollar to anyone who would shoot the French General occasioned the shot I have mentioned, the Hussar remaining behind his party and keeping concealed for the purpose. This was after their quitting the town. This force was pretty certainly known to amount to 8,000 men, with which not to have done more argued at least no very violent spirit of dash on their part. We had no Infantry at hand, but two companies of Cacadores who obeyed their orders to retire so soon as the determination of the enemy to pass the bridge was evident. A well posted battalion of Infantry might, had it happened to be there, have caused them infinite mischief. Junot, meeting his end in such a way, is consistent enough with his famous character, though he told Col. Murray at the capitulation of Cintra that he had given over the dash he had been celebrated for 'et qu'il ne sabreroit plus '.

Junot was not, in fact, killed, but he was incapacitated for the remainder of the campaign, and as for Romana, Wellington indeed regretted his death. He wrote with some exaggeration: 'Under existing circumstances his loss is the greatest which the cause could sustain, and I do not know how we can replace him.' Many years later Lord Ellesmere, who became a close friend of the Duke, recorded that he always spoke with affection and respect of Romana, but had no great opinion of his abilities.

The sally into Rio Maior was a short and isolated enterprise by Masséna, an outcome which Charles regretted.

Whether this advance had been merely for the purpose of reconnoitring, or whether it was for plunder, we do not know; the latter seems probable from the number of mules they brought with them, but took away equally light, there being nothing in store in the town. A visit to some salt pits in the neighbourhood is also given as a reason, while others say that they had heard of our having retired, a report which some appearances here had warranted. Whatever it was, they were disappointed, and as it customary with them hung their Portuguese informant.

We were, of course, upon the alert here, and I believe I may say that some of us were very sorry the French did not come on. The men were in the best of health and spirits, the weather fine, and the position a favourable one, the village being to a certain degree defensible. There is a bridge and causeway in its centre, a rivulet with steep banks covers its flanks for some distance, and immediately behind are commanding heights to which we could retire at our leisure. Our then left flank, by which we supposed the enemy would have continued their advance, was perfectly safe, while on the other side of the mountainous ridges on our right were the two other Brigades of the division who would have retired with us in parallel columns to a position to be halted or not as circumstances might have required. General Picton had drawn up a plan of operations which was so well understood that there could have been neither confusion nor risk, and everything was arranged so as to give the rest of the army time to retire in safety.

I should not be surprised, however, if the business of the other day alters in some measure the former determination of immediately taking up the retired position and that we shall not wait to see whether or not they bring up such a force as shall alone make it indispensable to take up stronger ground. Lord Wellington had been twice here reconnoitring and some works for Artillery, which we were without, are erecting. The Engineer in Chief thinks much more of the position than he at first did.

By 15 February, when he next wrote home from Alcoentre, there had still been no military activities of significance, but Charles was evidently having qualms about the potentially dangerous nature of the information he had been sending home.

My place of residence has become of greater importance since the strong reconnaissance made at Rio Maior on the 19th which cost Junot a broken nose. To avert any danger of surprise, the Commander of the forces has caused a good deal to be done to strengthen the position by batteries, abattis etc., so that our men, under the direction of the Engineers, have for the last three weeks been entirely given up to the spade, pick and felling axe. The appearance of the works is already very respectable, and they have this great advantage over those in rear that they have not cost the Government a farthing beyond the use of tools, whereas the others, upon which the peasantry were employed, have cost such sums that when the bill is presented to John Bull, as it will be one day or the other, it is certain to bring on an attack of the gout. He ought in reality to be thankful that his contributions avert from his own favoured isle all immediate danger of battle, famine, devastation of all kinds and disease to which the unfortunate people of this land are subject. I fear, however, that he thinks that what would be hard indeed for him might, when it happened to a Frenchman or a Portuguese, be good enough for the 'likes of they'. I cannot, however, after so severe a remark upon some of my countrymen, refrain from the pleasure of noticing the contrary feeling in others (perhaps improved by travel), when at this moment hundreds, I might say, thousands of the unfortunate peasantry are kept from starving by contributions from our soldiers' rations.

A letter of General Picton's descriptive of the battle of Busaco, with nothing but his name wanting to indicate by whom it had been written, has appeared in the papers, and though it is one of the best and most correct of the accounts, he is greatly annoyed at its publication. Several other provoking things of the kind have occurred: there is a letter attributed to the gentleman who is now my aide de camp, and another fixed upon a Captain of Grenadiers in my Brigade. I am sure my friends will not take amiss, if I ask them to exercise the greatest care in dealing with my letters.

Owing most probably to their confidence in their Chief, I never knew an army so little given to reports of intended operations etc. as this, and we hardly hear a conjecture even of what is to be done when we are re-inforced. Our army has at no period been so effective in this country as at this moment. Sickness during the winter (a very unusual thing) more attacked the officers than private men, and it is an easier thing to cure the former, though I am sorry to say many valuable officers have fallen within these few months. For my own part, I never was better.

Lord Wellington is seeing his army by Divisions, which gives us a little bustle. I believe he will see ours the day after tomorrow. A good many of the British brigades have established kitchens and other modes for feeding such of the Portuguese poor as for want of other refuge have preferred remaining among the hedges or other cover in our cantonments. The fund of my own Brigade proceeds from the heads, feet and insides of our fresh beef, with the exception of tongues and heart. Purchases of Indian wheat, corn and rice by subscription among the officers already gives ample relief to 120 people of all ages, and would do more had we better convenience for cooking.

The late Romana's corps, owing to their entire want of military conduct, have been nearly annihilated on the banks of the Guadiana in front of Badajos. For the ultimate fate of that place which is of great consequence from its depot of artillery etc. I have great fears.

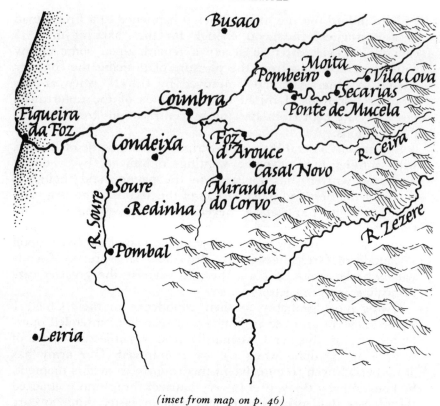

(inset from map on p. 46)

Fresh detachments arrived from England and Charles's brigade received the 2nd Battalion of the 88th Regiment. With these reinforcements Wellington proposed to attack unless Masséna withdrew; but starvation and lack of shelter was creating havoc among the French and they could hesitate no longer. On 3 March 1811 Masséna began to retreat northwards from Santarem and Tomar towards Coimbra and the River Mondego. Three days later Wellington's army set off in pursuit, the 3rd Division moving forward to Rio Maior and thence through rough, inhospitable country to Leiria. By the 11th they were at Pombal, close behind the French who had evacuated it the previous day. Marshal Ney, with the French 6th Corps, provided a rearguard, but he was unable to hold the bridge across the River Soure at Pombal. Masséna had hoped to cross the Mondego at Coimbra and stand fast in northern Portugal. However, when he reached the town of Condeixa, nine miles south of Coimbra, he decided to retire westwards towards the Spanish frontier. While relaxing at luncheon he was all but captured by a squadron of Wellington's Hussars. He escaped just in time, and Ney, after reducing Condeixa to ashes, took up a strong defensive position on the heights overlooking Casal Novo. The 3rd Division turned his flank and Ney withdrew, fighting all the way, until on 14 March he joined the main body of Masséna's army at Miranda do Corvo. There was no time for his men to rest. That very night Masséna set fire to Miranda and retired still further westwards, marching between the River Mondego and the mountains. He was forced to destroy much of his ammunition, stores and baggage to prevent their falling into British hands.

At 3.0 p.m. on the 14th, at the close of the action at Casal Novo, Charles found time to write this letter home:

> I take advantage of a halt of an hour, to give the other column time to come up in line with us, to say that, thus far, we have driven the French before us in fine style. Where to say I am, I cannot exactly do, but it is at the termination of a commanding ridge abreast of the Sierra Estrella on the way to Ponte de Mucela. The enemy have shown their abandonment of the last position they occupied by burning, as they always do, the villages as soon as they have no further use for them.
>
> In a village not two musket shots from where I now write they had for an hour or more 5,000 men at least, positioned up in a most crowded manner, but unluckily we had no Artillery to play on them. Shrapnel shells have, I understand, done their duty in other directions.
>
> We advanced this morning from the neighbourhood of Condeixa, from which place we had yesterday hurried out, it is said, their whole collected army by the move of the 3rd Division (by order of Lord W.) over a mountainous road they could hardly have thought we would have undertaken, and which alarmed them for their left flank. This was done without explosives on our part. This day we have also, as on the 12th in forcing the position of Redinha, had the right of the army and have, I think, done our business well. General Picton, I am perfectly satisfied with. The Division with the exception of the Light Battalion has given hardly any fire, but we have been a good deal under that of the enemy without, I am happy to say, any great loss.

Charles never ceased to like and respect Picton, a rich, eccentric and hot-tempered Welshman, twelve years older than himself, who usually rode into battle wearing a top hat. Wellington was not among Picton's greatest admirers and seldom gave him the praise that was his due; but he acknowledged his ability and forthright character. When one of the commissaries responsible for the army's food supplies complained that Picton had threatened to hang him, Wellington replied: 'Did he? Then I advise you to take care; for he is quite the man to do it.'

Picton was renowned for his personal courage which had first attracted attention, at an early stage in his military career, during the seizure of St. Lucia from the French in 1796. He did not, however, suffer from the rashness which sometimes accompanies gallantry and he proved himself, in battle after battle, a shrewd tactician. He was often severe; indeed, when temporarily governing Trinidad, he allowed the use of torture in accordance with the Spanish laws still in force on that island. For this he was tried before the Court of King's Bench. He was acquitted, not only by the court but also by the islanders, who subscribed a gift of £5,000 to mark their esteem of his governorship. A year later Port of Spain was destroyed by fire and Picton gave back the £5,000 to the people of Trinidad as his contribution to the rebuilding of the town.

In the 3rd Division, which became known in the Peninsular Army as 'The Fighting Division', and rivalled the famous Light Division in its exploits, he was loved by his men both for his unorthodox habits and his open-handed generosity. After the capture of Badajos he gave every survivor in the Division a golden guinea; and some years later, when Charles was in danger of being adjudged personally liable for a considerable sum on the discovery of an ancient defalcation in the regiment he had commanded, Picton wrote to him: 'I am extremely concerned to hear of the loss you are likely to sustain by the rascally conduct of the Quarter Master of the 13th Regiment. If it should eventually expose you to any kind of inconvenience, I hope, my dear General, you will not use any ceremony with one who will have great happiness in meeting your wishes on every occasion.'

Rough and outspoken in anger, Picton was affectionate as a friend and as unswerving in his loyalty to those who served under him as he was to his king and country. His martial distinction was not, like that of several other Peninsular generals, recognised by a peerage. This may have been because as a Member of Parliament he was inclined to take a line as independent as he sometimes did on the field of battle. Thus on one occasion he wrote to Charles: 'I believe those in power are not very solicitous of my attendance in the House as they find I am not *much* to be depended upon, and I shall not go out of what I conceive the right road to conciliate their favour.'

Posterity made amends for the tardiness with which the British Government rewarded Picton's merits. Severely wounded at Quatre Bras in 1815, he bandaged his own wound and with gangrene already apparent insisted on leading his men into action at Waterloo two days later. He was killed as his division charged the retreating French columns. He became in consequence a popular hero and a monument to his fame was eventually erected in St. Paul's Cathedral. Charles was his favourite and most trusted brigade commander while he served under him in the 3rd Division. So their friendship and mutual regard are of significance to this story.

The pursuit from Santarem had been hot and provisions were left far behind. The French crossed river after river in their flight. Bridges were destroyed and the River Ceira was in flood. On 16 March Wellington called a brief halt. On the 17th they were off again in two columns, one, including Charles's brigade, marching eastwards over a mountain track to the upper Alva river at Pombeiro, the other forcing Ney to evacuate Ponte de Mucela and retire hurriedly along the road to Moita. That village was soon occupied by the British, who captured large numbers of stragglers, and the 3rd Division then marched up the River Alva from Pombeiro to Secarias, bivouacking there on 19 March to await its slower-moving supplies. This gave Charles an opportunity to write the following letter:

Two hours after I had closed my letter of the 14th I posted my pickets in the village and found it the most intricate place I ever saw, and the most difficult for troops to file through. We had watched the French as they passed through it, and crossed it in various directions, and could see that those who had to wait their turn seemed to be sitting in the most woeful suspense.

Lord Wellington was unluckily not at hand, and no movement on this side could be made by General Picton without risk of breaking through the general combination. As I mentioned before, had the Artillery been up, we could have either made prisoners of the whole 5 or 6,000 men or have killed or wounded by our shrapnel one in five of them.

All continues to go on swimmingly. On blowing up the bridge at Foz d'Arouce on the Ceira two mornings ago on some sudden panic, they left on our side one of the three battalions which had been left to guard it. Of these, a great number were drowned in attempting to ford over. Major Dunn of the 2nd Batt. 88th assures me that on his march to join my Brigade, which he did that evening, he counted 50 bodies which had been fished up from a hole by the peasants, one of them a Colonel with a belt containing 150 doubloons about him, a treasure that perhaps caused his loss of life.

I heard that 600 prisoners were made yesterday without a shot fired, and a large proportion on the previous day, much in the same way, that is by the cavalry, and mostly, I understand, from the parties that have been detached for provisions and plunder or have sunk under fatigue. Their wounded, it is said, are provided for in a much safer way, that is shut up and burnt in the towns and villages which they have almost without exception consigned to the flames the moment they depart from them. When such is their conduct to their own people you may readily suppose what it has been to the unfortunate Portuguese.

The horror-fancying imagination of Monk Lewis* could not invent anything beyond it, so it suffices at present to say that the French army, beginning with Masséna, have totally forgotten that they have any claim to the title of human beings. The original orders of the General en Chef were found the day we marched through Leiria for detaching an officer and twenty men to burn the magnificent Abbey of Alcobaca. The walls and towers of Batalha, one of the noblest Gothical piles in the world, remain. I thought, as I surveyed them, I saw the grin of vexation on the Tiger's countenance that their ravages must be confined to the more fragile finds, monuments, altars, organs, etc., of the interior. All these are now confounded and mixed with the bones and dust of the Portuguese Kings and heroes of the Royal family who were alone entombed there, and without treading on which I could not walk along to obtain a sight of the building. By some accident, they have left behind King John II, who is besides a Saint. He is sitting, poor man, in a totally naked state in a cloister and might be mistaken for the ill-stuffed skin of a baboon.

My Brigade now consists of the 2nd Batts. of the 5th, 83rd and 88th, and the 1st Batt. 94th Regiment, and is a very effective and good one, though none of the Battalions exceed 500. Of

* This writer of blood-curdling plays was a member of the Holland House set. He was described by one of them as 'having a comic face and a horrid imagination'.

the three first, I have had 60 killed and wounded in the three affairs we have taken part in, that of Redinha on the 12th, which as a field day would be thought one of the finest sights possible; that of the 14th when we advanced from Condeixa, and which was also of an inspiriting animated nature; and that in front of the Foz d'Arouce, which for the part, at least, the 3rd Division took in it, to the right of the Light one, was of a more disagreeable species of warfare, the enemy hardly showing out of the woods which covered their main body, while as customary they kept constantly increasing their Tirailleurs.

We hope to seize Guarda, but at all events that the country beyond the Mondego is secure must be admitted a great point in England and Portugal.

The atrocities committed by the French armies in both Spain and Portugal during the Peninsular War equal those committed by the S.S. and the Gestapo 130 years later. In Spain their horror, and the revenge taken by the guerillas, can be glimpsed from Goya's drawings. In Portugal the hunt for hidden food included measures such as suspending a peasant woman and her children over a fire in the hope of extracting information where supplies might be hidden. The Portuguese peasants retaliated in kind, burning wounded Frenchmen in straw and crucifying others on the doors of houses. There was chivalry between the soldiers on either side; there were flags of truce and exchanges of newspapers. Indeed the French General Foy was constantly sending flags of truce for the sole purpose of obtaining the English papers, and when Wellington asked why he wanted them, the reply came that he had been speculating in the English funds and was anxious about the price of Consols. Doubtless he also found the English newspapers a useful source of intelligence, old though they must have been by the time they reached him. But whatever the courtesies shown by the opposing armies, between the French troops and the persecuted peasantry there developed a savagery unparalleled since the Dark Ages.

Masséna, with two corps at Celorico and one in Guarda, was now in touch with his supply bases at Ciudad Rodrigo and Almeida. However, he feared that re-entry into Spain, when he had been ordered to sweep the British army in Portugal into the sea, would anger Napoleon. So he decided to march south-east by Sabugal and Penamacor to the valley of the Tagus. His army was in a deplorable state: short of transport, lacking powder magazines, and heading for country devoid of food supplies. Ney objected to the plan and announced that he would march his corps to the strong fortress of Almeida. Masséna removed him from his command. But though insubordinate, Ney was undoubtedly right in believing that a southward march would be suicidal. In the end Masséna, after concentrating two of his corps at Sabugal, changed direction for Ciudad Rodrigo. The British occupied Celorico and set about the task of capturing Guarda, the 3rd Division moving across the mountains to Linhares while their artillery followed by road. On 27 March they halted at the village of Misarella, a few miles from Guarda.

The French did not stand and fight and thus, on 30 March, Charles was able to write from Guarda itself:

The operations of yesterday in this immediate neighbourhood have, I fancy, put an end to the campaign in this quarter successfully as to the great object, though perhaps not altogether to the satisfaction of John Bull or of his no less sanguine Ally.

In my last of the 20th, I mentioned my orders for a long march next day, but scarcity of provisions had by that time begun to be much felt by us, and our marches became of necessity shorter and our halts more frequent. My own route then became by Villa Cova, Torrozello, San Paio, Linhares; all in the mountains, and frequently walking three or four miles in the snowy part of the Estrella—to Misarella in a deep glen nearly at the head of the Val de Mondego, and one of the most romantic Alpine scenes possible, combining great fertility below with the boldest rocks, cataracts, picturesque bridges, fords, hills, etc. Being now within a league in a direct distance from Guarda, we came in contact again with the enemy; and their pickets, which were sent forward to reconnoitre our strength in the valley, made mine active for a time.

Lord W's information does not appear to have been very correct as to the strength of the enemy, but it was judged proper to hurry them as soon as possible out of the place, and in the hope of cutting off some of the detached parties assembling from different quarters previous to their departure. I have for the first time had something of a superior command, my Brigade alone advancing in front, while General Picton with the other two Brigades of the Division crossed the mountains to my right, and the 6th Division advanced by the main road on my left, supported by others on their left again. I was recommended to exercise caution and to wait in my final advance for the co-operation of the other corps, as the only troops of the enemy

44

known of a certainty were in a village called Cabo on my immediate front. After waiting accordingly a long time for the 6th
Division, respecting whose order of march it appears there had
been some mistake, I advanced close to their pickets strongly
distributed amongst rocks, but tantalised them by showing only
a few of my Light Infantry.

Their attention seemed totally occupied by us while, on the
contrary, I had the satisfaction of at last seeing General Picton
moving on and threatening their rear. I, then, giving him a
good time to do so, and having formed my people for the
attack and deployed out of their sight, threw the Light Infantry
rapidly forward, but the French by that time, having become
aware of their situation, retired with precipitation without firing
a shot, nor was one fired in the course of the day, except
in the subsequent pursuit by the Cavalry in the plain after
they had wholly withdrawn from their positions. This was another
very handsome Field Day to look at, but an unlucky one owing
to the late arrival of the troops on the left who, had they been
up in time, might have caused the enemy very great loss. As
it was we had the mortification on reaching the heights on
which the town stands to see them get clear off to the amount
of from 16 to 20,000 men (from 3 to 4,000 had been in my
front) but in great confusion, with baggage, cattle, etc. all inter-
mixed. They, in fact, seem to have been panic-struck and may
almost be said to have made a shameful retreat from not more
than a third of their numbers.

Marshal Masséna, who had lately commanded the rear himself,
since he sent away Marshal Ney under arrest (it is said that
the latter remonstrated against his atrocities), had told his people
he should not march before this day at the earliest and ordered
a general forage which has cost him the loss of a great many
stragglers.

[Guarda], March 31st

The 3rd Division, and Queens and 36th Regiment had alone
been left here, and we in expectation, or rather hopes, of being
shortly removed to more comfortable quarters had in the meantime set to work to clear out this Augean stable, but I have
to my great satisfaction just received intimation of the march
of the Division tomorrow in the direction of Sabugal. Whether
there are any of the enemy left in that neighbourhood or merely
to occupy the frontier, I know not. At all events, I am heartily
glad of the move. I had got a good house, but the situation

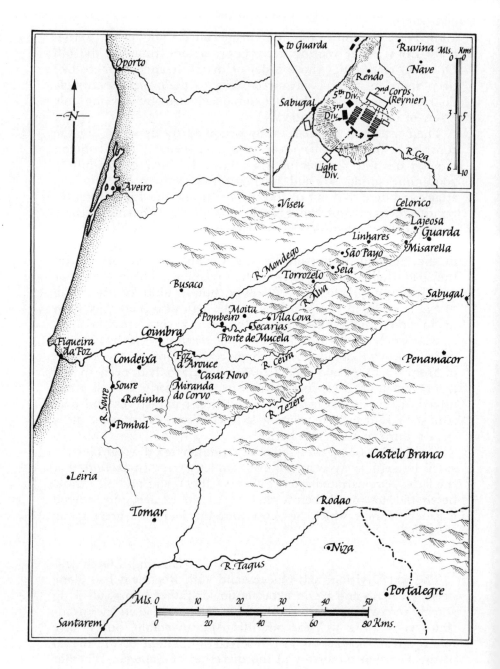

Masséna's Retreat

is cold and bleak to a degree, with scarcity of fuel and nothing eatable or drinkable but water for man or beast within many miles. The season seems two months more backward than I saw it ten miles off. Lord W's despatches to the Portuguese Secretary of State of the 14th and 16th inst. have just reached us in the Lisbon paper. They are not as correct as they might be made. I have (it seems) to be thankful to His Lordship for the introduction of my name in a manner gratifying enough, being the only one so particularised not in command of a Division.

Masséna's misadventures in Portugal ended with an engagement on the River Coa at Sabugal, where Charles distinguished himself. All three French corps were drawn up to defend the town and Wellington decided to attack on 3 April. Dawn broke with a thick fog which lasted well into the morning. Being unable to see anything, the commanders of the 3rd and 5th Division, which were to spearhead the assault, wisely awaited further instructions. However, General Erskine, in temporary command of the Light Division, launched one of his brigades across the river into the fog. This solitary brigade became embroiled with the entire French 2nd Corps and, but for the leadership of the Brigadier and the remarkable fighting qualities of his men, it must have been annihilated. In the nick of time the fog lifted and the 3rd Division, crossing the river, charged the heights to the left of the French General Reynier's Corps. Napier, in his history of the Peninsular War, records that 'General Colville, emerging from the woods on Reynier's right with the leading brigade of the 3rd Division opened fire on that side which instantly decided the fate of the day.' Wellington expressed himself highly delighted with the conduct of the troops; and Masséna had no alternative but to brave Napoleon's wrath and lead his battered army over the frontier into Spain. During his Portuguese campaign his army of 70,000 men had suffered 30,000 casualties.

Charles was gratified, but his pleasure was damped by the news that his eighty-seven-year-old father, the veteran of Fontenoy and Culloden, had died in March. His Division marched to the Portuguese frontier village of Alemadilla where, on 9 April, he wrote this letter to his brother John, the new Lord Colville of Culross:

I halted in this small village yesterday, and twenty times wished to sit down to write to you, and as often felt something that made me postpone it. I was called upon early this morning with an order of march for another village called Nove d'Aver,

47

four or five miles off and on the road to Almeida, the possession
of which will, I suppose, for the present complete our operation.
The French have at present three Regiments in the place, but
whether they will continue them in it upon our approach is
yet to be learnt. We have no battering train. Ciudad Rodrigo,
about five leagues from this, is also garrisoned, but I don't
suppose Lord W. will attempt anything in Spain till he is assured
of more cordial co-operation from the Spaniards themselves.
I think the hanging of the late Governor of Badajos, and the
General who commanded in the expedition from Cadiz, should
be the *sine qua non* of our further support. You will be glad
to see that His Lordship in his public despatches to the Portuguese Secretary has thrown off his former reserve in speaking
of the Spaniards as they deserve.

In my last I mentioned our intended advance in the direction
of Sabugal. This was attended with more important consequences
than we hoped for, and gave some brilliancy to the termination
of the chase we have been so long upon. Leaving it for the
present for Lord W's despatches more fully to describe the
affair, I shall only give you the satisfaction to know from myself
that my share in it, for the nature of the thing, was as gratifying
as either you or I could wish it, having by the opportune arrival
of my Brigade column, and rapid deployment of the leading
Battn., the 2nd of the 5th Regt. and their immediate and close
fire, repulsed and forced to retire the enemy, who at the moment
had done the same by the Light Infantry of our own Division
and hardly pressed the Light Division after a long and most
gallant (I believe in numbers unequal) conflict. The affair does
not come under the class of battles, or even actions of the
more distinguished sort, but in it as well as the others which
have occurred in the Campaign, my Brigade and Division with
which one naturally associates oneself, have fortunately had a
conspicuous share in which they appear to have acquitted themselves to general satisfaction. This makes up to me in my feeling
for previous disappointment which I have confided to you. Our
satisfaction would have been more complete, could our dear
Father have heard of the present success of his own General,
but it is still most sweet to me in my conviction of its being
so to the friends who yet remain to me.

While Masséna was losing his reputation in Portugal, Marshal
Soult had been effectively disposing of organised resistance in
the south of Spain. Andalusia, apart from Cadiz, was under his

control. The Spaniards failed to destroy any bridges across the rivers and Soult, joined by Marshal Mortier, was ordered to march to Masséna's aid. This he was about to do when Sir Thomas Graham made a sortie from Cadiz and threatened Seville. Soult was therefore delayed in his intended move to the north. However, the French captured Olivenza and on 11 March Badajos capitulated through the treachery of the Spanish Commander. His name was Imaz and it was he whom Charles would have liked to see hanged. then, on 21 March, the Portuguese town of Campo Maior fell to Mortier and Alburquerque, over the frontier in Spain, surrendered without offering resistance.

What the French did not know was that Beresford was advancing south of the Tagus with a strong Anglo-Portuguese force. On 25 March he drove the French garrison out of Campo Maior and Alburquerque was retaken. Having crossed the frontier into Spain, Beresford sent a division to capture Olivenza and by 11 April was at Albuera. The Portuguese campaign was over: the struggle for Spain was about to begin.

4

Tom Tiddler's Ground

Though the French never again ventured deep into Portuguese territory, the next eight months of 1811 were spent in a tantalising series of forays, excursions and occasional battles, Wellington alternately advancing into Spain and then withdrawing to the strong points he had established on the Portuguese side of the frontier.

During the last fortnight of April, Charles found Spanish living conditions an improvement, at least in some respects, on those to which he had grown accustomed in Portugal. In writing to his brother he commented on

> the variety from the Portuguese hovels to which we had been lately used, their customary filth rendered much worse by the recent wretchedness of the proprietors, the change to good weather, a pretty enough country, and the cheerful, civil manners of the poor people upon whom we were quartered: all this made me quite pleased with the change, and I was going on as fast in learning Spanish from my landlord, the Padre Vicar, as possible from an instructor who had only the one language to form his own ideas of another upon, and was consequently not very indulgent upon pronunciation etc. Our visit has turned out an unlucky one to these poor people. We paid them at a most exorbitant rate for whatever little thing they could spare us, while they had before been used to supply provisions upon *réquisition* to the French, but at the very moment they were selling us bread of one half peze at a shilling a pound, they were baking and concealing it in quantity to purchase the favour of these same people whom they had but too good reason to expect back again. In this, by the by, they showed that intercourse with those wordly reformists had a good deal changed the simplicity of manner the writers of romance formerly attributed to them.

Among the civil population of a country overrun by foreign armies such an element of self-protection is not unreasonable. Wellington himself was the first to admit the debt he owed to the Spanish people, maddening and corrupt as their Government at Cadiz might be and hopelessly led as, with a few exceptions, their regular forces certainly were. Bonaparte had, Wellington calculated, from first to last 600,000 men in Spain, and he knew that at the end of the campaign only 100,000 returned to France. Even those, apart from the small French army in Catalonia, were forced to leave their cannon and baggage behind. A great proportion of the credit must, he wrote, 'be ascribed to the emnity of the people of Spain. I have known of not less than 380,000 men of the French Army in Spain at one moment and yet with no Authority beyond the Spot where they stood and their time passed and their force exhausted by the mere effort of obtaining Subsistence'.

There were Spaniards fighting on both sides, thousands of patriots aligning themselves with the Anglo-Portuguese army and a corps of collaborators fighting with the French. There were francophile cliques among the upper and middle classes in most of the cities and fortresses, notably Madrid, Badajos and Salamanca. But the support and surreptitious assistance of the peasantry could be counted on by Wellington, while their hatred was always a hazard for the French. Under guerilla leaders such as Mina, Longa and the fierce Don Julian Sanchez they were far more effective fighting allies than the ill-supplied regular armies which were routed again and again by the French.

There were Italians, too, on each side of the fence, and though the King's German Legion and the Brunswickers fought for King George, they were balanced by other Germans and by Polish lancers fighting for Napoleon. These foreign contingents, uncertain in their loyalties, were a source of anxiety, for they included potential deserters who were a treasure-trove of tactical information to both sides. Thus Wellington and the French Marshals forbade their employment on outpost duties. Only the Portuguese were solid in their attachment to the Allied cause; but they, like the Spaniards, suffered under a proud, corrupt and inefficient Regency Government which was equivalent in value to a whole French army corps in its harassment of both its own subjects and of Wellington personally.

Early in May, 1811, Masséna ventured out of Ciudad Rodrigo. The painful retreat from Portugal had both dislocated his plans and sapped his army's morale. His reason for moving now was a desperate anxiety to save face. There could be little doubt of

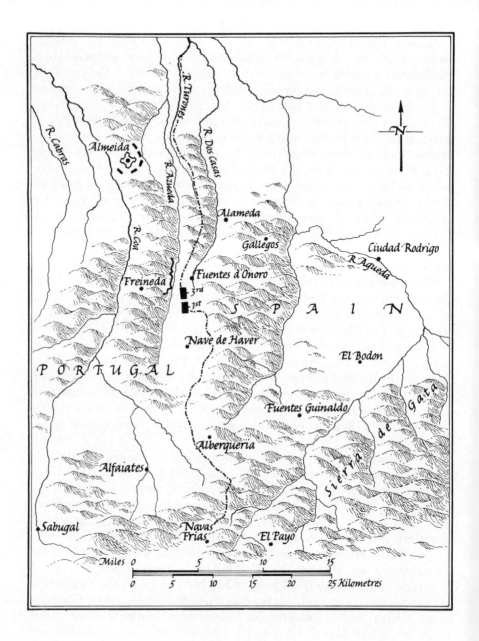

Fuentes d'Onoro

the indignation which Napoleon was feeling. Charles interpreted this surprising new French excursion as follows: ' Masséna's orders were to maintain the positions on the Coa and, should they have been forced, to maintain at all events Almeida and Ciudad Rodrigo to the last. The orders were evidently given in the idea that Masséna has possessed himself of Coimbra in the first instance. Their being, however, peremptory, it was necessary to do something; and waiting, as we suppose he may, further instructions when the true state of things is known, the French Commander returned upon us to see what could be done in the meantime, the greater part, if not the whole, of his exhausted cavalry exchanged for 1,500 perfectly fresh which had been collected for him by Bessières.' The result was the battle of Fuentes d'Onoro.

Wellington, who had been spending a fortnight in the Alentejo province in order to see how Beresford's divisions south of the Tagus were faring, returned just in time. His absence was criticised by Charles as 'an expedition beyond belief considering the business to be gone through', but by the time the French reached Fuentes d'Onoro, which lies a few miles south-west of Ciudad Rodrigo, right on the frontier, Wellington was back and in command again.

The British army was ensconced partly on the hills dominating the village and partly in Fuentes d'Onoro itself. One battalion of Charles's brigade was holding the village, jointly with two battalions of the 1st Division, when the attack began on the afternoon of 3 May. The fighting was severe, but the French were forced to withdraw. Masséna then tried to outflank the British, but Wellington forestalled him by wheeling his army round to face southwards between the two small rivers Turon and Dos Casas, while the safety of his left flank depended on holding Fuentes d'Onoro itself. In the event the village was nearly lost, for on 5 May the enemy attacked at two points in the line and in the early afternoon a French column passed right through Fuentes d'Onoro, gaining the heights behind it. However, one of the 3rd Division brigades, under Colonel McKinnon, counter-attacked and settled the day in favour of the British.

Charles devoted more space to describing the unfortunate demise of his horse than to his own battle experiences:

I myself was in the town on duty when the cannonade commenced, when and frequently else in the course of the day I have to be grateful for several hair breadth escapes which I will not omit to call providential. I have to regret, if such a thing is right, that in one of them I did not lose my 55

53

guinea horse upon which I was mounted during the day and who died the next of the staggers. In the one case I should have recovered nearly his price: as it is I do not get a farthing for him. It is remarkable that on alighting from him that day, I said to my servant 'there is a horse that as a sturdy charger is worth his weight in gold'. I think that I had never been better or more pleasantly carried by him than that day, and had not mounted him for three weeks before, having fagged him on the march.

I am under cover of a soldier's tent, which is more than many Generals have at present, and which good luck I owe to Col. Campbell of the 94th not allowing his brother, a Captain of the Regt., to pitch it when by rights it should have gone away with the baggage. You may be sure he shares of what is to be had in it, and is just gone away well blown out with as good soup and bouille and jugged hare as ever he ate in Scotland. You see I continue in some things to manage well, and a great comfort it is to be able to give a bellyful where it is so frequently needed.

Our own loss is, I fear, not much under 1,800. Poor Col. Cameron, son of the venerable chieftain, is I fear dead of his wounds. I left him within a pistol shot of where I am now writing on the morning of the 5th, after for some minutes sharing his dangers among shot and shell. He was in command of the town in perfect spirits and confidence as to retaining his post, and which were warranted by the consequences, as far at least as his command extended, but somebody gave way on the right (it is said the King's German Legion). At all events that side was the weakest, and upon the whole it was a gallant display of British spirit and discipline.

Meanwhile the enemy escaped from their surviving Portuguese stronghold at Almeida which the British were besieging. Wellington was enraged by the blunder which enabled the French garrison, after blowing up the fortress, to evade capture. He described it as 'the most disgraceful military event that has occurred to us'. Charles, too, lamented the episode:

The whole of the 7th having, contrary to expectation, passed off most quietly, we were surprised with the reports of a most extraordinary firing in the night from Almeida which most people judged to be the explosion of their works etc., but it turned out to be three rounds of great guns and musketry which they fired all round the fortress without hurting a man of our picquets. They were, it also afterwards appeared, answered by some unshotted guns from their hutted camp or bivouac of Alamada, opposite to the 6th Divn. on a height of the Dos Casas river which separated the greater part of the two armies. The red lights they fired were also, I am told, occasionally answered by others from us to confuse them. Similar signals were passing between the garrison and their army in the next two days, during which movements of retreat were observable in the latter, and on the morning of the 10th they were all off. They were followed shortly after by our cavalry and Light Divn. but without coming in contact. In the night between the 10th and 11th a similar noise to that of the 7th was heard, but in the morning the birds were found to have flown and, a message having unfortunately missed, which should have replaced in the Pass of Barba del Puerco the Regt. that was withdrawn during the advance of the enemy, 15 officers and 200 men are all that I yet hear have been recovered of the garrison, whose motto appears to have been 'sauve qui peut' over the fields and byways.

In the reduced state of my stud, I have not been able to ride over to Almeida, but I understand the destruction of the ordnance etc. has been more complete than that of the works themselves, and in the former we lose the means of undertaking the siege of Ciudad Rodrigo, had it even been before determined on, which I do not to a certainty know was, but think probable. One is difficulted to account for the explosions not having called the attention of the force immediately investing the place more particularly to it, and Genl. Pack who commanded has the character of a more than ordinarily zealous and alert officer. The circumstance is doubly vexatious in giving Masséna a handle to boast of the success of his advance, which however cost him at least 5,000 men.

When Masséna's last endeavour to restore his fortunes had failed, the one-time 'Darling Child of Victory' was recalled to Paris to face Napoleon's scathing displeasure. He was replaced by Marmont who, having no need of any immediate exploit to consolidate his reputation, moved the main body of the battered army to Salamanca to recuperate and reform. So, leaving three divisions of infantry, three brigades of cavalry and the Portuguese brigades to guard the crossings of the River Coa and keep a watchful eye on Ciudad Rodrigo, Wellington sent two of his best divisions, including the 3rd, south into the Estremadura province of Spain to reinforce the investment of Badajos, one of the most important Spanish frontier fortresses.

Before they reached their destination, Marshal Beresford, who had made little progress with the siege of Badajos, fought a battle at Albuera, south of the fortress, against Soult. It was one of the bloodiest battles of the war and one of the least decisive. Both sides lost heavily, the French rather more than the British, and neither gained any permanent advantage. It did, however, seem vital to take Badajos, which had been surrendered to the French in February through the treachery of the Spanish Commander. It was an exceptionally strong fortress with good natural defences as well as ancient walls of great height and thickness.

In a letter written from Campo Maior on 27 May, Charles described the march south with his usual disdain for the local inhabitants (although until now the suffering and the gallantry of the Portuguese had counteracted his British contempt for all foreigners):

My letter of the 13th, from Fuentes d'Onoro, would inform you of my expected march the next day for this place, and which we accomplished in 10 days without a halt: good marching, all things considered, being $37\frac{1}{2}$ leagues, or 17 miles a day on the average of four miles to the Portuguese league. Our route was by Alfaiates and Sabugal, formerly fortresses of considerable consequence for the defence of the borders, but now, especially the former, in addition to the ruined castle little but wretched hovels and made worse by the ravages of the two armies: for ours carry their scourge with them, tho' frequently, indeed as often as possible, counteracted by all that good discipline, and the more considerate habits of the officers over those of the troops, can do for the sufferers. This, aided by the generosity of the British Parliament and nation, will in a few years, I hope, efface every mark of the incursion of the modern Goths beyond the deep rooted impression of their wrong, which to the end of time must remain upon the hearts and minds of this nation. I have myself so bad an opinion of the Government and of the nobility and even gentry of the Kingdom, that I am convinced that in a year or two after the departure of the British, their army will be in as bad a state as ever, but the peasantry will never let another French army into Beira or Estremadura. The same mistrust of their Government would make me doubt the good to be expected for the real sufferers by the generous and munificent contributions I have alluded to, and in which I am borne out by the expressed mistrust of many of the Portuguese themselves, but that Lord Wellington, who has the same feeling, has the direction of the fund and seems to think himself in possession of the means of exercising its beneficial distribution.

Previously to crossing the Tagus by the Ferry of Villa Velha (the Bristol Hotwell cliffs on a grander scale), we passed through Penamacor, formerly a fortified place of great consequence and still of importance from its position, and a remarkable and picturesque feature in the rich and grand scenery underneath and around it. We also passed through Castel Branco, a Bishop's see; it stands high, but with the exception of a good episcopal palace and curious old-fashioned garden has little to recommend it. We had now, however, got into a country unvisited by the French since the first predatory excursion of Junot, but which is still held in sufficient remembrance and consequent abhorrence. We now, from Meimoa on, found the proprietors in general in their houses, but of the people alone would frequently have been better pleased to be without their company. Tho' civil in their way, the Portuguese are particularly vociferous, very filthy in their habits, and altogether, I think, very disagreeable people to live amongst. From the Tagus we came by Nisa, a good town, to Portalegre, one of the best cities, and most beautifully situated, in Portugal. I was quartered in the house of the Bishop and found him a liberal and well informed man as I am told the generality of their principal clergy are. Arronches was our next stage, a bad and now neglected piece of patchwork of modern upon ancient architecture with a tolerable town inclosed. On the 23rd we reached this place [Campo Maior] which has stood several sieges, the one the most to its honour that a few weeks since, and which, but for the behaviour they say of some militia from a distant quarter, would have been prolonged still further by the inhabitants and the Ardanenca, a kind of *local* militia (in their peasants' dresses) of the neighbourhood. The town is still a good one notwithstanding what it suffered during the bombardment and cannonade. As to the fortifications, a great deal of money and good work has been thrown away in addition to originally bad ones and a worse site. We found here the 7th Divn. who had preceded us on the march from the north, and who again left this two mornings ago to add to the investing force before Badajos which had latterly consisted of a Portuguese Divn alone, we ourselves expecting to follow tomorrow on the same duty.

57

I two days ago went to Elvas to see its celebrated fort of
La Lippe, the fortifications of the town itself being also very
respectable. It is at present Head Quarters, but with no other
British troops than the wounded, the long list of which you
are already acquainted with as well as the disastrous occasion
for it, for not otherwise are they in fact to be termed. The
greater loss and perhaps mismanagement (no! that is said to
be impossible) at Valverde than in front of St. Christopher's
causes the mention of the one to be almost sunk in that of
the other.

Charles's criticism of Beresford's conduct at Albuera (which
he called Valverde) was, in retrospect, unjust, but it reflected
the opinion prevalent in the British army at this time. He ended
his letter by expressing relief that General Hill had been chosen
to succeed Beresford, adding that 'the latter should never have
been taken from his immediate superintendence of the Portuguese
troops who, for want of it, have fallen off very much'.

St. Christopher's, to which he refers in his letter, was a fortress
on the northern side of the Guadiana river. It dominated Badajos
and whoever commanded the fortress also commanded the city.
Beresford had tried and failed to take it by storm and now it
was Wellington's turn to do the same.

On 28 May, the 3rd Division crossed the Guadiana and took
up its position for an attack on the castle in the town itself.
'I don't know', Charles wrote, 'whether the enemy will much
add to the heat or not, but that of the atmosphere is, I think,
nearly as great as ever I felt it. I hardly except the West Indies
(for many hours in the day), and but few only of the officers
have tents on an arid mountain side without a tree in sight except
some olives, which with us are sacred.'

Two assaults were intended. The 7th Division was allotted the
formidable task of assaulting Fort Christoval ('St. Christopher's')
on the right bank of the Guadiana, and the 3rd, on the other
bank, was directed against the castle. The preliminaries to the
assault were wearisome:

I have had two spells of 24 hours each in the trenches. I
shall have my third this evening because Generals of Divn.
do not share this duty, but Commanders of Brigades only, and
besides me there is one only of this rank viz. Genl. Hamilton.

Being the first siege by regular approach that I ever witnessed,
I am glad to be upon this; but otherwise it is a service of
no small discomfort, as you must either be exposed without

any cover at all to the almost incessant fire of shot and shells, or take what cover is offered behind the batteries or in the ditches, at best a partial one and especially for shells, and where in addition to the torrid heat by day and the dews of night, you are half suffocated between the dust kicked up by the afore named visitors and by the effluvia of three or four thousand men, half of them Portuguese, the filthiest nation upon earth. However, if I have but the satisfaction of informing you (as I trust I shall with whole bones) of the fall of Badajos, I shall think nothing of what inconvenience it has been individually to myself; for independently of the public advantage, I shall be fully compensated personally in a professional view by its practical exemplification of Vauban's system, and which like other arts and sciences is made more clear by actual occupation in it. The attack of my Divn. has been not upon that part which the French penetrated and have since carefully repaired and strengthened, but on very lofty and ancient walls: but though they look feeble they prove to be very tough, being formed of framework called 'tapia', against which our artillery, tho' equal to 26 pdrs. and 14 in number (besides two mortars and howitzers) have made but inconsiderable impression. Then our guns unfortunately are brass (a bad battering train), and being very old have so much windage that their direction is very uncertain. Our first parallel was made, as the engineers thought, at 550 yards, but on proof of our fire it turns out to be 800. Another parallel was therefore formed, 200 yards in advance, from which we fired all yesterday. From the appearance of the breach in St. Christopher we expected the storm to have been made last night, but it has not yet (1 p.m.) been attempted. Its fall is very desirable, especially as two flank guns, more than any others, annoy the right of our approaches. Dispatch is on every account important as French troops are on their march from the north to join Soult, when he will attempt at least to get off the garrison. The heat has been so great that I fear for the health of the troops. I have had the advantage of sharing with the commissariat the shade of a lofty building, a mile in the rear of the bivouac, an advantage which I duly appreciate and enjoy on the days I am off duty. My servants and horses are also best off of any in the investing army, being under a roof and only a quarter of a mile from the river.

As the hot June days of preparation wore on, Charles had plenty of time to continue writing letters. Indeed that quoted above was followed two days later by the following:

I went upon the duty of trenches again that evening and had but an unpleasant 24 hours of it, having in the first place the mortification to witness the failure of the assault made by the 7th Divn. on Fort St. Christopher's, which the beauty of the exhibition did not of course atone for. The fort is not half a mile from the right of our own trenches, the river which is between us being at this dry season about the breadth, in this part, of the Bath Avon in the broadest of Kingsmead Fields. The moon being only one day past the full, I saw the columns advance in apparently good order, and with rapidity, exactly at midnight under the musketry and some small shells from the fort itself, aided at times before and after the assault, as their position made them liable to it, by the fire of heavy shot and shell from Badajos and of the latter from the Tête de Pont, and of a new first opened battery at the end of the bridge on the town side. This was soon principally directed at the covering Brigade of light artillery, who returned it from their 9 pdrs. and howitzers very handsomely, and I was soon from this cross fire as well as that of the peasantry which, aimed high at the fort, came a long way in our direction, glad to retire a little from the river side where Capt. Spottiswoode and myself had taken our posts to witness the scene.

As our troops reached the crest of the glacis, a (but faint) Hurrah! was given when a fire of hand grenades was opened upon them from the interior of the fort, and kept up unceasingly and thickly, I suppose, a full quarter of an hour. I had never seen grenades used before, and hardly conceived their fire could be so well kept up, but it was smartly returned by our musketry, and perhaps too much so, to the neglect of the more useful weapon upon such occasions, the bayonet. After a time the fire seemed to proceed from our side alone, and my own idea was that the object had been attained and that this fire was only continued by the half frightened or disobedient, whom it is difficult to stop, especially at night. This seems confirmed by what I have since heard, that Lt. Foster of the Engineers with some small numbers of men had actually surmounted the breach. He, I fear, is since dead of the wound received, I understand, as he descended from it.

A period of nearly total silence in the neighbourhood of the fort had elapsed, and I was going to retire to my boat cloak, when the musketry recommenced sharply and with regret we saw it descend the hill.

On our side of the river things did not bear a much more

flattering appearance. The breach had hardly at all been added to in the last 24 hours, tho' the whole of our fire was directed almost exclusively to that object, but the guns turned out so bad that two alone were said to deserve the name, and when it was attempted to throw shells from the howitzers as shot, that they might burst in the rampart, they were found not to bear the quantity of powder necessary to carry them home. A new battery for five guns within 400 yards then constructing, and its approaches and communications, were also so much exposed that casualties were becoming numerous, a good deal owing to the direction that had been given them in the idea that Fort Christoval would have fallen two nights before, but which in fact continued to fire three guns smack in upon us as late as when I left the trenches yesterday evening. We, however, finished the battery in the night, and got in two guns and a howitzer from those more retired with which to keep doing something until the arrival of six *iron* guns, every hour expected from Lisbon.

Our trench miseries were not a little increased by the intense heat of the day, wind at south east. Among them must not be forgotten that one of 'Just as you have gone some little distance to the rear to take the gavel of a roofless house or the shade of a fig tree to eat your snack or take a nap under, up come some unnecessary servants or some more than usually respectful officer or sergeant, who soon betray the snug retreat of the General: and when two or three 24 pdrs. soon trundle by, as if to show what a good look out is kept'.

The much wished for guns have, I think, arrived to judge by the very much improved appearance of the breach as I see it (at this time, 2 p.m.) from my place of abode $2\frac{3}{4}$ miles from it, by calculation of sound. You will be glad to learn that the remaining fatigues of the siege are likely to be lessened for me by the addition of Col. McKinnon to the roster. McKinnon is a Colonel on our staff and commands the other British Brigade of our Dvn. He would have been put before perhaps to help us but for fear that the Portuguese Brigade and Corps should claim the same honour, which for many reasons it would not answer to allow them. The protraction of the siege beyond what was sanguinely expected pointed out, I suppose, to others that this help was necessary, but for my part I should have been as well pleased, having had so much of the fag, to continue it to the end in hope of proportionate credit. As it is, I take advantage of the complete day it gives me to myself, and by keeping out of the sun hope to be perfectly fresh again tomorrow evening for whatever more may be to be done. This General Hamilton is a very queer fish.

In a subsequent letter he summed up the reasons for the failure of the assault:

I am sorry to say that all our labours and now a considerable number of valuable lives have been thrown away upon Badejos, the siege of which is again converted into blockade. Advantage was yesterday taken of a three hours' suspense of hostilities to bury the dead and carry off the wounded of a second attempt upon St. Christoval, which I had witnessed the night before from the same spot I had the former one, and to commence upon the removal of the besieging apparatus. By this time I apprehend there is scarcely an article left in the trenches except what is wanted, also the two or three guns left in them for appearance sake to the last.

The ruins of the 'tapia' wall are now covered with soft black mould in which a man apparently would sink up to the chin, and deserters say that behind the breach itself is a solid rock which would take six months battering. The French Comman-dant, Philippon, is a Colonel of Engineers of celebrity, and seems to have left nothing undone that the defence of the place required. The breach of St. Christopher's had also, it is said, been well attended to, and its garrison appear, I can speak indeed as a spectator of it, of the greatest steadiness.

Reports are various as to the immediate causes of the failure, but I have always regretted that we did not from our side lay a couple of guns on the flank of the St. Christopher's breach, which would have assisted it and dismantled the guns I before mentioned as annoying our ideas so much. The victory we hope for in all humility will of course be followed by the surrender of this place, when the previous ill success will be sunk in the more important events, but I should be curious otherwise to hear what would be said of this want of knowledge of the proper points of attack of Badajos which had for six months been the Head Quarters of Lord W. I respect him too much not to regret his disappointment sincerely as well as that of his Chief Engineer, Col. Fletcher, an old acquaintance and very worthy man and good officer, much consulted by his Lordship. The fault has been our treating the place with too little respect, a thing the more extraordinary after the marked expression of his Lordship's displeasure at its surrender by the Spaniards after 40 days' open trenches during which the French lost 1,500 men.

It was time to leave Badajos. Soult was approaching with a force far outnumbering the British 3rd and 7th Divisions, and by remarkable exertions Marmont had reconstructed Masséna's beaten army so that by the beginning of June it was ready to take the field once again. On 17 June the 3rd Division recrossed the Guadiana and retired some ten miles to the Portuguese frontier towns of Elvas and Campo Maior. On the 20th Marshal Soult entered Badajos.

After two unsuccessful attempts to storm the fortress British pride, elated by victory after victory, was wounded. On 25 June Charles expressed the general disillusionment:

The second failure against Badajos must have been a great disappointment to our friends at home as to us, more immediately concerned in it, it was a most severe mortification. It was not however possible for Lord Wellington to conceive that the battering train of Elvas would prove so inefficient as it did, putting one in mind in fact of the arm of a giant in romance crippled by enchantment, or the sensation I have felt in a dream, when the charge of my fowling piece has proved harmless against the object it had struck. Various accounts are given for the ill success of the assaults on St. Christopher's. We had an active and intelligent enemy, who as early as possible in the night remedied in great part the injury done to the part of their work breached by day. But I do not think it was ever practicable. Unluckily its approach was too much exposed to the fire of the place (Badajos) to make the attempt on it advisable by day, and night attacks you know have many disadvantages. Our Engineers have learnt to hold old Moorish walls in more respect than they did, but were the attacks to be renewed I believe they would be on the same point, but taking the one upon the Castle of Badajos more to the left where the old works have had repairs of modern masonry, and against which Col. Fletcher says it was his intention the batteries should open. But a beginning having been made by the artillery elsewhere, Lord W. himself, I believe, did not wish it changed and the breach was the only object attended to. The batteries and approaches certainly did the Engineers great credit, as is proved by the small amount of our casualities.

He went on to mention, once again, the ineffectiveness of the old, inaccurate brass cannon supplied for the bombardment of the city. They were, it seems, artillery dating from the reign of King Philip II of Spain.

The full heat of summer began to be felt. Apart from cavalry patrols and skirmishes, the armies rested and the peasant farmers were provided with a much-needed respite. 'I should', Charles wrote from Campo Maior, 'be very sorry to abandon the harvests of this province, now reaping, without a sharp contest.' The Portuguese Government's neglect of its troops also aroused his indignation. He asserted that their commissariat was deplorably organised, that their sick were not cared for and that the Government 'even enforces the rejoining of deserters' instead, presumably, of shooting them or giving them a thousand lashes. He was also indignant when, 'observing upon the shameful state of rags the Portuguese infantry of the line are at present in, I was assured that the Government, being pressed for money due by them to their militia, had paid them with the cloth sent from England to clothe the regulars. In six months after the British leave Portugal their army will be as bad as ever, but I do not think that the peasantry of the middle and northern provinces will ever let the French or Spaniards in again.'

Charles was offended that his name was not mentioned in Wellington's despatch covering the recent fighting at Badajos. He was a brave soldier, but he was certainly not indifferent either to praise or to promotion. So he wrote privately to his brother, from whom he never concealed his inmost thoughts:

This is not the first time I have had to remark that in his public despatches his Lordship frequently gives as little satisfaction to individuals as he has lately done in his recommendations to the honorary promotions in his army, which have contented few and been a source of growl and complaint to many. In the despatch of the 13th June describing the operations before Badajos, you will, I am certain, be no less concerned than surprised at seeing honourable notice made of Major General Hamilton's name when my own is omitted, aware as you are of the duty being so equally taken between us, although the other does command a Divn. of Portuguese and in which account I suppose he was really included along with Picton and Houston, neither of whom were in much more danger during the siege than your Lordship in King Street. The instant I saw the omission, which was only yesterday (my horse at the door at the

64

time to go and make a bow of common compliment to his Lordship, and which was rewarded by an invitation to dine with him today ten miles off), I called on Genl. Picton with my request that he would explain to Lord W. my disappointment on the occasion, more particularly on your account who by my letter were acquainted with how I stood in regard to Genl. Hamilton. This he at first thought not altogether required from the loose nature of his Lordship's usual reports, but when coupled with the defective one in my case of the Sabugal action and other circumstances, he promised he would comply with my wish. I then requested he would make his Lordship acquainted, if he had not already done so, with my offer, originally made through himself, of commanding the party expected to make the assault on Badajos, but which on account of the similar claim of General Hamilton was in his, Genl. P's plan, allotted for the actual General of the day. Lord W. seems afterwards however to have himself allotted me that distinction, as in the plan settled by him for the storm, my Brigade with the light companies of the Divn. and I believe one Portuguese Battn. only, made the whole of the party. People don't always like to be told of their omissions, but I think his Lordship cannot be much displeased at the mention of a disappointment on so fair a subject of ambition. The circumstances must in the most favourable light appear a damper to those hopes which you from your partiality have ever, more than myself, entertained of any immediate favourable result to me from this campaign.

However, when shortly afterwards he dined with Wellington he had the good sense not to mention his disappointment:

I dined the day on which I last wrote with Lord W., the Portuguese Governor of Elvas, Leite, who spoke only his own language, being on his right and myself on his left. I had a great deal of interesting and unreserved conversation with him, a good deal about Badajos, but of my own affairs of course not a word.

The campaigning season was over. The armies, sweating under the summer sun in the same heavy cloth uniforms that were designed to protect them against the wet and cold of winter, retired into cantonments while Wellington made leisurely arrangements for the siege of Ciudad Rodrigo with the help of a new 'battering train' sent from England and the steady arrival of reinforcements.

Charles and his brigade settled for a few weeks' rest in the town of Castello Branco.

In August Wellington moved his headquarters northwards to Fuentes de Guinaldo, some fifteen miles west of his next objective, Ciudad Rodrigo, where he believed the French garrison to be running short of supplies. From a temporary bivouac at Albergaria, in the northern foothills of the Spanish Sierra da Gata, and only twelve miles south of Fuentes d'Onoro, Charles wrote to his brother on 13 August:

I hope you have by this got mine of the 17th ult., the day previous to our leaving Campo Maior for Castel Branco, which place we reached on the 24th by easy marching, and with the expectation of being stationary there for the remainder of the hot season, being however, notwithstanding the great height of its situation, a very hot place, badly off for water and other essentials to the comfort of ourselves and horses. We were not sorry when moved off on the 1st August further to the northward by the same route we pursued on our way down the country in May last. We at first thought this might be only for the purpose of an extension of cantonments for the better health of the troops and getting provisioned from the northern Provinces, but were soon overtaken by Head Qurs., tho' it was before pretty certain that Lord W. was to have gone for a month to Lisbon, if not to England; and the march of other Divns. denoted that some object of greater interest was in view.

It now appears that the Army of Portugal (Marmont's), having comfortably seated themselves in a plentiful country with Talavera for the Head Quarters, had set to work in establishing magazines and strengthening their communications between the north and centre of Spain by the valley of the Tagus. From this state of things his Lordship thought it fitting the enemy should be disturbed. The chord of the march on which we moved within the Sierra de Gata, that of the Penade Francia and an interior one of still greater height covered with snow, giving us so much the advantage in point of distance, some of us were sanguine enough to hope to be by this time in Salamanca, leaving the rear Divn. to invest, or if necessary carry on the siege of Ciudad Rodrigo. But many things conspire against such rapidity of movement as this would have required, and it seems problematical if any greater advantage from the movement will take place than the harassing of the enemy by the long march they must take after us and bringing them from a plentiful

66

into an impoverished country. Time however will show whether Marmont separated from Soult will be strong enough to meet us in the field.

Generally the weather has been not only dry but pleasantly cool after the scorchings we got in the Alentejo. But there has been here, as indeed in the climate of Portugal in general, too frequent and violent contrasts to be perfectly healthful, especially to people under bad cover. The thermometer under a tree at my front door yesterday morning at half past five was at 46, and at 4 in the afternoon, at the same place, at 81, and now at this moment, 2 p.m., at 85. I have myself, as have many of the officers, a small single canvas tent, and which, when we meet with trees to place them under, I find much more pleasant at this season than going into most of the quarters one gets in this side of Portugal. At least in Spain, the instant you passed the border, they improved in cleanliness, tho' it is seldom that more than a cottage offers for the accommodation of even the General Officer.

The French, too, were regrouping their forces and it became clear that Marmont would soon have the strength to lift the threat to Ciudad Rodrigo. On 24 September he did so, assembling 60,000 men in the plain near the fortress and preparing to attack the British. This was no surprise. Two days previously Wellington had already concentrated his divisions to meet the French advance, the 3rd Division being posted along a line of heights stretching from the Agueda river (on which Ciudad Rodrigo stands) to the village of El Bodon, which is six miles south of Ciudad Rodrigo and equidistant from Wellington's Headquarters at Fuentes Guinaldo. The road between the two passed through this sector of the British front and it was here that the brunt of the French attack fell.

It was described as 'the Affair near El Bodon', for it was not a full-scale battle. But it is notable in that after the British guns had been overrun by French cavalry and recaptured, on Wellington's direct orders, by the steady advance in line of the 'Fighting Fifth', Charles executed a six miles' withdrawal of his men in squares, a defensive formation on which the massive surges of French cavalry were unable to make the least impression. It was, in its small way, a foretaste of the squares versus the cavalry which was such a distinct feature of the Battle of Waterloo; and Wellington was sufficiently impressed to record that 'the conduct of Major General Colville was beyond all praise'. On 29 September,

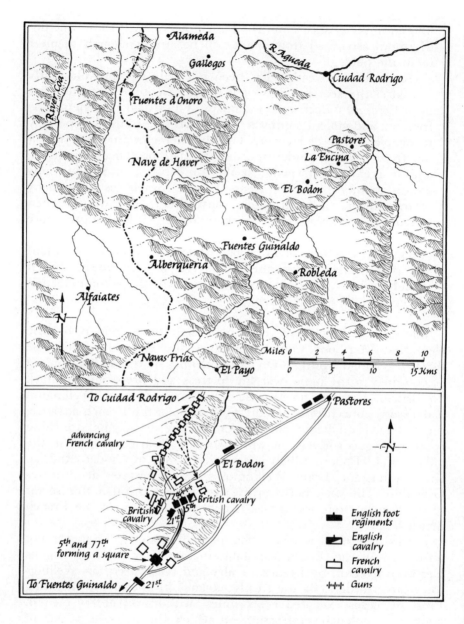

'The Affair at El Bodon'

after the British had retired to impregnable positions between the Coa and Azueda rivers, and Marmont, fearing to risk a frontal attack, had withdrawn his army to Plasencia, Charles sent home his own account of 'the Affair at El Bodon':

On the morning early of the 25th we had been under arms for precaution sake, but dismissed when I rode up to the spot occupied by our Portuguese Artillery (five 9 pdrs., three 5 inch and one 5½ inch howitzers) guarded by the 5th Regiment. Finding all quiet there, I rode along the ridge in front, over which a good road runs to the advanced post of our Cavalry about three miles off, when I perceived two French regiments of Cavalry moving to our left at Carpio. I also perceived the enemy passing the fords below and above Ciudad Rodrigo in great force. Making all despatch, I gave what directions were necessary to the 5th Regiment in passing, and went on to El Bodon to join the rest of the Brigade with whom discretionary orders had been left by General Picton to move to the right if the alarm should take place in that direction, he himself having gone to visit the Brigades at Encina and Pastores.

I found that the Brigade had moved and met them posted on an advantageous height at the head of a ravine which the enemy were then moving up in great force. Our Portuguese Brigade were nearly similarly posted on their left. I had just commenced the operations which I thought necessary when Lord Wellington arrived. It was a most fortunate moment for in that space of time he perceived the enemy were moving off to their right and he, after giving directions for the 77th and one Portuguese regiment to follow and join the 5th, galloped off at full speed. I followed as well as I could on Duchess, a good old creature.

His Lordship's first idea was that the enemy only meant a reconnaissance, but we soon found the contrary, for our measures of defence were not completed when the French Cavalry with dismounted sharpshooters advanced rapidly up the ridge, threatening us in front and on the right flank. Lord Wellington sent away the Portuguese regiment to a height on that flank some way retired, while I placed the 5th in rear of the nine pounders on the right and the 77th (the two only making 620 rank and file) in a position to support the nine pounders on the left, while five weak squadrons of the 11th Dragoons and 1st Hussars under General Alten occupied the centre. But the whole, with the exception of the Artillery, were retired under the slope of the hill to be out of sight of the enemy's six pieces.

I was in the middle of fixing points for the 77th to move up to when necessary, and while two of the 9 pdrs. were detaching to the right, when hearing a noise I turned round and saw, as I thought, Don Julian's guerrillas in the midst of the Artillery and the 5th advancing with ported arms against them. I flew to prevent (as I thought) mischief, but as soon found that they were advancing by Lord Wellington's orders against a body of French Dragoons and Polish Lancers who had most surprisingly got possession of the guns, but who, seeing the Infantry, could not be persuaded to advance further by their officers. They fled at our advance, and we soon got them down the hill again, peppering them smartly as they attempted the thing a second time.

Very shortly afterwards we saw a regiment of their regular cavalry to the left of our guns on the left. The 77th gave them a volley, which made them turn about in the greatest disorder, which our cavalry, who charged them vigorously, took full advantage of.

I have only time to say that after repeated attempts of the kind in which the British always shone with the greatest credit, a huge mass of Infantry was seen rapidly coming up the ridge. On this our Infantry were ordered to retire to Guinaldo. I formed my two battalions in column at quarter distance, ready to form square, and moved off. We were soon followed by our Cavalry, driven on at full speed by a great superiority of the enemy, who were so close to them that I much feared that the fire which we gave as the two bodies passed our square would involve in its effects friends as well as foes; but the men were cautious and no accident of that kind happened, while on the other hand we completely sickened such of the enemy as had been up with us, so that we were able to continue our retirement in safety, though frequently threatened and annoyed by their cannon. We marched sometimes in echelon of battalion squares and sometimes in line as the ground suited. My other two battalions joined us on the march.*

I have now but to add that Lord Wellington expressed himself in the highest terms of approbation of my two regiments, and

---

*In the *Dictionary of National Biography* the credit for this remarkable retreat in battalion squares is given to General Picton, as Commander of the 3rd Division; but it was in fact Charles who organised, supervised and participated in it.

if he is satisfied with their Major General, which I trust he is, I at the same time must be ever thankful that he was at hand to direct, as he did, the general movements which his uncommon quickness and experience enables him to do with such happy effects, and by his presence authorising measures of defence and of partial offence when without such authority retreat alone would have been justified.

When his brother, John, wrote to ask further details, Charles replied as follows:

What this new square is, which you and the papers mention, I know not, but none I think can be more expeditiously or safely formed than those practised by the 5th and 77th on the 25th Sept. They were so closely together that Lord Wellington thought they were in one.

The square is the Light Infantry or Sir John Moore's. The column marching in wheeling distance gets the order to form 'square' four deep, on which the leading company halts, the next moves up close to it, the remainder (with the exception of the last two who only close up), as they arrive at quarter distance, wheel outwards, two and two by sections, the rear then closing to the front. You are then four deep all round without any intervals, officers being all within the 'square'.

If men are only steady, no force of Cavalry can, I think, hurt the square, supposing it not at the time exposed to Artillery which it can hardly be at the moment of the enemy's making their immediate charge.

There was not only an efficacious, but to lookers on, a beautiful manoeuvre (not mentioned in the Despatch) when I fell in with the other two battalions of my Brigade; that of the retreat in echelon of battalion squares, each one supporting the other. That of the 83rd being formed from close column and not as the others were, which would have given it a larger area, received a shell which killed and wounded 23 people.

Some years later, Major Spottiswoode, who was one of Charles's A.D.C.s at the time, wrote the following account of the Affair:

I well remember being present with General Colville in his quarters at El Bodon, on the evening of the 24th of Sept. 1811, when it was notified to him that the 2nd Batt. of the 5th Regiment, instead of rejoining the Brigade that day, had been ordered to proceed from Fuentes Guinaldo to support the guns. I well remember the General's anxiety to communicate with his detached and I may say favourite battalion. His first care the following morning was to visit it. At daybreak I attended him and he went first to the hill where the Regiment was and afterwards to the front on the Rodrigo road. On our way we met the officer commanding at the post, who reported to the General that he had discovered the enemy coming on in force. We still rode forward until we could clearly see them advancing both from the fords of the Agueda and also from the bridge.

The General then hastened back to rejoin his brigade, and to give notice of what he had seen. On his way however he gave such defensive orders as appeared necessary.

The alarm had been given before the General reached El Bodon; and the officer commanding in his absence had moved the troops forward to defend the approaches to the town. It was for some time doubtful which way the enemy would come: but just at this moment, their column appeared to be moving directly towards El Bodon, and General Colville ordered me to bring one of the guns from the hill to enfilade the road.

I went thither and, having received a gun from the officer commanding the Artillery, I had not proceeded more than 50 or 60 yds with it, when Lord Wellington came up from the right, enquired whither I was taking the gun, and ordered it to stop where it was. After he had observed the movements of the enemy for a few minutes, he said, 'Ah! I thought so. They are coming up here. Bring back the gun' or words to that effect. I could then clearly distinguish that the head of the enemy's Column of Cavalry had turned off the El Bodon road to their right, along a ridge which led up directly towards us. The British cavalry were skirmishing and retiring before them; but they were still beyond the reach of our guns.

His Lordship bid me stay where I was, adding 'General Colville is bringing up more troops and will be here directly'. I remained on the hill until the final retreat. Before his Lordship left the ground, General Colville came up at full speed and received from him some directions relative to the defence. When the 77th Regt. arrived M. General Colville formed it across the Rodrigo road, and placed the 5th Regt. to its right, and behind the knoll where the guns were. The guns opened as soon as they could do so with effect, and the affair had continued some time before the enemy succeeded in taking them.

I was very near and an eyewitness to the charge of the 5th

Regt. in which the guns were retaken. The officer then commanding, the lamented Major Ridge, knew well his duty upon such
an occasion and to the present hour I recollect, with feelings
of unabated admiration, the decision with which he gave the
word of command and the spirits and energy with which he
led on his men.

There were some who believed that even with the winter months
approaching, Wellington would now again lay siege to Ciudad
Rodrigo, but a sizeable element of the French army was at Plasencia,
within comfortable range of interrupting a siege, and so the British
Divisions were ordered into winter quarters. On 8 October, Charles
wrote from the Spanish village of Navas Frias:

We had a rainy march on the 28th but it cleared in the
afternoon, and the troops were all I hope under some kind
of cover before the 3rd, 4th and 5th inst., when tremendous
storms of rain, wind and hail ushered in a most delightful contrast,
which we hope to enjoy for some weeks longer, and which
I make the most of in riding about the romantic forests and
mountainous scenery in which I am situated. My Brigade is
at present cantoned as much for cover as anything else in the
four towns of Payo, Navas Frias, Lajeosa and Fojos, the two
former Spanish, the latter Portuguese, and all poor places. We
are also intended to support the Cavalry who patrol to the
villages in front of the passes of the Sierra de Gata.
I had a laborious, more than a pleasing, ride yesterday in
visiting the two former, but the day before had my labour
well recompensed by the sight of a most beautiful romantic
ravine and fertile valley beyond, with that of a tolerably large
and populous Spanish town with everything about it of a stamp
of original native, or at least centuries behind the alterations
introduced anywhere else that I have been. The women, young
and old, many of the former very handsome wore large black
patches on their temples, like the ladies of a certain description
in Hogarth. The exercise in mind and body and the change
of season have stopped, as was expected, the fevers that were
before so lamentably prevalent in the army. A few agues and
dysentries may still be expected, but we have every reason to
hope that our effective numbers will now every day increase.
The French are completely removed from this immediate neighbourhood, their latest offensive having been in small numbers
to carry off bread they had ordered at different places as they

retired and a good deal of which we have disappointed them of, by eating it ourselves on our occupations of the villages, but not forgetting to pay for it.

We had a report yesterday of their removing in force to the southward; if so, it would not be long before we move also. Lord Wellington's Despatches will inform you of what we at present are in the dark about.

There were a few abortive cattle raids, with the intention of capturing those supplies on the hoof which the French persisted in grazing on the plain in front of Ciudad Rodrigo. However, despite sunny days when 'the weather is delightful and there is a superb view of the north end of the valley between the passes' (and 'how our dear father would have enjoyed a December day's walk on the terrace of the house I am quartered at'), the prevailing snow and melting ice made a return to cantonments welcome. After one offensive excursion Charles wrote to his brother, by then commanding a man-of-war patrolling the English Channel:

At present it freezes smartly with a fine clear sky and a most bitter North East wind, which I think it not unlikely you yourself are experiencing in full force off Cherbourg. We were desired to leave our baggage behind, and expect to return, when the present service is over one way or other, to our former cantonments. I shall be well pleased to get back to Navas Frias, which to be sure had not many things to recommend it as a residence in common time, but it is at least as good as most of the villages or small towns for many leagues round and after some doubt as to its possibility, I undertook and succeeded in building myself a chimney, certainly one of the greatest desiderata in this climate and season. Out of doors, I have employed the regiment quartered with me in widening and improving the avenues to the town and the roads of principal communication in such way as to improve our rides and obviate the evils we had to expect from floods, snow, etc. in course of the winter. Navas Frias means in Spanish 'cold plains', while our adjoining Sierra de Gata is the 'mountain of the clouds' and to the Westward we shall have full share of the cool breezes from the Sierra de Estrella, that of the 'Stars'.

Shortly before Christmas an unsuccessful cattle raid, which Charles describes in the following letter, was the occasion of his providing Wellington with the first intelligence that the French had withdrawn from Plasencia. Marmont had felt obliged to do so on being ordered to detach 16,000 men to reinforce his hard-pressed fellow Marshal, Suchet, at Valencia, where the Spanish generals, Blake and Ballesteros, showed signs of mounting an offensive.

Major Grey, of the 5th, who had accompanied a flag of truce carrying letters to the enemy's outposts from Plasencia at Val de Obispo upon the Alagon River, reported to Lord Wellington his having seen some way this side of it cattle to the amount of twelve or thirteen hundred in two herds, which he thought might easily be brought off. On hearing this his Lordship, contrary to the system we have hitherto observed on that side of the country, resolved that an attempt should be made to secure them as although the cattle were the property of the Spaniards, they might be made subservient to the use of the French.

I accordingly on the morning of the 13th passed over from Payo, at a very early hour, 500 Infantry and a troop of Dragoons and followed myself at daylight through the Paroles pass which to the bottom of the hill is about three Portuguese leagues from the former town.

By the way we learnt that the enemy had moved off from Val de Obisbo and their other neighbouring cantonments, which enabled my Infantry to proceed as far as Villa Buenos. Whether or not the information gained by the recent flag of truce of their ill prepared state had caused the move we do not know.

Soon afterwards, overtaking Major Grey and the Cavalry further in front, I had the mortification to learn that of the larger herd expected to be found upon the bank of the Arago, a little river running nearly parallel with the Alagon, not one was to be seen, while the other smaller one, and nearer to us, had dispersed in all directions on the first attempt to enclose them, though we had brought two and twenty regular bullock drivers with us. Unluckily not one of their own conductors was to be seen, or perhaps on the promise of good payment the cattle might, like those which overthrew Don Quixote, have all been brought within our passes at full gallop following that single man on horseback.

Our object having failed, we had then but to get back the troops as soon as possible into quarters, so the 5th and Cavalry returned the way they came to Payo, while I accompanied the 200 of the 83rd, who had been the most advanced of the Infantry, up the pass of Gata, the nearest to us. We were very comfortably lodged for the night at the town of that name, which was some half way up the pass. I was glad to take this mode of seeing the place, having been deterred from doing so before by the very bad character of the last three miles of the road up to the top of the Sierra, which it is easier to ascend than to go down; we did it mostly on foot . . .

I find great comfort in the chimney and other improvements I have made to my house, not forgetting my oiled-paper windows, and have laid in from the other side of the Sierra a good stock of hay, chaff, straw, which in most of the other cantonments they are in great want of, and we hope to keep as Merry a Christmas as we can.

Charles' xenophobic comments yielded temporarily to admiration of the efforts made by the Spanish Generals Blake and Ballesteros in Catalonia, and also of 'Don Carlos d'Espana, who is of French origin and one of the most intelligent, active and decisive of the Spanish Generals. His Corps does not exceed 6,000, nor are they well advanced in organisation, but with the assistance of Don Julian's guerrillas they are useful in repressing the enemy between Salamanca and Ciudad Rodrigo and will do for the garrison of that place, and other duties, when we get possession of it.' On reflection, however, his disdain for our allies won the upper hand:

I do not indeed hear a character of anything like good organisation among any of the Spanish corps and it is consequently melancholy to see the numbers of fine young fellows got together almost to certain sacrifice, as must continue to be the case as long as they are brought forward in that indisciplined state. Even Blake's troops at Albuera could not be trusted in a movement, though Suchet seems to have found them improved. Blake's own greatest merit seems to be a good spirit, on which a constant succession of mishaps has no power of depression. Lord W. having in our own Ministry and that of the Portuguese the advantage the Duke of Marlborough possessed with Queen Anne and the Dutch, what a thousand pities there should not be a Prince Eugene found among the Spaniards, but a thing unexampled I believe in the history of Revolutions is that, in the present one of Spain and Portugal, so far from a really great man hardly more than one of 'Jog Trot' abilities has appeared in either Kingdom.

76

With Marmont withdrawn, the way was open for Wellington to convert his blockade of Ciudad Rodrigo into a siege and assault. But, meanwhile, Christmas 1811 was for Charles a season of exceptional good cheer as this letter, written to Lord Colville on New Year's Day from Alameda on the banks of the Dos Casas river, explains:

A day or two after my last letter, I received through General Picton a request from Lord Wellington that I would be so obliging as to take the command of the 4th Division during the three months leave of absence of your old shipmate General Cole, promising me, lest he should not by the expiration of that time be able to give me a permanent command I should like better, to keep my former Brigade vacant for me to return to, concluding very justly I should prefer them to any other.

I accordingly left Navas Frias on the 24th, spending the rest of that day with General Picton at Alberqueria. Next day after coursing three or four hares with him, 'chemin faisant', we arrived (my aide de camp and I) in time to eat our Christmas dinner with an old acquaintance at an adjoining contonment, Major General Kemmis of the 40th, who commands one of the British Brigades of the Division consisting of the 3rd Batt, 27th, and 40th Regiment. In the other Brigade, which is Major Pakenham's (he himself now sick and absent in England) are the 7th and 23rd Fusiliers and 48th Regiment. The Portuguese Brigade is your acquaintance General Harvey's and the Artillery a Brigade of the King's German Legion. The Division is nearly a couple of thousand stronger than the 3rd and until cut up at Albuera and by subsequent sickness was without exception the finest in this army. The total of Rank and File in the country is 9,021, but our effectives present only 5,009, having sick 2,570.

General Harvey has great credit for the state of his Brigade, which in numbers and condition is at this moment, I believe, by far the best of the Portuguese army.

Here, notwithstanding the season, everything betokens an early commencement of the siege of Ciudad Rodrigo. In about a week more, a bridge for the transport of the heavy Artillery and stores will be completed over the Agueda about six miles from this, being at the ford of Molino de Flores in front of Galegos, while gabions, fascines, etc. are preparing fast and in great quantities at the cantonments of the divisions in the front line. The possession of that fortess is certainly a most momentous object, but a great though temporary object would also be obtained by the threat alone of an immediate siege, should it bring back Marmont from the junction he seems to intend forming with Suchet.

I waited upon Lord W. two days ago, but found him in his stable, and had little other conversation than about the stud and hounds with which he goes out twice a week. In coming home from a long search for them yesterday, I got a tally ho, but there were few dogs up with the chase, having separated in a large covert, it being a bad scenting day from the frost: the huntsman was at the time calling them in and in any case I had only meant to be a looker-on.

My present family consists of A.D.C., Major Brooke (A.Q.M.G.), Captain James, son of Sir Walter, (A.A.G.), and Captain Mulcaster of the Royal Engineers. In addition to these I have hitherto got on very comfortably with three visitors at dinner, General Cole having left a very good cook behind him, whom I have taken in addition to my former establishment. The party of eight made up by Chaplain, Staff Surgeon, and the Commissary of the Division did on this day of festival partake of one out of half a dozen fine turkeys I purchased at three dollars each, out of a flock which had found their way a few days since from the hands of the Philistines in the Sierra de Salamanca, a district, it seems, very famous for that bird.

The gentlemen I have mentioned as of my family are very pleasant, and I believe very 'au fait' and correct in their departments.

I finished the year by dinner yesterday with General Harvey at his cantonment between three and four miles off, walking there and back by fine moonlight in a hard frost, which you may think a good symptom of my present health.

5

Fall of the Fortresses

Although in August 1811 there were 370,000 French soldiers in Spain, with over 50,000 horses, they were dispersed on a variety of fronts and they were harassed by indomitable Spanish insurgents. Moreover, some of the best troops, including a contingent of the Imperial Guard, were soon recalled to France to swell the Grande Armée which Napoleon was assembling for his march on Moscow. The time for a British offensive might soon be ripe, but before Wellington could advance into Spain, he must recapture and hold the two strong border fortresses of Ciudad Rodrigo and Badajos.

The French had occupied Ciudad Rodrigo in July 1810, after a long and gallant resistance by 6,000 Spaniards under the Governor, Andreas Herrasti. At that time Masséna, with an overwhelming superiority of men, had hoped to lure Wellington to the city's relief and destroy his army in the flat, open country through which he must approach it. Wellington, though anxious to help Herrasti, had avoided falling into the trap and ever since then Ciudad Rodrigo had been a strong, well-defended French advance post. In September 1811, after the French failure at El Bodon, Wellington was at last in a position to blockade the city, preparatory to besieging it if the covering French forces were moved or reduced in size; and all the while a huge siege-train, recently arrived from England, was making its slow journey eastwards from Oporto. Five thousand bullocks wearily dragged sixty-eight new iron guns across the mountain ranges while a thousand Portuguese militia repaired the roads ahead of them.

Ciudad Rodrigo lies on the east bank of the Agueda river, a strong-flowing tributary of the Douro, running parallel to the River Coa which is twenty miles to the west of it. By December 1811 Wellington's opportunity had come when, on orders from Napoleon, Marmont was required to send a substantial part of his army from Placentia to reinforce Marshal Suchet at Valencia. The garrison of Ciudad Rodrigo, though amply supplied with artillery and ammunition, was reduced to less than 2,000 men.

So in January 1812 Wellington moved forward to take the fortress by assault, resolved to spare neither effort nor lives in completing the task before Marmont was again strong enough to relieve it. Four of his divisions, encamped behind the Coa, moved to an assembly point six miles north of the city. The attack was delayed two days not, as Charles thought, on account of bad weather, but because the Portuguese muleteers, entrusted with the transport of supplies and ammunition, were so dilatory. As Napier put it, little more than twenty years later: 'The native carters were two days moving over ten miles of flat and excellent road with empty carts; the operation was thus delayed, and it was dangerous to find fault with these people, because they deserted on the slightest offence.' Low productivity is not a phenomenon confined to the twentieth century.

However, all difficulties were finally overcome and a bridge was successfully built over the Agueda. Charles's next letter describes the beginning of the siege:

> Salices, right bank of the Agueda six miles
> to N.W. of Ciudad Rodrigo. Jan. 15th, 1812
>
> I am this moment returned with fingers cramped with the morning's frost from my second twenty-four hours' duty in the trenches before Ciudad Rodrigo, and as the post goes from Headquarters this evening, will have it in my power to give you but a hasty sketch of our proceedings hitherto; but that you will, I trust, think better than none at this interesting moment.
>
> A few days of bad weather prevented our commencing the investment before the afternoon of the 8th inst. It began very auspiciously by a portion of the Light Division early in the night taking possession in assault, in gallant style, of a redoubt with three guns in it and fifty men who were made prisoners. It had been erected by the French at between 5 and 600 yards from the body of the works and, had it been regularly approached, would have taken at least four days; this at any rate is said to have been the enemy's opinion of its value. Under its cover, our first parallel was immediately begun rather in advance of where the French had theirs, but partly making use of their approaches for the easier working of the ground which is generally very shingly.
>
> On the night of the 13th, a ruined convent on the right

of our trenches, occupied by the enemy, though open, was got possession of by the 1st Division, in return for which the French yesterday, as the trench duties were about relieving, very handsomely sortied and before they could be driven back, succeeded in doing some small mischief to a sap, which in the course of a night had been commenced in approach to what is to be our breaching battery. The battery is to be on an elevation which was used by the French for the same purpose, at a distance, so it is said, of no more than 120 yards from the walls.

The point selected for attack is that part of the work which is semi circular in shape or is perhaps better described as forming a very obtuse angle. It was breached in the French siege and is supposed to be weak on that account. The wall is apparently a very good one but with some stone embrasures.

We opened our fire yesterday afternoon, but too late for any effect and a flanking battery of two 18 pdrs could not be used as the platforms had not been laid. We were unable to silence a field piece on the top of a square tower and a howitzer in the garden underneath the convent of San Francisco. From this garden, so celebrated in Masséna's siege, part of our approaches could be enfiladed and other projected works taken in rear, so Lord Wellington gave me, having command of the trenches, directions for the assault of the fortified suburb in which it stands, to our left of the town.

We were able with the assistance of ladders and tools to open a breach in a high loop-holed wall, through which we succeeded in getting in a proportion of men to a post which turned their position. The enemy in the convent and immediately adjoining defences took fright and set off, leaving me in quiet possession of the convent, two pieces of cannon, and the whole fortified suburb in the same state as when it cost them, I believe, thousands to take it. On the former occasion the numbers were very considerable on both sides; on this night they had only 100 men there; while on our side the three companies, which were alone employed of the battalion allotted for the duty, had one man slightly wounded.

We immediately set to work with our tools, and lodged the Battn. safely within 300 yards of the place. The choice of spot and mode of attack was all his Lordship's own, in which however we were favoured by the information obtained from a peasant without and of the gardener of the convent taken in a house in the suburb. I left our batteries, which are calculated to be at a distance of 520 yards, playing from twenty-two 24 pdrs.

One sector has already been driven in, and matters altogether promise well. More guns will be mounted today in the same line of batteries, the total ordnance employed being thirty-two English 24 pdrs and four or five Portuguese. Neither mortars nor howitzers are employed, I suppose to save labour in the first case, though I should like to see the howitzers from the field Brigades used.

Our casualties average about fifty in the day, the enemy firing mostly from their mortars and howitzers with a great deal of teasing musketry. We have no time to lose, as Lord W. himself, before we commenced, calculated on Marmont's joining again with Dorsenne by the 21st inst. and this opinion there has been, I believe, no reason to change.

We began the siege with four divisions only, taking the duties day about. Our cantonments are all very distant, some of them as far as fifteen miles off, but we return to them on the completion of our tours of duty. The work is hard, but three divisions more are moving up, which will enable us, I trust to cover our siege should the place not have fallen before the enemy comes up. The weather has been very much in our favour, hard frost at night but with beautiful clear sunshine for these three days past.

Our bridge, which I mentioned in my last, is a masterpiece of its kind and is at the ford of Molino de Flores, about three miles in front of Galegos, a place you will see in the map. When I before spoke of howitzers I forgot to say that we have now a new piece of ordnance, much approved of, iron chambered carronades. They have about four hundred yards longer range than the five inch brass ones, and are still lighter. I have one attached to the Brigade of guns attached to the division I command. There are eighteen of them, five inch and eight inch, on travelling carriages in depot at Almeida, so if necessary they can soon be brought up.

It was one of the few assaults at this stage of the war made with comparatively little bloodshed. It was, none the less, a spectacular affair, as Napier, who saw it happen, wrote in his most purple prose:

Then was beheld a spectacle at once fearful and sublime. The enemy replied to the assailants' fire with more than fifty pieces, the bellowing of eighty large guns shook the ground far and wide, the smoke rested in heavy volumes upon the battlements of the place, or curled in light wreaths about the numerous spires, the shells, hissing through the air, seemed fiery serpents leaping from the darkness, the walls crashed to the stroke of the bullet, and the distant mountains, faintly returning the sound, appeared to moan over the falling city. And when night put an end to this turmoil, the quick clatter of musketry was heard like the pattering of hail after a peal of thunder, for the fortieth regiment assaulted and carried the convent of Francisco and established itself in the suburb on the left of the attack.

Ciudad Rodrigo finally succumbed after a twelve days' siege, which was only half the duration Wellington had expected. Charles's old division, the 3rd, was in the trenches on the 19th January and thus, with the Light Division, bore the brunt of the assault. The 4th were spectators of the attack on the two breaches in the walls and Charles wrote this account of it, three days after the fall of the city:

On my return to the duty of the trenches on the morning of the 18th I found the breach of both the main wall and its fausse braye well advanced from the fire of the batteries mentioned in my last, although they had contrived to clear it during the night, a measure we guarded better against on the ensuing one. We had also opened another seven gun battery to our left where the ground declines to the convent of San Francisco.

On the other hand the fire of shot and shell from the enemy's batteries directed at this battery, and at the second parallel and their sap approaches, was very destructive, as our own fire was entirely directed at the breach. The Chief Engineer naturally became anxious and asked for a change of system in that respect or for an assault as soon as the breach became practicable. The Governor had been summoned to surrender, but in the true style of the vile Fanfaron he has turned out to be, answered that, rather than do so, he should bury himself in the ruins of the place. Lord Wellington on leaving the ground that evening said that he expected the fellow would stand the assault, but authorised me to promise the usual honours of war, should he, in his absence, offer the immediate surrender of the garrison on seeing that, the breach being now practicable, he could do so with honour.

On the morning of the 19th we opened the seven gun battery

upon the square tower and its fausse braye, which flanked with two guns the original breach, and with such good effect that in a few hours it became the best breach of the two. Arrangements were then made for the assault which took place in the evening, but for an account of which I shall leave you to his Lordship's Despatches, he having the best verbal information. Both he and I were eye witnesses from the batteries, but what one gets as an eye witness is very imperfect in so defective a light as that obtained by a young moon and the flashes of light from the small arms and grenades and the accidental explosion of heaps of shells, which took place, I think, in six considerable instances and to which, I believe, we owe the greatest part of our loss.

Neither breach was defended exactly from the top, though a considerable fire was thrown, especially on the large one, from the windows and other cover afforded by ruined buildings on a level with the rampart, but separated from it. I all along felt anxious that part of our artillery should be directed against the enemy's defences, and the effect it had for the few hours it was allowed to play on them previous to the assault confirms me in my opinion, differing for once, as I presume to do, with my Commander. The fire of the enemy's Artillery was very considerable and well directed. I hear they fired no less than 11,000 shells.

The four Divisions having in the siege lost upon the average under fifty a day, and the assault having as I understand cost about 250, makes a total of about 800,* but I should hope that not more than a third of these are irrecoverable to the service. The officers have suffered in large proportion, including the Engineers, who among others lost Captain Ross, a man of much talent and science, who had lately been employed in improving the navigation of the Douro with much promise of advantage, not only to us in the forwarding of supplies from Oporto, but in the future exercise of the wine trade on that river. It is not perhaps generally known that the Oporto Company did at some distant period effect a great undertaking of the same kind, but unfortunately the rights of the improved navigation were made over by the Crown to a family who did not take advantage of it (though they are now planting vines in the neighbourhood) and I understand that bold as the boatmen are in the troubled waters of the river generally, their superstitious

* Charles underestimated the casualties.

fears are so great that they do not like to engage in the new channels.

The late Governor of Ciudad Rodrigo abuses his garrison, and says that had they been all French he would never have been taken. Against this we have to say that, though there may have been a large proportion of Italians among them, they were fine healthy-looking young men, and as far as we can judge, did their duty, bad as was the example he set them; for instead of heading them at the breach he stationed himself very snugly with a Guard of Honour of an hundred men in the Citadel ready to capitulate, and thus is very angry that these Italians did not sacrifice themselves to a man for his sake and for the love of his French Imperial Majesty.

The Brigade of the 3rd Division, which Charles had led until three weeks previously, suffered badly in the breaches, as Colonel Cambell of the 94th and Major Ridge of the 2nd/5th described in letters they wrote to their former Commanding Officer:

The 94th were the first that ascended the great breach, and had cleared the sides of the breach when the 5th and 77th joined us. Captain Williamson, Lang and myself were the first to reach the summit. The first was shot through the heart by my side while cheering to the charge of the guns and the second severely wounded through the arm. I believe I was the only one of the front rank that was not knocked down. I must confess that I never was so much staggered in all my life between admiration and horror at the awful tragedy that presented itself. The conduct of the 94th Regiment cannot ever be surpassed. Their obedience, and steady brave conduct will always command my most grateful admiration, as will also the behaviour of the whole of the brigade.

I also transmit a return of the killed and wounded and am in hopes you will excuse this hurried scrawl. I remain etc.,

J. A. CAMPBELL

P.S. I hope you have quite recovered the bad effects you experienced from the explosion of the shell.

Major Ridge, Commanding the 'Fighting 5th' wrote as follows:

Accept, my dear General, the sincere thanks of myself and brothers of the 5th for yours of the 21st, and believe me it is a real satisfaction that our conduct has met your approbation, feeling as we do that you were the first to bring the 2nd/5th into notice.

After forcing the gate in the ditch, scaling the wall of the fausse braye, rendering the guns innocent by disposing of the gunners, and proceeding along the fausse braye to the breach, I halted the battalion according to orders and was there joined by the 94th, the 77th supporting us. This junction was no sooner formed at the foot of the breach than the enemy's destructive fire opened, which of course pointed out the only plan to be adopted as the shells, grenades, and every kind of combustible devilment came so thick amongst us that in the ditch we could not live, and we were not sent there to go back.

The two regiments therefore, as by one consent, rushed up the breach which was very soon carried, and it fortunately happened that the French were so closely pursued as to prevent them pulling away the planks thrown over the ditches which they had cut across the ramparts, and thereby we were enabled to cross and drive them from behind the traverse and clear the ramparts to the right, as well as partially on the left, and on the whole kept them in check until the arrival of General McKinnon's Brigade which soon decided the business.

Our loss has indeed been severe but it is great satisfaction to know it must have been infinitely greater had the enemy not been taken by surprise, as we were actually in the fausse braye before a single sentry took the alarm, when their drums beat most furiously. I have succeeded in completing all my drummers present with French drums and would have done more had they been wanted. Our George and Dragon has been carried from the King's Colour by a shell passing through it, but if his figure is extinct, his spirit I trust still remains. I am etc.

H. RIDGE

After the capture of the city, the British ran wild. All control was temporarily lost by the officers, cellars were emptied of their casks and bottles, and a drunken horde of lascivious soldiery committed excesses against the Spanish inhabitants, friends and allies, which were a disgrace to their flag and uniform. As the two generals commanding the assault, Crauford and McKinnon, were killed in leading their men to victory, it may be that the necessary restraining hands were absent. Men from Charles's division were not among the guilty, for they had taken no part in the storming.

The sacking of cities which were summoned to surrender and disdained the summons was long held to be a traditional right of victorious troops, just as the body of a fox, killed at the end of a long run, is thrown to the hounds to stimulate their zeal for the chase. However, this tradition was falling into disrepute and both Wellington and Marmont (though not Masséna) had issued stringent orders against plundering. Wellington, who was severe with looters, was doubtless distressed; but he took no disciplinary action. He had the satisfaction of capturing 150 pieces of artillery, including Marmont's entire battering train. The French lost only 300 men killed, the remainder surrendering, while 1,300 British soldiers fell, more than 700 of them in the breaches.

The Spanish Cortez, overlooking the atrocities committed against their fellow citizens when the town was sacked, created Wellington Duke of Ciudad Rodrigo and a Grandee of Spain. The Portuguese followed suit with the marquessate of Torres Vedras, and the British, not to be outdone, made Wellington an earl.

Charles regretted the death in action of Crauford, the brilliant if sometimes wayward martinet who had commanded the Light Division; but the tragedy might have provided opportunities.

I returned two days ago from poor General Crauford's auction at Headquarters, without making a single purchase. I saw nothing I absolutely required, so resisted temptation as although his complete dinner service of Sheffield plate was divided into desirable lots, I determined to go on with my old block tin (of which I have a re-inforcement, however, arrived as far as Lisbon) until I shall at least have a division called my own.

There was a short pause while the battered walls and redoubts of Ciudad Rodrigo were repaired and strengthened against a possible French endeavour to recover it.

After the finest weather we could possibly have expected (though at times very cold) for our winter siege and subsequent operations (repairs to the fortress as well as demolition of our works, and renewal of stores and Artillery), the rain set in in earnest upon the 29th, after a previous heavy fall of snow, and has continued for part of every day since. The Agueda is full and become a mighty torrent which would have covered, if not carried away, our temporary bridge had it not been removed just in time. Our only communication from this with the other bank is on our right, by the bridge of Barba del Puerco, five miles off, and having for the cattle a break heart hill to go up and down from it; on the left by that of Ciudad Rodrigo seven miles from this, and to this even, an officer tells me, he was obliged to swim his horse over some flooded place, but as this river, like others supplied principally by mountain torrents, is rapid in filling so it as suddenly decreases in depth.

The country people have a mode of carrying themselves as well as their corn across by a wooden triangle, which they haul along a cable, fastened as taut as a rope dancer's, across the narrow straits of the river. This differs from my aerial trip to the Fungus Island from Gozo, which you may remember my mentioning, and which was by a chair running on two slack ropes, the impetus of the descent sending it half way up the declivity. Both were perhaps adopted from the American Indians, if we may judge from the plates in Moore's Voyages, but why indeed should they not be natural to each country thus similarly circumstanced.

The city was to be garrisoned by the Spaniards, and then the army would be free for its next objective, the subjection of Badajos.

Previous to giving it to the Spaniards we are to victual the place for them and the garrison will be furnished from Castanos's army, if his unorganised rabble can be so termed. I should think that the whole of our force will then be disposable for active operations.

These, there is every reason to apprehend, will commence with another siege of Badajos. The mortars and carronades of the battering train that I before mentioned as being at Almeida, are already half way on their road thither, as are the carriages of the 24 pounders we lately used here. We even send shot from here by the means of mules, (which carry about eight each) of the number of fifty or sixty, which are generally attached to every division for the carriage of reserve musket ammunition. This, as well as all superfluities in the Field Artillery department, is being deposited in Almeida which is now in a good defensive state, the guns rebouched etc., etc. The Cavalry are already sent off, as are some of the Infantry who have taken steps, for the purpose of saving transport, to get their clothing etc. from Abrantes on the way. I expect we shall follow in a few days. Depots are establishing at Elvas and Paramante, where I suppose a bridge will again be thrown across the Guadiana.

This important fortress of Badajos, stronger than Ciudad Rodrigo, had already withstood two British sieges and, indeed, the French had only succeeded in occupying it in the first place because of the treachery of Governor Imas, who had taken command when his more resolute predecessor was killed in action. Before a new attempt was made, it was important to ensure that two French armies, under Marshal Soult and General Drouet, Comte d'Erlon, were prevented from interrupting the operation. They both lay at a comparatively short distance from Badajos, and Wellington

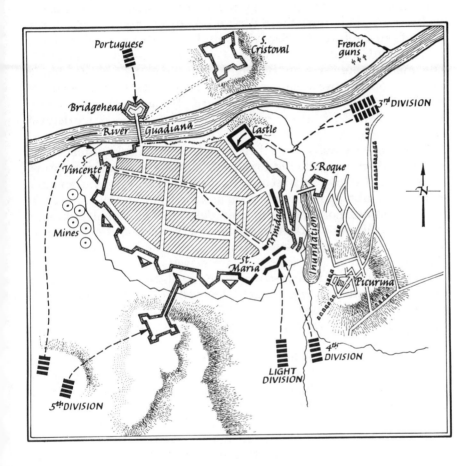

Badajos

89

later told Lord Ellesmere that he believed Soult to be the best strategist with whom he ever had to deal. So while the 3rd, 4th and Light Divisions were selected to attack the fortress, the remainder of the army, under Generals Graham and Hill, was sent to watch and restrain any French divisions marching to its relief. They were assisted by a Spanish army which temporarily deflected Soult by means of a threatened attack on Seville.

There were 5,000 defenders of Badajos, under the command of the brilliant French Governor, Philippon, who showed energy and ingenuity in strengthening the defences and erecting lethal booby-traps. This time there was to be no repetition of the futile attempts to capture the San Christoval fort: the city itself, lying on the south bank of the River Guadiana, was to be stormed. The main assault was to be on the Trinidad and Santa Maria bastions, on the west side of the city and close to the Castle which Charles and his brigade of the 3rd Division had unavailingly beleaguered in May 1811, while they waited for San Christoval to fall.

Before the city walls, with their ravelins, curtains, counter-scarps and deep ditches, could be breached, it was necessary to capture an outlying, heavily defended fort called the Picurina and another smaller redoubt, closer to the walls, called San Roque. Between these two strong points and the main defences ran a small tributary of the Guadiana, which Philippon had caused to be dammed, thus creating a deeply flooded area to add to the hazards of attack. The initial task of the investing army was to dig trenches, saps and parallels, and to construct solid, well-protected sites from which the artillery could breach the walls. The task was much hampered by the arrival and persistence of heavy equinoctial rains which turned the trenches into quagmires as fast as they were dug.

Wellington was in a hurry, for there was no saying how long Soult and Drouet could be held at bay; but the Portuguese Regency Government, which had been a thorn in his flesh for months past, was entirely unhelpful in providing transport to move his supplies and ammunition. Nor were the British Government anything but dilatory in supplying the money required. Thus, as Napier put it: 'Here, as at Ciudad Rodrigo, time was necessarily paid for by the loss of life; or rather the crimes of politicians were atoned for by the blood of the soldiers.' This is a cry which was echoed many times in later years, on the blood-stained fields of the Crimea and as a background to the catastrophic losses of the Somme and Passchendaele. Perhaps it has always been so except when a Chatham or a Churchill is in power, or a Marlborough can afford to disregard the political intrigues at home.

On the night of 17 March 1812 the investment began. On the 26th Charles wrote to his brother from 'The Camp before Badajos':

I left Galegos with the 4th Division on the 27th of February. I had myself got leave to gratify my curiosity of seeing a new country, and instead of coming through Castel Branco, on which road I had been twice before, kept to the right and traversing the pass of Talleardes and other strong defences of Portugal on that side, got to Abrantes, a place very well worth seeing for the beautiful scenery about it as well as for its military importance. From Abrantes I moved across to Portalegre and arrived there the same day as the Division.

We reached Elvas on the 15th inst. and on the 16th, along with the 3rd and Light Divisions, crossed by one pontoon bridge and invested this place. We found the enemy had been most busily employed in improving and adding to their works here ever since we left them, and their appearance most respectable with, by all accounts, a strong garrison.

I commanded at the advance and breaking of ground on the first night, the 17th, when it rained for the first twelve hours without ceasing a moment, but as at times it was not very heavy the weather may have been rather favourable, as that, and my not allowing the men to load, enabled us to proceed without discovery and by morning we were under good cover in our first parallel within 250 yards of the Picurina redoubt, which is about 400 yards from the body of the place.

On the second day the enemy made a sortie, in which Colonel Fletcher, the Chief Engineer, was wounded (I trust it will turn out slightly). The laborious duty of the siege has again fallen on the 3rd, 4th and Light Divisions and this compliment has kept us from being more agreeably employed with Generals Graham and Hill, who are in advance on the look out with the 1st, 2nd, 6th and 7th Divisions with directions to bring Drouet to action or force him into the Sierra Morena and thus prevent his junction with Marmont on the North or Soult on the South, both of whom, it is to be supposed, will not be long in advancing in this direction. I understand that even should they unite with the 10,000 men which Soult had asked from Suchet, our numbers would be greater than theirs; but any interruption of the siege is to be deprecated.

The 5th Division is at Campo Mayor, ready to look at the

north eastern frontier, with two battalions investing on the St. Christopher's side of the fortress: but on this work it is not designed to make any real attack, as besides what we before learnt of its difficulty, they have much strengthened it and erected another in front of it of a very respectable description. I am happy to say that with the exception of the loss of many valuable lives, among them Captain Mulcaster of the Engineers, attached to the 4th Division and one of my family, things are going on favourably notwithstanding the weather we have had to contend with, it having rained heavily for eight days which has of course much impeded our work and rendered our trenches hardly possible. We from this cause could only open our fire yesterday, which we did from four batteries, in all I believe, 20 guns and iron howitzers. It was directed against the enemy's defences in various directions, but principally against the outwork of Picurina which it was necessary to obtain possession of previous to advancing further on our present front of attack. Being of earth, our shot has little or no effect upon it, but it was stormed in the evening and taken, I fear with considerable loss, the party employed being again of the 3rd Division in their regular turn of duty under Major General Kempt, successor to poor Mackinnon's Brigade in it.

I understand that there were two French officers taken in their shirts as if having gone regularly to bed, a confidence most extraordinary and which, along with its undamaged state from our fire, shows that it might as well have been taken the first night as now, which would have saved us a great deal of the work we have since been employed upon, and have enabled us to commence upon it our first parallel, where is now our second. It was however entitled to more respect than the redoubt in front of Ciudad Rodrigo, and the force before the place not enabling us to make another attack, false or real, Lord W. was I presume unwilling to risk too much.

I go on duty again this afternoon for the fourth time, taking it with M. General Bowes and Kempt. General Picton has a nominal superintendence, but his Lordship is himself on the ground and when that is the case little is done in the way of direction but by himself, and the Brigadiers, as before, give us no assistance for fear of being obliged to give those of the Portuguese nation a situation it is not thought proper to trust them with. The weather has, however, yesterday and today been fine, and has the appearance of continuing such, and not having taken even the slightest cold I think nothing of the fag, hoping that the fewer our numbers the greater will be the credit given us, though I know by experience how it sometimes goes in the contrary.

The time poor Mulcaster gave for the duration of the siege was 27 days; if the calculation was a just one three more may be added for the weather we have suffered, and by which our pontoons were sunk and a flying bridge washed away. Luckily the Ordnance had all been got on this side before the accident. Excuse the trouble this will give you in decyphering, being written with my blotting book resting on my knee, for though I have a comfortable marquee over my head, my table is a couple of boards resting on my canteen, this not being a time to encumber oneself with baggage when, independent of the present, we have an active and, I trust, brilliant and successful course of operations opening before us.

P.S. I have broken open my wafer to correct two of my expressions. In the first place, I think the intimidation of the enemy from our taking possession in a moment, as it were, of the Picurina redoubt, which turns out to be much stronger than was ever suspected, must shorten the siege much within the period I before thought probable.

As to the French officers being stripped to their shirts, one of them, whom I have just seen, says that whoever told me so made a mistake, but that in fact he was stripped to his pantaloons by the English, a custom now too common, sometimes not leaving even that article of dress.

On 3 April, he wrote again:

I broke off to prepare for my sixth spell of 24 hours in the trenches where I found them hard at work with two breaches, one of the right face of the Trinidad bastion, and the other on the left flank of that of San Maria: they are both in a good progressive state of decay but have been found of better masonry than was expected. At the last look I gave to the latter one, it seemed already practicable for a small front, and after a little more battering at the former's revetment, as low down as possible, we shall be able to thrown shells into the uncovered parapet. A few hours might make them both practicable but the assault I imagine will not take place till tomorrow night, though some are sanguine enough to think it will take place tonight. Another breaching battery of six guns was ready this morning to open against the curtain between San Pedro and the Trinidad, but I suppose it will not be tried until it is ascertained whether we shall be able to reach the curtain from our approaches, as an inundation covers that front. The wall is presumed to be a weak one. An unsuccessful attempt was made last night to blow up the great dam, but it could not, I understand, be got at: an explosion which was effected against the smaller dam was unsuccessful, not letting out any water.

The battering of the gorge of the raveline of San Roque which is now going on as it covers the dam, though its own fire of Artillery has been silenced for some days, betokens another attempt this night, when I hope the good old way of mining will be resorted to as the most certain. Last night's attempt was made upon a new principle, said to be much acted on by the French.

We enfilade the flank of the bastion of San Pedro and have fired a ricochet apparently with some success, as they have been pretty silent there today. This flank joins the work of the Castle. On the other side there is a flank of six embrassures bearing upon our batteries, who are also fired on from the flank of the Pardeleros against which we have not strength enough to turn anything.

We have for the third time undertaken the siege of this place, deficient of means. Half of the guns employed are only 18 pdrs.

We have not a single mortar, but it appears that our shrapnel shell of $5\frac{1}{2}$ inches from our iron carronades must have, where employed, done good service, as from the accounts from a deserter the enemy has already had a thousand killed and wounded in the sortie, the assault of Picurina and the other operations of the Siege; a great number, but to which I fear our own loss is already commensurate, for we have laboured under the great disadvantage of a heavy flank fire on both sides.

When the assault comes the two main breaches fall naturally, from our actual position, to the 4th Division, while the 3rd and Light Divisions might be employed in false or real attack by escalade in situations which offer favourably enough for it on the Castle side on our right, and on the line walls in the rear of the crown works of Pardeleros; but Lord Wellington keeps all his plans so well to himself that it is impossible to say who will be employed and who will not.

Several ineffectual attempts have been made by the cavalry to cut off Drouet's communications, but I believe Sir Thomas Graham has come back to San Martha six leagues off. Sir R.

Hill is at Merida. Soult, it is expected, would himself leave Seville on the 31st of March, and his brother collects the troops from Granada and Cordova, but Suchet is, I understand, besieging Alicante and Marmont is making a show at least of an attack on Ciudad Rodrigo.

Our own force in the field a few days since was, exclusive of Artillery, 50,000 men, of these 31,000 British including, I think, 4,800 Cavalry; a force I hope we shall find sufficient for all our purposes, and flatter myself I shall soon again have to write to you of other successes in our glorious cause, looking I trust with no more than a just confidence to the early and happy termination of the present operations.

Sunday, 6 April, was Easter Day. The Moslems respect Ramadan, but the most sacred festivals of the Christian religion are seldom taken into consideration by generals or politicians when *raison d'état* can be enlisted in support of military action. Did not Mussolini invade Albania on Good Friday, 1938, and the Germans launch a final, fierce assault on the Americans in Bastogne on Christmas Day, 1944? Marlborough fought and won the battle of Ramillies on Whitsunday, 1706. The horrors of Badajos, 'a combat', as Napier described it, 'so fiercely fought, so terribly won, so dreadful in all its circumstances, that posterity can scarcely be expected to credit the tale'—those horrors began at 10 p.m. on Easter Sunday when the 4th and the Light Divisions marched in column towards the breaches, still insufficiently wide, that the artillery had pounded in the Trinidad and Santa Maria bastions.

There was a ditch, eighteen feet deep, into which water from the flooded area had seeped, the recent heavy rainfall increasing its depth. Many of the Fusiliers, leading the 4th Division, were drowned as they plunged headlong into the abyss. In the resulting confusion the men of the Light Division, who were supposed to be attacking the Santa Maria, mingled with the 4th at the Trinidad, and the reserves, which had been ordered to wait in the rear, rushed forward to add to the serried ranks fighting to clamber on to the ramparts. The French rolled barrels of gunpowder down on their assailants and those survivors who managed to climb the ramparts found awaiting them one of Philippon's most effective devices, a row of sharp sword-blades embedded in heavy beams. In front of these sharp deterrents were loose planks, studded with iron points, so that the front rank stumbled as they advanced and were pushed on to the sword points by the pressure of their

95

comrades behind. The succeeding waves advanced across a ditch now carpeted by the bodies of the dead and wounded, only to find that even if they circumvented the murderous sword-blades they fell into deep holes, cunningly dug to protect the 'curtain' and parapet, and a final enemy entrenchment.

After a holocaust lasting two hours, the 4th and the Light Divisions withdrew, their attack an expensive failure. However, Badajos fell, because despite an initial check and grave loss the 3rd Division finally captured the Castle, to the right of the Trinidad bastion, and the 5th Division forced an entry into the city far to the left of the main breaches.

The aftermath was scarcely less fearful than the assault: 5,000 British and Portuguese soldiers had fallen, one tenth of Wellington's entire army. In Charles's division alone 51 officers, 40 sergeants and 560 rank and file were killed in the storming, and nearly 2,500 of all ranks were wounded. On this occasion it was the British who suffered, for Charles's Portuguese only lost one officer and three rank and file killed, and sixteen wounded. The survivors sacked Badajos with even greater ferocity than at Ciudad Rodrigo. 'Shameless rapacity,' wrote Napier, 'brutal intemperance, savage lust, cruelty, and murder, shrieks and piteous lamentations, groans, shouts, imprecations, the hissing of fires bursting from the houses, the crashing of doors and windows, and the reports of muskets used in violence resounded for two days and nights in the streets of Badajos.'

That Easter weekend takes its place in history alongside the worst excesses of Attila the Hun; nor can the unsurpassed bravery of the attacking soldiers, nor the fact that the Spanish inhabitants of Badajos (unlike those of Ciudad Rodrigo) included a number of collaborators with the enemy, be an excuse for conduct as disgraceful as that for which Soult's and Masséna's troops have been censured in their infamous treatment of the Portuguese peasants during the French retreats from Oporto and Santarem.

Charles can be acquitted of any responsibility for failing to restrain his men. All five generals taking part in the assault were wounded, three of them severely, and though he and Picton were the two whose injuries were the least serious, Charles was twice hit early in the attack on the Trinidad bastion, just as he was about to descend into the stygian ditch. Two days later he was able, despite the amputation of a joint of the third finger of his right hand, to write to his brother-in-law, the Rev. Roger Frankland. The letter, of 8 April 1812, is written from 'Camp before Badajos'.

My dear Frankland,

Badajos has been a very dear purchase to us, but leaving you to the public accounts for the details of its capture, I shall only say that in my own case I think myself very fortunate in having escaped in the assault with the loss of the upper joint of my third finger, and a musket shot through the thick part of my thigh, which has most providentially kept clear of the bone, and I may with truth say, I believe, that there is every chance of my soon recovering from both. I shall be moved this evening into Badajos.

I exceedingly regret having to inform you, that there is hardly any possibility of the recovery of that very valuable young man and excellent officer, your nephew, Captain Nicholas of the Royal Engineers, who was attached to me on that night to lead the column to the assault. He met the various wounds he received in the ditch, where his voice in energetically doing his duty was the last heard previous to myself being knocked down in the Place d'Armes. Of my own staff and other officers attached to me, Captain Lathom of the Artillery was killed; Major Brooke A.Q.M.G., Captain James of the Adjutant General's Department and Captain Spottiswoode A.D.C. were severely wounded, but I hope will soon recover. My friends of the 3rd Division as well as of the Light also suffered much, and you will particularly feel for the loss of my friend Col. Ridge of the 5th, knowing how much we have been together on former services.

The 4th Division may be considered for the present 'hors de combat' from loss of officers. Among those which I have to regret of the wounded, are M. General Bowes, Brig. General Harvey, and Lt. Col. Harcourt, who commanded the three Brigades of the Division. From the loss of Regimental Field Officers the Division is now under the command of a Portuguese Lt. Col. Fortunately it is thought that Soult, hearing of the loss of the place, will not prosecute his intention of engaging us.

I shall not write to my brother or any other friends by this opportunity, but leave you do to it for me.

CH. COLVILLE

In a letter to Wellington he said: 'At the time when I was totally disqualified from giving my superintendence to the Division, I was delighted to witness the exertions of Capt. James, Asst. Adjt. General, to maintain order and bring on the troops.' It seems that, wounded though he was, Charles remained where he

97

had fallen and did his best to maintain contact with his battalions through the officers on his staff. Most of his 'family' were themselves wounded and so, as the night wore on, were the officers commanding all three of the brigades which formed the 4th Division.

It was as dangerous to be a general in Wellington's army as to be a private soldier, though it was certainly less uncomfortable. There was never any question of leading the regiment from behind, like the Duke of Plaza Toro or, in the more sophisticated battles of the twentieth century, the commanders in both World Wars. A major-general, sword in hand, led his division or brigade in the attack and as the years went by Crauford, Picton and many others died at the head of their troops. Wellington himself was seldom out of the mêlée and on a number of occasions he had the narrowest of shaves. Men serving in the ranks led a hard life, but their courage and determination never to recoil owed much to the personal example of their officers, including those of the highest field rank. There was no safety on the staff.

To be wounded in days before the advent of anaesthetics, antiseptics, antibiotics and blood transfusions, when the infections carried by the surgeon's knife and probe were as dangerous as an enemy cannon-ball, was a hazard so great that it is surprising how many recovered. The explanation must lie in the strength of those who outlived their birth and early childhood. The population of the United Kingdom in the Napoleonic Wars was little bigger than it had been a hundred years earlier when Marlborough fought the armies of Louis XIV. It was but half that of France. With none but the crudest methods of birth-control available to their husbands, and none at all to themselves, women bore children annually; but as late as the 1790s nine out of every ten babies born in London died before their second birthday.

Pain, too, was borne with a resignation by which men and women of modern times, at any rate those fortunate enough to live in civilised lands, must be astounded. Women suffered the full, unmitigated torture of childbirth, which was almost sure to be mortal if any complications arose, and men were subjected to sufferings which would possibly kill their descendants or at least unhinge them mentally. Thus the amputation of a limb or the removal of a deeply embedded musket ball or shell fragment was borne with phlegmatic patience, with gritted teeth and frequently with scarcely a cry or a groan. To show cowardice during an operation was unmanly, though few would decline a stiff tot of rum before the ordeal and a long course of pain-alleviating laudanum when it was over.

There is little suggestion in the records of the time that soldiers were prone to what we call shock, however great their suffering or terrifying their experience. They complained more of physical conditions than of physical pain, and their reaction to the nightmare of Badajos was to get drunk and to pillage rather than to succumb to nervous breakdowns. It would be rash to suggest that psychological disorders were unknown, but they cannot have occurred with the frequency or intensity which became familiar in both World Wars, in Korea and in Vietnam. There was no room for weaklings in Wellington's army or Nelson's navy, although there was no shortage of scroungers, social misfits and criminals. They may have been 'the scum of the earth', but they were a remarkably gallant scum.

Emotion, too, was seldom shown, except in the privacy of letters. Wellington did, indeed, break down and weep when he saw what had befallen his men at Badajos. Lord Clinton, who was on his staff, said that on this occasion he betrayed more anxiety than anyone about him had ever witnessed. Picton, on the other hand, was an unmoved and astonished witness of what he considered Wellington's weakness, while Charles, for his part, was far more impressed by the bravery of the troops than by the slaughter of thousands in circumstances which must, by modern standards, be judged hideous in the extreme. The losses which he deplored were those of officers in his 'family' and a few friends of long standing. Probably we are more aghast at the carnage of Badajos than ever were those who saw it happen or who read about it in the newspapers at home. Wellington was, it seems, an exception, at least on this occasion.

6

Interlude

Charles recuperated from his wounds first at Badajos and then at Estremoz, in Portugal. While he was at Estremoz, news came that the British Prime Minister, Spencer Perceval, had been murdered in the Lobby of the House of Commons. Perceval's Government was much criticised by the Peninsular army for the slowness with which money was remitted to pay its essential expenses. Thus, 'we owe 15 months' pay to our Spanish muleteers', Charles wrote, 'and the amount I have heard it estimated at I am afraid to mention.' They were offered, instead of cash, three-year British Government bonds bearing interest at 5%; but the poor muleteers had to live and, as the Spanish General Alava told Charles, 'they have such a contemptible opinion of their own Government, that it shakes their respect for ours. However, he and others are expatiating to them on the difference.'

Whatever the financial inadequacies of the British Administration, Wellington, who had more cause to worry and complain than anybody, wrote many years later to Perceval's son that 'a more honest, zealous and able Minister never served the King'. This was a polite exaggeration, written in a distant after-glow; but the immediate fear was that the Prince Regent, who was now exercising George III's powers, might invite the Whigs to form a Government. In such an event, with 'peace at any price' the new policy, the Peninsular army, however confident of its ability to enter Spain and beat the French, would be withdrawn to Britain. Fortunately the Regent sent for Lord Liverpool, whose close alliance with Castlereagh and Canning reassured the soldiers that the struggle to thwart Napoleon's ambitions would be prosecuted with the utmost vigour. The ill temper of the Whigs was displayed by a motion in the names of Samuel Whitbread and Sir Francis Burdett opposing the grant of a small pension to the murdered Perceval's widow and children.

Charles's relations kept him well posted on political trends at home; but their primary concern was that he should return to England to convalesce, whereas he, with the almost certain prospect of succeeding Picton in command of his beloved 3rd Division, was resolute in his determination to stay at the centre of operations. The amputated finger was healing and he made valiant efforts to play down the seriousness of the wound in his thigh.

He suffered acute pain in his leg and foot—'perhaps indicative', he optimistically wrote, 'of returning tone to the nerves', though he admitted that the pain was 'sometimes setting laudanum at defiance'. Badajos, on a field-bed, was unpleasant for the wounded. It was noisy and must 'shortly become very unhealthy, the dead being only half-buried and the inundations made by the French a great addition to the usual drawbacks on that score—and a Spanish garrison being also soon expected'. So he jolted thirty miles in a hospital waggon ('a most vile mode of conveyance') to Estremoz. It was, he said, 'one of the great hospital stations: they had no less than two thousand cases of wounds here, but eight hundred are already fit for duty'.

Once there he had time to reflect on the loss of his 'family' in the Badajos assault. His A.D.C., Spottiswoode, had been wounded; Captain James and Captain Mulcaster were killed and his brigade major, Potter, died after the amputation of a leg. The gallant Captain Nicholas, whose bravery had been conspicuous in the assault, was dead too.

He was killed, poor fellow, five minutes, I suppose, after he had asked my opinion in the covered way if the scene was not the grandest that could be fancied; to which I naturally answered that were it possible to divest one's mind of the horrors consequent on it, it must be acknowledged such, particularly alluding to the uninterrupted blaze of light from the various explosions which made the works appear twice their proper height.

He was nevertheless gratified to read in Wellington's official despatch that 'the arrangements made by Major-General Colville for the attack of the 4th Division were very judicious and he led them in the most gallant manner'. If only he could be passed medically fit, there were good hopes of rapid preferment. 'I have a letter, a most kind one, from General Picton to say that he has postponed his leave of absence until he can turn over the 3rd Div. to me, meaning "entre nous" to do so altogether, so far as he himself is concerned, but he does not say whether or not he has had any conversation with Lord Wellington on my subject, who may perhaps have some other plans for my employment, though I see none more probable than this.'

So, in the hope of accelerating recovery, 'I suddenly determined on setting out for Caldas da Rainha, the baths of which had been before recommended to me, taking Lisbon by the way for the purpose of first trying electricity.' Meanwhile, other warriors were enjoying themselves. Colonel J. A. Campbell, in charge of Charles's old brigade while he was seconded to command the 4th Division, wrote from the north of Portugal to describe a jaunt to Oporto:

General Picton and Col. Williams started the same day as I did and we all met at Oporto, the General's party going by land, and mine down by water, and I think we had the best of it, for poor Williams, whose wound is still open, complained much of the fatigue he suffered. I returned by Penafice, Amarante and Lamego, and was highly gratified with everything, and no person ought to form his opinion of Portugal till he has made the same trip, as it differs totally from the rest of the country we have been through. The banks of the Douro are highly cultivated on both sides to the very summit of the mountains, and it is in fact a beautiful garden the whole way, with numerous villages and quintas interspersed, which appear very neat, clean and romantic. The river runs very rapid, and carried us in a large boat, with a strong breeze against us at some places, two leagues an hour. The country I returned through as far as Lamego was equally delightful, and I am at a loss which to praise most. We all received the utmost hospitality and kindness from the Governor, as well as the whole of the inhabitants of Oporto, who fed us sumptuously, and we danced all night with all the beauty and fashion of the place who turned out to show themselves to us, and among them were really some fine girls. Genl. Picton was beset by all the ladies, who vied with each other most warmly to obtain his smiles, and the General surpassed us all in the amusement of the fantastic toe. Williams fell in line in all directions, and it will be a hard job to dislodge him. Oporto is by far the cleanest and most beautiful place I have seen in Portugal, and the houses elegant and superb; in fact I was very sorry to leave it, as must be the case with everyone.

Charles's hopes of being passed fit were dashed. He did not even reach Caldas, for at Lisbon he was hauled before a medical board, examined and ordered home. 'Further pertinacity', he wrote to John, 'was useless when I was assured by the medical men that I could not expect to mend in the fast approaching heat of a Portuguese summer.' So on 8 June he sailed for England where he stayed in Somerset with his sister, Catherine Frankland, paid a three weeks' visit to Plymouth to see John, whose ship put in there in August, and after a course of vapour and hot sea-water baths, prescribed by the naval surgeon on alternate days, he soon felt well enough to travel to London and plan his return to Lisbon. He secured a passage in the frigate *Niemen*, but while awaiting her departure from Portsmouth, he was stricken with an attack of rheumatism so violent that he had to be carried on board in a sedan chair.

He took with him his nephew Frederick Frankland, who aspired to become an officer in the Peninsular army. This is Frederick's account of the voyage, written some years later:

In the month of November 1812, I received a summons from my uncle to join him at Portsmouth, to embark with him for Lisbon, to join the army of Lord Wellington. I found him in lodgings, very unwell with rheumatism. As the wind was foul, we did not embark for a day or two. I was not much acquainted with my uncle, and my introduction to him under the irritating influence of the twinges of rheumatism was not favourable. It amuses me when I remember how tormented I was by his remarks at dinner time because I was awkward at carving. However I took it all quietly, as I saw that in the main he was very kind and friendly, and afterwards throughout life he proved the best friend I ever had.

After three or four days the wind appeared to be changing to fair; a gun was fired and the Blue Peter run up to the fore of the *Niemen* frigate, Capt. Pym, on board which ship the General and myself were to embark. We accordingly packed up and moved down to the point, where we found the frigate's boats taking people off, amongst others Major Genl. Stopford of the Guards, who was to take his passage with my uncle. Our trip to Spithead was anything but agreeable, for it blew half a gale of wind in our faces, and rained cats and dogs, or little pigs, which you please.

We had not been two hours on board the rolling, pitching

ship (during which I was lying on deck half dead with sea sickness) when the Captain decided that the wind would not take us down Channel, and we went on shore again to my great relief. It was still blowing very hard with a high sea. 'Lie down every one of you' was the word given by the master who commanded the boat to the crew. We ran into the harbour on the crest of a magnificent wave, square-sail full and wind right aft.

Previous to our first attempt to put to sea, the General's horses and a splendid pony he had purchased for me were embarked in one of the horse transports, conveying the Blues and one Regt. of Life Guards to Portugal.

After a few days more the wind became fair, and we went again aboard the *Niemen*. There was a tremendous sea up at Spithead, for although the wind was fair, it blew a gale. The sight of the hundreds of ships all under weigh was magnificent beyond description, for there was a large force of infantry as well as the household troops in our fleet, which was convoyed by the *Niemen* (32) and two other men-of-war of smaller force.

I was so very ill that I believe I did not go on deck until the third day, on which day soon after breakfast the man at the mast head sung out 'A strange sail on the weather bow.' She was made out to be a man-of-war, and the officers in the gun-room seemed to think she was a Yankee frigate: and supposing we should have to fight her, I became tremendously excited, turned out of my berth, dressed myself in uniform, buckled on my sword, and went on deck to the astonishment of everyone, quite cured of my sea sickness.

It was not at all wonderful that I should have been so ill, for the sea was so high that one night the frigate was pooped, the cabin windows stove in, and my uncle and Genl. Stopford were completely sluiced in their cots! In fact, although the wind was fair, it blew a gale all through the Bay of Biscay, to the great injury of the poor horses of the household troops; many of them died, and we could see them hoisted up from the holds of the transports and dropped over board every day.

Being now quite cured of my sea sickness I was able to go and dine every day with the Generals and Captain, which I enjoyed very much, for good dinners we had. One day, however, a couple of roast ducks were sent to table very much burnt, which put the Captain in a terrible rage, the cook being reported to be drunk at the same time. I shall never forget the sight which presented itself to our dinner party as we came out of the Captain's cabin on to the quarter-deck. There was a great hulking fellow fastened up to the weather rigging by the wrists and ankles, looking as if he were crucified, but he was so very drunk that he appeared to me not to know what had happened to him. It was, however, a shocking sight, for at last his head began to droop, and he appeared to be fainting, on seeing which the Generals, as much shocked as I was at the cruel punishment, begged the Captain to have the unfortunate devil taken down, which was done at once with this warning, 'Don't over roast your ducks again.' It is needless to say further that the sufferer was the Captain's cook. This, I am sorry to say, is but a mild specimen of the cruelty exercised with impunity by Captains of men-of-war in those days. Captain Pym was a fine, tall, powerful man, very dark, and with a voice like a lion, and when heard through his speaking trumpet it made the men jump. It was his custom to use this implement as a cudgel also; and when the marines were hauling on the main sheet, he used to stand by licking into them like fun, calling out 'Run away with it, run away with it.' Notwithstanding his savage manner on board, he was a gentlemanlike man ashore, this Captain Pym, and considered a crack officer. He was always very kind to me during the passage, and I believe he was pleased at my turning out in full rig when I thought we were going to engage a Yankee frigate.

We were nearly through the Bay of Biscay before the gale abated, and when we were able to look about us, we found our immediate fleet of transports very much scattered; then came firing of guns and making of signals, and well do I remember the Captain's fine powerful word of command 'Fire another gun in the waist'.

At last, after passing Cape Finisterre, we had fine weather, and I enjoyed the sensation of coming into a warmer climate. I think we reached the mouth of the Tagus in about three weeks from our departure from Spithead.

While Charles was recuperating, Wellington fought and defeated Marmont at Salamanca, after which he occupied Madrid. However, he failed to capture Burgos and in November 1812 he found that he was faced by the combined forces of Soult, the French army of the north and King Joseph's large contingent from Valencia. These exceeded Wellington's total strength by 25,000 men and he was obliged to fall back, in considerable disorder, on Ciudad Rodrigo. The French did not follow with much enthusiasm, for

Salamanca was fresh in their memory, and they preferred to go into winter quarters.

Thus, when Charles landed on Portuguese soil once again he found there was no need to hurry:

> Finding on my arrival in Lisbon that the army had gone into cantonments, I was glad to halt there for six weeks to recover my strength. I recovered fast from my rheumatic attack in a three weeks very tempestuous passage, during which however I was perhaps rather benefited than otherwise by the shock of a wave, which while we were under bare poles awaiting the convoy, broke in three of the cabin windows and soused me in my cot as completely as if I had been keel hauled.

It was disappointing that Picton was, after all, intending to return to Portugal and to the 3rd Division, but in his absence Charles was given temporary command.

On 6 January 1813, he and Frederick Frankland, with four horses and seven mules, set off for the northern province of Beira, travelling by way of Tomar, Leiria, Pombal, Coimbra and Viseu, along a road fringed with the bleached skeletons of mules, oxen and horses which had died of fatigue and starvation during Masséna's retreat. They passed through the ruins of villages blackened by fire, where the houses had neither roofs, nor doors, nor windows. However, beyond Coimbra there was a dramatic change of scenery. The north of Portugal was and still is of rare beauty. This is how Charles, writing from his headquarters at Moimento de Beira, described the journey:

> I arrived here on the 21st, halting one day at Leiria and two at Coimbra. From Condeixa, where in pursuit of Masséna we had turned to our right, I came through a country quite new to me, and with much of which, especially about Coimbra, on account of the magnificent beauty of its scenery I was much pleased, though we had frequently most diabolical roads to encounter. The most interesting was of course the country about Busaco where I spent the night with the Mendicant Friars. The convent, which is situated in a large enclosure of wood, mostly very fine cedars, in any other country would be considered (in summer weather) a paradise.

The mendicant friars, according to Frederick Frankland, at first declined to shelter the soldiers' wives (of whom more anon) accompanying the party; but Charles sternly demanded that they be admitted and finally, with an ill grace, the friars agreed to this irregular and unwelcome invasion of their masculine privacy. Charles continued:

Notwithstanding occasional bad stabling and forage and the villainy of the roads, frequently as dangerous for a horse to move upon as a broken flight of steps would be, I brought up my stud without accident and in very tolerable condition. As for myself, I bore the journey particularly well, seldom sitting down after my ride of 16 or 20 miles until the setting in of darkness obliged me to return from the walk I usually took to see my surroundings.

I found the 3rd Division 8,400 rank and file on paper, but with only 4,602 effectives present, and of these 1,736 Portuguese.

My family consists for the present of the A.A.G. Stovin, who had been A.D.C. to General Picton, and of an A.D.C. in Spottiswoode's absence, Lt. Jackson of the 83rd, a smart gentlemanly lad, whom I saw a good deal of in former times, and who shewed much kindness and interest in me when wounded. His brother is Colonel of the North Mayo Militia. He is like most of his countrymen, let them be ever so well connected, defective in attainments which Spottiswoode possesses, but I think he promises to be more generally active and useful in housekeeping and I must not omit the superintendence of the stabling as well, which the former had no turn for, though it is a thing of great consequence to his General.

My A.Q.M. General has at present his wife at Quarters.

The division is dispersed in villages with not more than one Regiment in each, which gives me a great deal of riding, but to this I have no other objection than what arises from the badness of the roads. The country is extremely picturesque, having all the great features to make it beautiful in summer.

I bear horseback exercise pretty well, though I perhaps have at times overdone it, and after trying different modes of saving the hollow of my foot from the pressure of the stirrup I find the best is a clog in addition to the boot.

The Assistant Quartermaster General was not the only soldier with a campaigning wife. The baggage party, under the command of a sergeant, which preceded Charles on his journey north included several women married to men in the ranks. They were determined to join their husbands encamped north of the Douro.

Half a day's march from Leiria Charles came upon a Spaniard trudging southwards towards Lisbon. This traveller said that he had just heard 'great shrieking' from a woman whom be believed to be English. She was a little way off the road, but he had been afraid to approach her in case, being a foreigner, he might be accused of having molested her. Charles sent Frederick Frankland to investigate.

Frederick cantered ahead. Hearing loud groans among the olive trees some way off the road, he discovered a soldier's wife in an advanced stage of labour. None of the other women with the baggage party had been willing to stay with her and they had callously left her to her fate in a ravaged and deserted countryside where packs of wolves abounded. Neither Charles nor Frederick were prepared to try their hands at midwifery, but Frederick, searching for help in the nearby forest, at last found an aged Portuguese crone. He took a piece of money from his purse and with this as an inducement led her to the sufferer. She immediately grasped the situation and the soldier's wife assured Frederick that she was content to be entrusted to the old woman's care. So, making signs to indicate that more money would be paid if she eventually brought her patient to their next stop, Pombal, Frederick spurred on in pursuit of his uncle, who congratulated him on acting the part of the Good Samaritan.

The next morning, as Charles and Frederick were mounting their horses in Pombal for the day's journey to Condeixa, they were surprised to see the soldier's wife enter the town with a healthy baby in her arms and the Portuguese woman at her side. She told them that after delivering the child among the olive trees, the old woman had disappeared into the forest. Returning later with two other women and some food, she had escorted the mother and baby to a forest hut for protection from the wolves. At dawn they had set out to walk seven miles to Pombal. Charles made a handsome payment to the Portuguese woman, whose solicitude was so much greater than that of the soldiers' wives, and arranged for the mother and child to be given food and shelter in Pombal until such times as a further detachment of British troops should arrive and escort them on their way northwards. Evidently the women of the Peninsular War generation were as tough, resilient and impervious to hardship as their husbands.

In March Charles had time to pay a visit to Oporto, though with less opportunity for gaiety than General Picton and Colonel Campbell had found the previous May.

I arrived here the evening before last from Regua in one of the great Douro wine boats now in the service of the Commissariat of our army. The distance of 14 leagues (of four miles each) we did in twelve hours, without a sail but occasionally using our oars, or rather sweeps, which are as large as would be required for a frigate. Our rudder was a machine about thirty foot long poised on a pivot, having but two or three feet immersed in the water; it was worked by occasionally one, and at other times, six men on a high stage elevated nearly amidships. The management of this unwieldy machine was very dexterous when going down the narrow rapids which we frequently met with in the first four or five leagues. When towing the craft upstream in those parts of the river where the banks do not admit of towing paths, you will see twelve or sixteen men in a row, bare footed, skipping with their tow ropes from rock to rock in a way only to be matched by so many monkeys. The work these men do shows the Portuguese of this part of the country in a very favourable light as regards industry and perseverance.

The scenery of the river is very good the whole way and in the most romantic parts the most extraordinary artificial effects are also exhibited. In the neighbourhood of Regua, where the best wine is made, the vines are in terraces up to the summit of lofty mountains. Other parts admit of hardly the smallest vegetation, the river being narrowed between masses of rocks. The day was as fine and warm as one could wish for, but a barge for the last eight leagues would have been a good exchange for the heavy barca. I am just returned from a ride to the mouth of the river, and saw two brigs pass over the bar, but it was a perfect mill pond to what it generally is. I think it would be a pity were I not to order a pipe of wine from here. It will not, I apprehend, be much less than £70 for wine of four or five years old, for the prices have not yet fallen though the last vintage was a particularly good one.

I shall return in four or five days, by the right bank of the river, which is the best road to Lamego. Mr Jackson is alone with me, and we brought mules and horses to the amount of seven in the boat with us. We are particularly fortunate in the weather, but are otherwise in point of time for society, not only as being the beginning of Lent, but that the Prince of Orange, in a six weeks' residence, had drawn too hard on the hospitality of the inhabitants for them not to require a respite from dancing etc. to 4 o'clock every morning. However I am glad to see the place and country when I can and thought it best not to postpone the attempt.

When the rains and gales of April 1813 subsided, preparations were made for an offensive. 'This year', said Charles, 'we shall take tents with us and I believe we shall start in a better state of equipment than has been done for some seasons and in numerical force greater than any years yet.' Hitherto, whatever the weather conditions, the troops had, except during the siege of Badajos, been expected to spend their campaigning nights on the cold, bare earth when there was no village to give them shelter. Only a few officers, who were able to provide themselves with the requisite transport, had enjoyed the luxury of sleeping in a tent.

In May Picton returned, having the grace to tell Charles that 'I am much concerned to deprive you of a command in which I am sure you would have achieved much honour and reputation.' He welcomed him back to his old brigade and expressed the hope that they might 'divide the laurels which I have no doubt will be the result of our joint exertions'. This was a disappointment, but Charles's example in leadership and his training of the brigade to which he now returned had contributed much to the heroic reputation it had earned in the attacks on Ciudad Rodrigo and Badajos. It was like returning home, to a smaller house but to one which was well equipped and deeply loved.

Wellington's army was now concentrated in northern Portugal. At the end of May 1813, a British force of some 80,000 men was ready to advance eastwards across the River Douro and to embark on the great enterprise of liberating Spain from the French. It was to be a last farewell to Portugal, for whose people and countryside Charles and his fellow soldiers had developed a basic affection and admiration, however corrupt and incompetent its Regency Government and however much the British sought to disguise their feelings by supercilious references to the dirt and poverty of the wretched, exploited and war-scarred Portuguese peasantry.

7

Vitoria

Spring came late in 1813 and it would have been imprudent to move against the enemy until the countryside through which the army was to advance could provide forage for the horses. It would also have been imprudent to move the whole army along the well-worn route through Ciudad Rodrigo and Salamanca against new French defences guarding the fords of the Tormes and Duero rivers in Spain. So Wellington divided his army in two and made a deception plan. Towards the end of May, he marched from Ciudad Rodrigo with Sir Rowland Hill and 20,000 men and easily drove a weak French garrison out of Salamanca. He then left Hill in command and set off to join the main body of his troops to the north.

This main body, including the 3rd Division, had been concentrated in the Portuguese province of Tras os Montes, which is in the north-eastern extremity of the country and contains some of the most beautiful scenery in Europe. It is as rugged as it is beautiful: to march through its deep defiles meant guns must be lowered by ropes over steep precipices, cavalry, infantry and pack-animals must be directed along ravines which seldom offered so much as the amenity of a cart-track. Under the command of Sir Thomas Graham, an Anglo-Portuguese army of 80,000 men achieved this formidable task and crossed the Douro from Portuguese soil. Charles did not conceal his disappointment that circumstances had denied him the substantive command of the 3rd Division, for he had believed that Picton, who had returned to England disgruntled by what he considered lack of recognition, would stay there and attend to his duties as a Member of Parliament. However the Order of the Bath had removed Picton's grievance and resolved his doubts. On 26 May Charles wrote from Vimioso on the north-eastern frontier:

My last from Moimento of the 2nd inst. mentioned that I expected to write my next from Tras os Montes and I accordingly now write from very nearly the northern point of it while we halt a couple of days on our way to the bank of the Esla, a strong feature which covers the enemy's right from above Benavente to Zamora, near to which it falls into the Douro. As I don't think the preparations for the advance of the army were in sufficient forwardness to admit of its well taking place at an earlier period, we were fortunate in the rains commencing just when they did, lasting for nearly a month to the 16th when the Divisions in general broke up from their cantonements. The 1st, 3rd, 4th, 5th, 6th and 7th Divisions with Pack's and Bradford's unattached Portuguese Brigades of Infantry crossed the Douro at different points from Oporto to Torre del Moncorvo, while Lord W. employed the Light Division and General Hill's corps upon the old ground, being himself in the first instance with them. The troops on our side advance in three columns under the general direction of Sir Thomas Graham. The 3rd Division is in the centre arc, which will consist of about 15,000 men when we meet together, which we have not yet done, under Sir Thomas Picton. He arrived only three or four days before our march, and had subsequently so smart a fit of illness as caused him again to resign the command to me, but he rejoined us two or three days ago, I am glad to say to all appearances perfectly recovered and in excellent spirits. No one would believe me where I to say that I did not feel regret at losing the command of the Division at such a moment, and more especially one that I know so well and which I have had the satisfaction to see improved so much in health and general fitness for service during the time I have commanded them, being now 6,000 effectives. But I certainly have much satisfaction in seeing my old commander again with the army to which he is such an acquisition, and it would be a very ungrateful return for his kindness were I to wish for aggrandisement at the expense of his health or convenience.

My present command consists of the 1st Batt. of the 5th, reduced from about 900 men with which they left Lisbon this time twelve months to half that number, and of these the moiety of my old little 2nd Batt. men, but with a woeful falling off in value of their officers; the 2nd Batt. of the 87th, the Prince of Wales Own Irish, or Sir John Doyle's hunters, about the same strength as the 5th, with my two other old corps, the

2nd Batt., 83rd and 94th, both weak and making an ensemble of 1,800, which is as many as I can at any time count upon in action. Weak however as they are in comparison with many other Brigades, I have a natural attachment to the remains and would not exchange them for the best similar command in the army.

On 30 May, the army, in exact accordance with its time-table, reached the River Esla, a turbulent tributary of the Duero flowing southwards from Leon and the mountains of the Asturias. At the village of Lucilla, Charles took advantage of renewed postal facilities to report progress and his own living conditions:

> Our column encamped here yesterday. I am myself in the village in a really Spanish cottage (with the exception of cleanliness) calculated exclusively for heat, and with one window only just four times the size of my hand. It is well that it rained yesterday as I can open the door today to give some light or you would have had occasion to think me neglectful of writing. We hear that Lord W. has got possession of Salamanca with little opposition and he has this day, as I expected he would, come to this side of the country to judge of the measures to be pursued here, and his neighbourhood will now, I suppose, reopen to us the usual communications of the post.

Crossing the Esla presented problems, but none that were sufficient to damp the spirits of men well-fed, well-trained and by now experienced in the adventures of campaigning. The enemy forces confronting them were scattered. Joseph Buonaparte, commanded the French armies with the advice and assistance of Marshal Jourdan, hero of the early Revolutionary army of the Sambre et Meuse. They were still in doubt where the main attack might be directed. The French cavalry did their best, but on 2 June the British 10th Hussars, with the 15th and 18th in support, fought and destroyed a regiment of French Dragoons.

> La Mota, June 4th, 1813
>
> I broke off my last letter to go and pay some visits at Headquarters, but one of the first persons I met was the D.Q.M.G. who informed me that a route was just setting off for the march that evening. I returned upon my steps and leaving our tents standing, being then in sight of the enemy from the other side of the river, we marched at 8 with orders to pass, along with

two Brigades of Cavalry and some more Infantry, a ford which had that day been reported practicable. We found however that it had increased two feet in depth from the melting of the snow in the mountains and that it was otherwise a very bad one, and we were in consequence obliged to give up the attempt; but the Cavalry persevered and succeeded with the loss of several men drowned. Some others of the Division found equal difficulty at another ford lower down, and we ourselves and the rest passed by a pontoon bridge the next day.

Our advanced Cavalry, the new Hussar Brigade, has been very dashing and fortunate in the commencement of their career; everybody is in high spirits and the army healthy.

It was reported yesterday that we were likely to commemorate our good old King's birthday by coming in contact with five Divisions of the enemy posted on one of the small rivers we have to pass on our way to the Pisuergo, but there are none of them I now learn nearer than Valladolid, so instead I shall be satisfied to drink his Majesty's health in Lord W's claret from whom I had the honour of a hearty shake of the hand today, being the first time I had seen him since my return.

The 3rd are this day in one column with the Light and 4th Divisions. The Hussar and three other Brigades of Cavalry are in our front. The Household and two Brigades of Reserve Artillery are in our rear. The formation of this 'Corps d'Elite', as we conceive it, and his Lordship's presence makes us suppose that we are to have the honour of the first attempt upon the enemy. I hope soon to send you good news.

The British army marched north-eastwards from the Esla, across several smaller streams, in the direction of the next formidable water-barrier, 150 miles ahead, the river Ebro. When King Joseph at last discovered what was afoot, he sent distress signals to his generals in the hope of concentrating his forces at Burgos. This plan had to be abandoned, for the fortress had no adequate provisions, and so the French, having done all they could to destroy the castle and the city, retreated eastwards. In London both the Admiralty and the Horse Guards (as the War Office was then called) showed an administrative competence for which they are seldom given credit in organising the despatch of supplies and reinforcements. The indefatigable guerillas did their best to keep some northern Spanish ports open, but these were neither large nor secure enough for the army's requirements and it was another three months before Wellington could dispense with Lisbon and Oporto as supply bases.

The march to the Ebro required as much vigour and endurance as that in Tras os Montes, for the route was equally wild and mountainous. The guns were manhandled through the gullies and ravines for six exhausting days while band after band of Spanish guerillas appeared over the mountain tops to join the advancing forces of liberation. The army marched in three strong columns. By 18 June they had reached and crossed the Ebro, a fact of which the French were entirely ignorant until British formations appeared on the Bilbao-Burgos road and there was a skirmish in which the French were worsted.

Two tributaries of the Ebro, the Bayas and the broader Zadora, flow west of Vitoria,* a city standing in a basin enclosed by hills. By 20 June the French were behind the Zadora and the British, having discarded their tents and their baggage, spent the night some two miles away on the banks of the Bayas, divided from the Zadora by a steep ridge of hills. Picton's 3rd Division was one of the four which together with most of the artillery and the heavy cavalry formed the centre of the British line under Wellington's direct command. Numerically, the Allies for once held the advantage, with 60,000 British and Portuguese troops and 20,000 recently arrived Spanish auxiliaries. The French had only 60,000 men in all, but they had 150 cannon against Wellington's 90.

At daybreak on the wet misty morning of 21 June, the British forded the river Bayas and began their advance towards the enemy lines. There were seven bridges over the Zadora and the French, perhaps themselves intending to attack, had destroyed none of them. On the right of the British army, two miles from Wellington's centre, General Hill commanded a mixed column of Spaniards and British, and on the far left, scarcely a mile from Vitoria itself, General Graham approached a well-defended stretch of the river with the 5th British Division and a strong force of Portuguese and Spaniards. However, the main attack was to be in the centre, which embraced four bridges leading to a series of undulating hills and finally to a fertile plain of standing corn surrounding Vitoria itself.

The left-hand section of Wellington's centre was composed of the 3rd and the 7th Divisions under Lieutenant-General the Earl

* I have adopted the modern spelling—originally Vittoria, in Charles's and other contemporary accounts of the battle.

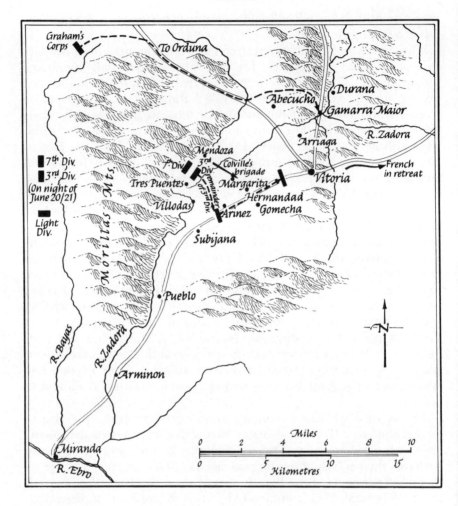

The Battle of Vitoria

of Dalhousie, Commander of the 7th Division, who was senior
to Sir Thomas Picton. It was obviously important for these divisions
to keep in touch, not only with each other but with the formations
on their right and left. When they marched out of their camp
on the Bayas river and began their arduous ascent of the ridge
which separated them from the Zadora, the early morning mist
still clung to the hills. Contact was lost; nor was it regained
as the mist dispersed. First, as Charles declared, General Graham's
men on the left flank were at fault.

A bad look-out was kept by his people, and though our column, consisting of the 3rd and 7th, saw his very plain as we reached the top of the mountain, they did not see ours, which was to have been the signal for his advance, and I believe consequently he did not march for three hours afterwards.

Worse was to follow; for most of Lord Dalhousie's men vanished. When at 8 a.m. the 3rd Division, having surmounted the ridge, began moving down to the villages in the valley below, they found only one brigade of the 7th Division and the divisional artillery alongside them. Dalhousie's other two brigades tried to be clever and take a short cut through the mountains. In consequence they lost their way and only arrived on the scene of action several hours later. It was thus that Charles's brigade was called upon to play a part in the battle which had been no part of the original plan.

His letters tell his own story, but this becomes clearer if a brief account is given of the action fought by the neighbouring divisions. There is a loop in the river Zadora which juts sharply westwards towards the mountain range across which the British had advanced that morning. There King Joseph placed an advance post of artillery. On each side of the loop were bridges. One was at Villodas, where the Light Division advanced under cover of woods and rugged ground almost to the river bank. The other, north of the loop, was at Tres Puentes, and it was unguarded. When Wellington learned of this, he despatched a brigade of the Light Division which crossed the Tres Puentes bridge at the double, outflanked King Joseph's advanced artillery in the loop, ran up a hill and lay on the crest a few hundred yards from the main French line. They were followed by the 15th Hussars who galloped across in single file.

Meanwhile, still further upstream, the 3rd Division patiently awaited the arrival of Lord Dalhousie's errant brigades. When these failed to appear, the 3rd were ordered to advance on the heavily guarded bridge at Mendoza where they were met by concentrated artillery fire and a hail of musket-balls from a strong body of French light infantry. A mass of heavy cavalry also awaited them, but a daring colonel of the Light Division, seeing the losses which the 3rd Division must suffer against such opposition, led his riflemen to the rescue from their position on the crest of the hill above the Tres Puentes bridge. Running between the river and the French cavalry, they made a flank attack on the French gunners and light infantry. Under the cover of this diversion the leading brigades of the 3rd Division crossed the Mendoza bridge, and Charles's four regiments, followed by Dalhousie's only available brigade, forded the river to their left.

It was now 1 p.m. and the whole line of the River Zadora, from Hill's column on the extreme right to Graham's several miles upstream to the left, was a blaze of cannon-fire and musketry. The French retreated to their second line of defence and Wellington, seeing the importance of taking the village of Arinez, astride the main road to Vitoria, sent Picton and two brigades of the 3rd Division to the right, diagonally between the British and French lines, to help in the assault on that village. Picton, says Rifleman Kincaid, was 'dressed in a blue coat and round hat and swore as roundly all the way as if he had been wearing two cocked ones'. Thus Charles was left alone in the face of a greatly superior enemy force, although on his left he had the comfort of that solitary brigade of the 7th Division which had not lost its way. Dalhousie summoned him to join this brigade in an attack on the strongly held villages of Margarita and Hermandad and, once they were taken, to advance through the standing corn on the left bank of the Zadora towards the last French line of defence a mile outside the city walls. Meanwhile, when Picton departed, there was a dangerous gap on Charles's right where he was, to all intents and purposes, unsupported.

His brigade, containing 1,500 rank and file, advanced over banks and deep ditches under heavy artillery fire from the heights above Margarita and Hermandad. In the fields the crops grew so high that the men had corn up to their chins. Charles sent the 83rd Regiment in front and, with the three other regiments in support, they drove the French from Margarita and Hermandad, occupied by a French Division over 4,000 strong. Later in the day they were to capture Marshal Jourdan's baton which he let fall in the turmoil of retreat. Charles was in the thick of things. He had two horses shot under him, and was himself hit by a musket ball between the thumb and wrist. This shot, which fortunately missed both artery and tendon, came, he said, 'from a fellow who with some others took us in flank from behind the village church'.

On the day after the battle he wrote to his sister Catherine Frankland to say that being detained on the left, while Picton and the rest of the division were detached to attack Arinez, 'soon made me become the principal engaged on that side and for the many hours it lasted I had a kind of distinct battle on my own with infantry only, opposed to an infinitely superior number of the enemy in my front and flank, assisted by a numerous artillery. My loss could not but be considerable.' A few days later he amplified his account in a letter to his brother John:

A general action was what the enemy, we had all along understood, wished to avoid, but which you in England would naturally suppose Lord Wellington would be equally anxious to bring on after the efforts he had made to collect a force competent to the purpose and the success of combinations so honorable to his foresight, judgement and energy.

We here consider the battle of Vitoria, including of course its previous combinations, perhaps the finest thing ever done by a British Allied Army; as a deroute of the enemy it was most complete, but the difficulties of the ground even for infantry (for very little of the cavalry could, or at least did, come into action), being besides banks and hedges, to be expected in a richly cultivated place, cut by drains and ditches in the cornfields in which we occasionally marched up to our chins. All these gave the enemy an advantage of keeping at just such a distance from us as they pleased, and prevented our making such a number of prisoners as would otherwise have followed such a success, a paucity indeed, not amounting for two or three days after to above 2,000, which I doubt that they will allege in diminution of their defeat: their killed and wounded too, left on the ground by no means being in proportion to ours, I am sorry to say. But we have subsequently heard that they have carried off towards France many thousands of the latter. They take more pains to conceal their dead, and are cleverer in carrying off their wounded than we are.

Our loss arose from the great superiority of the enemy's artillery actually engaged; for instance my Brigade was heavily cannonaded for the greater part of the time we were engaged without having a single gun to give them in return direct from ourselves.

As my letter to Catherine mentioned, mine was altogether that day on detached service, not having received from anybody an order from the time I commenced till the time I discontinued action, then taking up a defensive position on account of my being threatened with being turned by an overwhelming force, when Lord Dalhousie sent me a Brigade of the 7th Divn. to support my right. As far as my observation and feeling went at the time, I should say indeed that this was the only support I directly received the whole day, though this of course does not argue against my being otherwise assisted by the attacks made relatively to my position, though without being immediately in concert with me.

His Lordship, I am told, had a good view of us at one time and expressed much anxiety on account of the preponderating numbers against us. He was just, I am told, sending orders for something to be done, when he observed his wish was anticipated. He was as usual, I understand, here, there, and everywhere, and as he never minds how heavy the fire if he wants to have a nearer view of things, his numerous escapes are as extraordinary as they are fortunate for the army under him. I had a hearty shake of the hand from him next day as Genl. Picton and I met him on our way in to see the town of Vitoria, having on the night before lain *à la belle étoile* about a league in front of it, rejoining my Lt. General about 8 o'clock, after having been separated from him at eleven in the morning.

His Lordship seemed highly gratified, but entered into no particulars, and even in a message to Sir Thos. desiring him to send in the names of such officers of the Divn. as he wished to recommend for promotion, declined having any details of occurrences.

I had another instance of providencial escape, for which I cannot be sufficiently grateful: for it appears to me that had the ball pierced only a line or two deeper, I must have lost my thumb and with it most probably my hand. The bruised flesh sloughed off two days since and wholesome granulations are throwing themselves out, which by the bye is the most painful part of the process of the wound, but only occasionally felt. In another fortnight I shold hope it will entirely have healed over. Rest would be preferable, but still having the use of my fingers, I dress myself and go on much as usual, and with my hand generally in a sling of my sash, and have taken my daily marches, nearly sometimes eight and ten hours on horseback, without inconvenience. I had the scabbard of my sword in my hand at the time I received the blow, which came sideways, and which probably by swelling out the muscles accounts for the depth of the wound without material injury. I was at the time on foot, my horse, one I bought in Lisbon, being just before disabled for the time (I believe he will recover) by a shot in his leg and another in his throat. I shortly after mounted one of my Brigade Major's, but from which I was glad to alight without a fall, as his eye, poor ˙creature, was knocked out by a shot which, without meeting some such obstacle, would probably have encountered some part of myself.

Wellington made no public or private acknowledgment of Picton's diagonal attack on the French forces at Arinez, which has been warmly praised by military historians. This may be evidence that he felt a certain personal antipathy towards Picton and sometimes deliberately omitted to give him the credit that was his due. He did not even ask for an account of the 3rd Division's contribution to the victory.

Charles, for his part, sent Picton a detailed and official report of his action on that eventful day:

Camp near Vitoria, June 22nd, 1813

Sir,

My Brigade of the 3rd Divn., having been detached from under your immediate superintendence during the operations of yesterday, I do myself the honor of submitting to you a statement of the way in which we were employed: a pleasing task as far as the conduct of the officers and troops is the subject, but which I lament to say is embittered by the loss in killed and wounded of very many of each.

Immediately on passing the bridge of Mendoza, being then as you are aware the rear Brigade of the Divn., I received an order from Lt. Genl. Lord Dalhousie to proceed to the left in support of the light companies under Lt. Col. Lloyd, and soon after had a message from that officer himself pressing for assistance, he being warmly engaged. The advance of the Brigade soon made it the principal object of the enemy's attention in that quarter. The ground over which I had to advance was much intersected with banks and drains and otherwise intricate, so that the deployment I made (as early as possible on account of the enemy's cannonade from the heights opposite) did not admit of more than a Battn. at a time, and these, in the instance of the first two, I was obliged to separate into wings, that the leading ones, while they were supported by those that followed, might inclose a village immediately in our front, and into which the French, as they fell back from before the light companies as we advanced, had thrown themselves.

Having with the left wing of the 83rd. (the leading Battn.) turned the village on that side, I posted them in a lane, perpendicular to the march of the Battalions in line, and where by their fire upon a large body of the enemy opposite they would have much facilitated the advance of the former, but that some more of the retiring enemy, coming the furthest from the left,

121

threw themselves into another village and galled us much by an enfilade fire at the distance of not more than sixty or seventy yards (see Note 1).

To put a stop to this, the men falling fast from the fire in our front as well as flank, I ordered a charge with the few men that could the readiest be collected out of the lane and ditch, and the measure succeeded, the enemy retiring in very superior force in a great hurry from that and a third village from which we also forced them, but not without a considerable proportion of loss in that part of this weak Battn. (see Note 2).

The right wing having continued their flank march, rejoined us at this period, which enabled me to go to the other Regts. of the Brigade. These I found advancing much in the order I had left them (but with sharp shooters on their right flank), and also engaged with very superior numbers in front and flank, with a smart fire of round and grape shot and occasional shells upon them. The appearance of the enemy on the right being particularly imposing and threatening, in an attempt to surround us, I placed the 5th regt. *en potence* behind a bank from which their fire could keep the enemy in check on that side, while with the other two Battns, 87th and 94th, I determined trying the same experiments that had succeeded on the villages, but on a larger scale and with more regular formation which the ground now admitted of, and the enemy consequently gave way, retiring in very good line of infinitely more than our numbers (and covered by *tirailleurs*) before the good countenance of our men rapidly advancing for a charge. (See Note 3.)

Upon this occasion the ground offered most favourably for the 87th Regt., and I should do injustice to them and fail to express my own grateful feelings, were I not to mention that Lt. Col. Gough and his Battn. availed themselves of it in a style of gallantry and good order that in my opinion nothing could excel. Having proceeded in this manner as far as I thought prudent, or as might be consistent with the movements of the rest of the army, I looked out for ground to place the Brigade under cover from the enemy's cannonade, at the time very heavy, and succeeded in the cases of the 83rd and 94th Regt., but unfortunately could not in those of the 5th and 87th and they continued to suffer much.

In a little time the enemy, apparently disappointed at not having been able to tempt me further on, broke off in a strong column, or rather I believe two, with the evident intention of turning my left. This measure would have been much assisted by their occupation of a village and mill dam on that flank.

I had at first hoped that the village was in possession of the light companies under Lt. Col. Lloyd, but on closing to it found it not to be the case, and that it was too late for me to attempt it with fatigued troops, as the enemy had already arrived at it. I therefore satisfied myself for the time with only securing the Brigade by placing it's left on the river, and covering its front by the light infantry (who now for the first time joined me in very small numbers) placed behind trees and on the mill dam.

My Lord Dalhousie shortly after sent Major Genl. Barnes's Brigade of the 7th Divn. to the support of my right, and in about half an hour more the enemy retired apparently on the advance of Sir Thos. Graham's column, and which I followed in the direction of the village attacked by that Corps. Before I had reached it, the heads of my Brigade columns keeping line with the march of the 7th Divn., the enemy were driven out.

The charge of our Hussars now taking place, and the reserve Brigades of artillery coming up, I halted my Brigade and was shortly after met by your Aide de Camp, who pointed out where I could again rejoin the Divn., and with your orders to do so.

Note 1: It was here my horse (one I bought at Lisbon) and which at the time I held by the bridle, was wounded, first in the neck, and then in the leg, upon which, giving him to my orderly Dragoon who was also on foot by me, he, the Dragoon, got his wound in the side.

Note 2: It was here I received the shot in my hand from a fellow, who with some others, took us in flank behind the village church.

Note 3: It was now that my Brigade Major's horse, on which I was mounted, had his left eye knocked out, a sad thing for him, poor fellow, but which most probably saved me from an equally severe casualty.

The notes were not written for Sir Thomas Picton's edification, but for that of Charles's brother-in-law, the Rev. R. F. Frankland, to whom he sent a copy of his despatch. Meanwhile Frankland had himself written to condole on the wounded thumb, of which he had read in the *Official Gazette*.

It seems to be your destiny to be always found in the brunt of the battle. A friend of mine, who was every day shaved by his old Scotch gardener, used as constantly to be cut by Sawney's operation, who as regularly exclaimed when he broke the skin, 'I never saw any one so free to bleed as you are.' So one may say of you: you are very free to bleed! To have been the only General wounded in the victory of Vitoria is no small honour; and if you could have been as well known at St. James's as by the army, and had been as intimate with Princes as you have been with the yellow fever, this circumstance would not have passed unnoticed in Court and Parliament.

The City of London, however, was not slow to record its approval. On 13 July a Common Council 'holden in the Chamber of the Guildhall' poured an encomium of praise on all concerned in the 'splendid and decisive victory', conferred the Freedom of the City on Generals Graham and Hill, and included Charles among those whose 'skill, bravery, and exertions' deserved particular mention. Picton and Charles seem to have been doubtful whether Lieutenant-General Sir Thomas Graham deserved either the Freedom or the gold box, 'of the value of 100 guineas', in which the City Fathers saw fit to enclose it. Picton, for his part, was aggrieved by Wellington's official despatch:

The Gazette of the battle is (like most of the despatches of the Noble Marquis) anything but a correct likeness of the events which it purposes to relate, and it uncandidly (I think) endeavours to attribute to combinations and manoeuvre what was really effected by hard fighting. The preparative arrangements were excellent and perfect, and entitled the planner to every degree of credit. But the fact is that the French obstinately disputed every foot and were driven back, by sheer hard fighting of the 3rd Division, from a succession of strong positions. Yet it would not appear from the official account that we were at all engaged except General Colville's Brigade. This is not quite fair but the army will do us justice.

Charles, though gratified by the references to his own 'firmness and resolute gallantry' in the despatches of Wellington, Dalhousie and Picton, also felt that the 3rd Division had not received due recognition:

Heavy loss is not always a proof of merit on the part of

either the troops or their Commander, but when success against very superior numbers crowns their exertions, their country and friends must not grudge their loss, and as this is admitted to have been the case with mine in the battle of Vitoria, I need not be ashamed to own that it cost me 553 in killed and wounded, amounting to a third of the Brigade that day in the field.

The service I was employed on was quite of a detached nature, never receiving an order from the time I commenced till I left off action, nor having, that I was aware of, any direct support, but it seems that those who were looking on, among others our most noble Commander, took better care of me than I thought of. The other two Brigades of the Division, I may be allowed to say, equally distinguished themselves; the Portuguese one in particular had the full admiration of everyone who saw them for active as well as passive bravery and steadiness. The Division lost 1,760 men, a third of their own numbers, and I think equal to one half of the loss of the whole on that day.

Under these circumstances our vanity, if our friends will allow it to be so called, was not a little hurt at seeing ourselves lumped in the Despatch with the Light and 4th Divisions who had very little to do, and with the 7th who, with the exception of the Brigade that supported me, lost their way late in the day in the mountains and never pulled a trigger or lost a man. Individually and even for my Brigade I have reason to be satisfied with what was said, but Sir Thomas Picton and the Division think far otherwise. It is highly mortifying to have the description of such a day's business entrusted to so unequal or partial a judge as Lord Bathurst who in the House of Lords, without a word of the 3rd Division, said Sir Thomas Graham carried all before him, whereas the business of his column, which commenced too late, was confined to the freeing of one village which was done almost entirely by his Artillery.

The end of the battle was thus described by Napier:

At six o'clock the French reached the last defensible height, one mile in front of Vitoria. Behind them was the plain in which the city stood, and beyond the city thousands of carriages and animals and non-combatants, men, women and children, were crowding together in all the madness of terror, and as the English shot went booming over-head the vast crowd started and swerved with a convulsive movement, while a dull and

125

horrid sound of distress arose; but there was no hope, no stay for army or multitude. It was the wreck of a nation.

It was, in fact, to be another two years before the nation was finally wrecked, but there has seldom been a greater rout. All the French army's stores, baggage and papers had to be abandoned. King Joseph's baggage train, containing many of Spain's finest treasures which he had personally annexed, was captured. Nearly all the enemy guns were taken, the French managing to save but two out of their whole (and, greatly superior) ammunition train. There could now be only a brief delay before the French were driven out of Spain altogether as the result of a six weeks' campaign in which Wellington marched his army of 100,000 men nearly six hundred miles, over steep mountains, from the Portuguese frontier to the Pyrenees, crossing river after river, often in flood, investing strong fortresses as he went and fatally dividing and disrupting a French battle-trained force which had been in total over 120,000 strong.

8

The Pyrenees

The French have always proved themselves capable of swift recovery. Few nations have endured more shattering defeats in war and more cataclysmic upheavals in peace. None have been quicker to revive their strength and restore their prosperity.

After the rout at Vitoria, the only intact French divisions in northern Spain were those of General Clausel, numbering 18,000 men. Arriving too late to take part in the battle, he had recoiled undamaged and was still at large. The way therefore seemed clear for an immediate Allied invasion of France, even if Napoleon refused to accept the apparently inevitable. Britain's continental allies, beaten a month previously at Lützen and Bauzen, had been cheered by the news of Vitoria; it was even more important, in Napoleon's view, to deceive his own countrymen about the prospects before them. He could be a prodigious liar when he found it convenient. Like Hitler, who shared many of his defects but few of his qualities, he treated truth and falsehood as handmaidens to be employed as best suited the occasion. He issued totally false announcements about a brisk but indecisive engagement. He recalled his discredited brother, Joseph, and the crestfallen, baton-less Marshal Jourdan; and he took instant action to restore the position on his south-west frontier.

The Emperor ordered Nicolas Jean Soult, Duke of Dalmatia (known to the British Army as 'Johnny'), to go to Bayonne and take immediate command. That skilful Marshal, whose taste for viceregal splendour had led him to prefer luxury to military exertions at Oporto and Seville, now girded his loins with all the energy and enthusiasm of his early days. Three weeks after the sun had set on 'the wreck of a nation' at Vitoria, he reached Bayonne, assumed full authority and applied himself to organising an army of 80,000 men dedicated to throwing Wellington back from the foothills of the Pyrenees.

Soult was much assisted by the tenacity of the French garrisons at Pampeluna and San Sebastian. Perhaps Wellington could have swept past those fortresses, as Eisenhower by-passed Brest and Havre in 1944. He might have left his guerilla friends, Longa and Mina, together with units of the Spanish army under his command, to blockade the garrisons. He might thus have crossed the river Bidassoa, which is the frontier between France and Spain, before Soult had time to organise his defences. But the British army was exhausted after its long march across swift-flowing rivers and steep mountain ranges. Supplies were only trickling through the ports of Santander and Passages; and until San Sebastian should be available to the Royal Navy, much had still to be brought the whole way from Lisbon and Oporto. In Catalonia there was an undefeated French army, under Marshal Suchet, which might join forces with Soult or attack Wellington's flank. Worse still, after the triumph at Vitoria, over 12,000 of Wellington's victorious veterans had absented themselves in search of plunder. The British soldiers, incomparable in battle, were incorrigible in victory. Their discipline was iron-clad under fire, and in normal circumstances they were compassionate to the wretched Portuguese and Spanish peasantry; but nothing could deter them from pillage and drunken licence when a blood-stained siege or battle was over. Lord Melville, lately First Lord of the Admiralty, had said that 'the worst men were the fittest for soldiers', a remark which seems hard to contradict, even though it was made by the last British statesman ever to be impeached by Parliament for peculation.

So it was that for a whole month Wellington consolidated his position in the southern foothills of the Pyrenees, collected his erring sheep and laid siege to San Sebastian and Pampeluna. By the time that month had passed, Soult had reorganised the battered French divisions and stood prepared to re-enter Spain with his 80,000 men by whichever mountain passes he might choose. There followed, between 25 July 1813 and 2 August, ten battles fought in nine days, during which over 20,000 men were killed or wounded. Wellington expected Soult to concentrate his forces for the relief of San Sebastian. He therefore established his headquarters within easy distance of that city, and in an effort to forestall the French an ill-conceived assault on the fortress was attempted on 25 July. It was an expensive failure. Meanwhile Soult had moved powerful forces to the eastern end of the forty-mile front and, attacking where Wellington least expected him, came close to relieving Pampeluna.

Those ten engagements are collectively known as the Battle

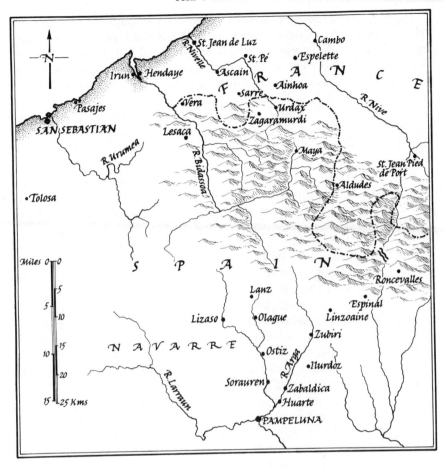

of the Pyrenees. They were fought as fiercely as any in the Peninsular War. Indeed, Wellington is on record as saying that the finest feat of arms he witnessed in Spain was in the Pyrenees, when the 40th Regiment alone repulsed 20,000 men. Partly because of the complexity of the military situation and partly because the nine days' campaign was overshadowed by subsequent events, it is seldom described in detail in the history books; nor is it relevant to this story to refer to the activities of any but the 3rd Division.

Between the eastern end of the forty-mile battlefront and the sea, the main range of the Pyrenees runs diagonally from north-east to south-west, casting out rugged spurs which are separated by valleys. These spurs gradually decline south-eastwards into the farm lands of Navarre. It was, in those days, a wild and sparsely inhabited region.

129

During the preceding month, after a few days at Salvatierra, where Wellington concentrated such of his men as were not away marauding in the surrounding hills, the 3rd Division had been included in an abortive endeavour to intercept the elusive General Clausel, whose 'Army of the North' was believed to be near Pampeluna. At least Clausel was not driven far enough eastwards to join forces with Marshal Suchet's Catalonian army. Instead, he escaped into France and the 3rd Division was diverted to take part in the siege of Pampeluna. At the end of June Charles wrote:

My letter of the 23rd from Salvatierra mentioned our being in hopes of cutting off the divisions of Clausel and Abbé. On their march together to join Joseph at Vitoria, not knowing what had taken place there, they had nearly fallen into the snare Lord Wellington had prepared for them with the 6th Div. and Spaniards, when they received information that made them put about. It was then supposed they would make for Jaca, the pass of the Pyrenees on the direct road from Saragossa.

After halting one night near Pamplona to take up the investment until the arrival of the 2nd Division, the Light, 3rd, 4th and 7th Divs and Mina's corps were sent by mountain roads in different directions to cross them. I myself saw from the top of a mountain three days ago the smoke of a cannonade which took place on Mina's falling in with them about Tudela on the Ebro; his having done so, it is said, has made them move off to Saragossa, where it is to be hoped one of the regular Spanish armies will be at hand to receive them. So I hope Suchet has enough to do on his side.

We have had a halt here today, and tomorrow proceed back on the Pamplona road to Monreal, where we expect at least four or five days' rest for the purpose of refreshment, which we much want. What is to become of us afterwards I know now, but as we (the 3rd Div) are too much reduced for a siege except to be employed in the covering army, I shall not be sorry if my next is dated still nearer to the Pyrenees, as when the sun does break out from amidst the deluges of rain we have had, it is very oppressive.

I have not time to speak of the beautiful country, very like Switzerland, which we have been in for the last month. Here the population seem very honest, coarse people, but very civil and fortunately adverse to the French on account of their severities in retaliation for the injuries Mina and his people have done them. He is held in particular respect by his countrymen.

I am sorry to conclude with a very bad piece of news just arrived, namely that Sir J. Murray has raised the siege of Tarragona, I fear very shabbily leaving his cannon etc. behind.

Poor Frederick was out of the battle which he might have seen and remained unhurt, as the 4th Division were not engaged. He is now, he sends me word, well again and on his way to join.

Wellington ('The Lord', as the army had taken to calling him) decided to concentrate on capturing San Sebastian, to station those divisions not required for the assault in the most prominent Pyrenean passes and to turn the siege of Pampeluna into a blockade by the Andalusian Army of Reserve, which was commanded by Henry O'Donnell, Conde de La Bispal. So the 3rd Division was directed to the village of Huarte, some five miles north-west of Pampeluna and on the main road which leads from the city up the Zubiri valley to the famous pass of Roncevalles. From Huarte, Charles wrote home on 8 July:

From Sanguessa on the Aragon, we returned here on the 3rd in two days, and with the 4th, 6th and 7th Divisions have taken the duty of investing the fortress, while the 2nd and Light Divisions have gone to assist Sir Thomas Graham in forcing the French into their own territory. Already we have some few of our troops in it towards St. Jean Pied de Port, while to our left some opposition has been made which has taken the Lord himself to look after things. We shall have probably two or three sieges on the sea coast, while at present there seems no idea of attempting that of this place, which would require very great means such as we should have a difficulty in commanding. We hope it will fall from want of provisions; 'nous verrons'.

The Spaniards are to take over the blockade, leaving the British to more active service if required. We are now throwing up redoubts to keep the French sorties in check as it is well known that the Spaniards would not take the trouble of doing this. The first expression of O'Donnell's on coming up was one of surprise at seeing us toil at them instead of employing peasants upon them. At present we here are comparatively reposing ourselves in a pleasant and plentiful country, but the weather has suddenly set in from very cold to very hot. This rest has been of use to my hand, which will I hope in a week more be healed over.

When dismounted from different causes on the day of action, my poor foot did me much service but it was the force of mind upon the body, and the next day I was as lame again as ever, that is as I have lately been, but am by no means unhopeful of ultimate cure.

Charles was not alone in being critical of O'Donnell. That proud Spanish general of Irish descent begged Wellington not to employ his men on active operations because they were in no condition to do more than blockade Pampeluna. Wellington complied, but he later saw O'Donnell's despatch to the Spanish Government in which he said that he and his army would never forget the insult to them. After the war, when Wellington visited Madrid, O'Donnell called to pay his respects. The Duke received him alone. Those who saw O'Donnell leave described him as 'pale, nearly fainting, and clinging to the banisters of the stair for support'. Wellington could be formidable in peace as well as in war.

After a fortnight at Huarte, during which Picton and his brigade commanders reconnoitred the country thoroughly, the 3rd Division was moved to Olague, halfway up the Lanz valley, whence they could rally to the support either of General Byng's brigade and General Cole's 4th Division, which held the pass of Roncevalles, or of General Hill's corps which held the Maya pass.

On 25th July Soult, who had quietly concentrated 35,000 men at St. Jean Pied de Port, put himself at the head of Clausel's divisions and attacked Byng in the Roncevalles pass. Simultaneously Marshal Drouet, Comte d'Erlon, well remembered from Badajos days, attacked Hill's men in the Col de Maya. D'Erlon carried the day, partly because one of Hill's brigade commanders, General Stewart, was some miles away at the critical time; but Byng, with the combined assistance of the Portuguese and a thick fog, halted the French attack in the Roncevalles pass against overwhelming odds. Wellington was primarily concerned with the assault on San Sebastian which took place, and failed, on the same day. His headquarters, at Lesaca, were far from the scene of action and his staff arrangements were faulty to the extent that there was no rapid means of communication with the western end of the line. So it was that Soult came close to his objective, which was to relieve Pampeluna and then, turning eastwards, envelop the beleaguered San Sebastian in a pincer movement from north and west.

Despite Byng's gallant defence of the Roncevalles pass, General Cole decided that a retreat of the 4th Division towards Pampeluna was the only sure guarantee against being outflanked. Picton rode over the mountain ridge from Olague to join Cole at Linzoain in the adjoining Zubiri valley and, as the senior general, took charge. He had received no orders from Wellington, who belatedly sent him instructions to hold fast at Zubiri, and so he and Cole agreed to fall back towards Pampeluna. This they successfully did, with the French in hot pursuit, until they reached a defensive position along a ridge of hills a few miles short of Pampeluna. It was here that the great and sanguinary battle of Sorauren was fought on 27 and 28th July, the 4th Division bearing the brunt on the left, with the eventual and timely help of the 6th Division, and Picton's 3rd Division covering Huarte and the main road from Roncevalles.

A few days later Charles had time to send his brother this account of the affair:

Having about a week before given up the blockade of Pamplona to the Spaniards we were at Olague, a central position between that place and the passes of the Pyrenees, when hearing of General Cole's being obliged to retire from Roncesvalles, Sir Thomas Picton moved us up to his support and we joined him on the afternoon of the 26th of July. He was then in action in front of Zubiri and hard pressed. Having however been forced from a better position in front, the Lt. General did not think the one we were then on tenable against the superior and ever increasing force of the enemy and we retired by a night march on Huarte, my former station, less than a league from Pamplona and which was the first ground which afforded anything like a position to prevent the enemy's advance upon that place. The quickness and judgement with which Sir Thomas took up this position with the two Divisions and Byng's Brigade atoned, I believe, to the Lord for the greater degree of promptitude than he had counted on in the retrograde movements so far, and it turned out that with his usual celerity he had himself marched the preceding night to support us. Lord Wellington joined us in our new position, a few hours after we had taken it up. We had by that time been joined by some Spaniards and General Campbell's Portuguese Brigade, which had followed us from a pass they had also been obliged to retire from, with the enemy so close to their heels that it was for a little time doubtful which of the two would first obtain the summit of one of those mountains, on which the great contest took place on the 28th, as necessary for subsequent

offence on the part of the French as for our own defence.
All the fighting from the 27th to the 30th took place on the
left of the position while the right, which was the post of the
3rd Division, was never seriously attacked, though on comparatively low ground and at first very weakly provided in troops.
The enemy contented themselves with demonstrations which,
when pushed too far, we made them repent with our Artillery.
Three Brigades of Cavalry subsequently joined us where they
could act with effect, and I should have been very well pleased
had they really in anything like proportionate force attacked
us.

On the 30th we had the mortification to see them move regularly off from ground where we could not incommode them,
while they formed their junction with their main body. We,
however, had shortly after orders to follow but with caution,
as at first his Lordship could not be certain whether their retreat
was real or a feint with intent to turn his left. The confusion
and evident consternation among the enemy soon showed the
former to be the case and we hemmed them in by a parallel
march, principally on the high road, while the 4th and 6th
Divisions pressed their rear and left flank so that at times they
were perfectly bandied about. At one time Sir Thomas brought
his Brigade of nine pdrs to bear upon them, supported by
two regiments of General Brisbane's Brigade, and Colonel
Keane's Light Corps annoyed them so much that great numbers
surrendered prisoners.

In these operations the 3rd Division had the good fortune
to be as usual highly useful, suffering at the same time a very
trifling loss. Of my own Brigade not a man.

I was sent for that evening to Headquarters, but was so knocked
up I could not go. The next day the 3rd and 6th marched
upon the same point and thus has ended for the time at least
my services immediately with the former corps, for on reaching
Roncesvalles I received orders to join and take command of
the 6th Division, Sir H. Clinton having returned to England
in bad health. The two divisions have been since, and will
I hope continue to be, neighbours perhaps forming one column
under Sir Thomas Picton.

Although Charles's brigade did not lose a single man in the
fighting at Sorauren, they did, as he claimed, play a useful part
in the battle. However, when in September 1814 clasps to be
worn on the ribbon of the Peninsular War medal were issued

by command of the Prince Regent, the officers of Charles's brigade were not included in the list of those entitled to a clasp for the Battle of the Pyrenees. This seemed unjust to Picton, although he was himself a recipient, and it was much resented both by Charles and the dashing Colonel Gough, a future Victorian hero. In January 1815, Picton, temporarily retired in Wales, wrote this to Charles:

> The case is certainly hard on our friend Gough, who appears to have great sensibility on such occasions, and he most truly remarks that the appearance of the 3rd Division in those days round Pampeluna gave a decisive turn to the campaign; for if we had not arrived to take up a position on the heights of Zubiri and stop the Duke of Dalmatia for that evening, Pampeluna would infallibly have been relieved and the whole army must have fallen behind the Ebro, which they would have reached with difficulty. I look upon it to have been one of the most important occurrences of our campaigns in the Peninsula.

The Battle of the Pyrenees had come nearer to an expensive calamity than could be happily contemplated; but despite Soult's daring, his subordinates made mistakes and the vagaries of the weather, unusual in July, were of great help to the British. The passes in the Pyrenees were so numerous that an attacker from the French side had every opportunity to spring surprises. As Wellington wrote to the Prime Minister, Lord Liverpool, on 28 July: 'The Pyrenees are a very long line: there are no fewer than seventy passes through the mountains and the communication, so far as I have been able to learn hitherto, is on the side of the enemy.'

All the same, perhaps he was thinking of these events when he modestly remarked: 'If other generals commit an error their army is lost by it and they are sure to be beaten; when I get into a scrape, my army gets me out of it.'

With Soult thrown back into France, his army seriously depleted by heavy casualties and the loss of over 3,000 prisoners, Charles encamped with the 6th Division in the valley of the Aldudes, a few miles from St. Jean Pied de Port. Thence, on 6 August, he wrote to describe his new command:

> The 6th is one of the finest divisions of the army, and notwithstanding a severe loss on the 28th and 30th ultimo are still

5,110 operatives present in rank and file, a strength which indeed I fear is more than equal, after what they have lately suffered, to that of any other division of the army. I have had a private intimation that I am not likely to be superseded again in this command, but it may happen that I may return, should I wish it when the opportunity offers, to the 3rd Div., Sir Thomas Picton being frequently ailing, and what is more, little pleased with the slight manner in which himself and division are passed over in the despatch of the battle of Vitoria. He is talking of remaining in the country but a short time longer. However, all people are liable to change their minds, and my present possession is better than any probable attainings.

My present Generals of Brigades are Pack, reckoned as an excellent officer, and whose wound being slight, though on the head, has returned to quarters; Lambart not yet joined from the Guards on promotion to Major General; Tryon, a fine fellow and good officer, who was with me as Major of Brigade in the 4th Div. Pack's is a Highland Brigade, composed of the 42nd, 79th and 91st Regiments; Lambart's of the 11th, 32nd and 61st Regiments. The Portuguese are the 8th and 12th of the Line and 9th Cacadores. Though they suffered much on that day, the Division are flushed with their success otherwise, having after a long march come up opportunely, and being very judiciously posted (by Pack I believe) contributed much to the failure of a fresh and very strong column of the enemy's, from which much was to have been apprehended. If the news of the first successes of the French had reached England before that of their final discomfiture, it would have caused unpleasant feelings and inclined people to doubt the benefit of our victory of Vittoria. As it is, the final success, which has rewarded the gallantry of the troops and the skill of the Commander, will probably gloss over with John Bull the scrape itself, which the Prince of Orange's carrying the Despatches may assist.

The French must be a good deal affected by such a complete discomfiture under an undoubtedly good General so soon following the other. The extent of their advance is, however, much to be regretted; in the first place, for our great loss of men, which in British and Portuguese alone cannot be less than 7,000. That of the enemy is not triple in numbers, but cannot be much less. Secondly, the immediate loss of the very powerful pass of Maya was occasioned by something too like a surprise, to repair the effects of which the bravery and lives of many a noble fellow was unavailingly thrown away.

Lastly, the loss of all the passes proceeded most likely from an opinion of their strength too hastily formed, whereas, stupendous as are the heights, and deep as are their abysses, there is nothing of either kind which French and British are not now in the habit of attempting, frequently with success; at the same time they are all liable to be turned.

The mails still come and go by Lisbon; we are promised they shall do so by St. Sebastian when that place is taken, but when that is to be I cannot guess any more than why naval co-operation has not hitherto been made use of against it. Pamplona has not yet fallen, but from all accounts it must very shortly do so from scarcity of provisions. As the late vigorous measures to relieve it have failed in so complete a manner all hope of a repetition of a similar attempt in sufficient time must have been given up and all appetite for dog's and cat's flesh must have gone.

On 18 August, he wrote again from Maya:

I came here a week since from the Passes of Roncesvalles and the Aldudes to guard the adjoining one, having my old Division the 3rd in support under my orders from the illness, I am sorry to say, of Sir Thomas Picton on whose quitting the country, as I fancy he must and where he will not return, I shall perhaps be given the choice of one of the two permanently. If so, I shall of course go back to my old friends though this is a much stronger Division having in it some of the finest regiments in the army. I have however no right to object to, however much I may lament, the weakness of the 3rd.

The marching we have had since the battle of Vitoria, though I cannot call it without intermission, has been considerable and connected with circumstances so contrary to the quiet required for letter writing, that it is not easy to bring oneself back to the habit of it, as even now in a clean, comfortable Padré Curé's house on a delightful day. With the click of a corn mill within twenty yards, I do not find the occupation a very congenial one, though I am glad of a little leisure to give my foot a respite from the stirrup.

The village of Maya from which I write is in the fine, but to us at present unproductive, vale of Bastan. The pass, or only regular road, is about two miles off, running through a lofty ridge which we occupy as a position to cover the road as well as smaller paths; for the principal pass itself is, like that of Roncesvalles, to be turned by half a dozen others. The loftiest part of all, which is on the right, is the spot to which the French ascended on the 25th of July unperceived.

When by chance it is at all clear we see Bayonne, St. Jean de Luz, St. Jean Pied de Port, but the fogs are so thick and the rains so frequent that the beauties of the scenery, which would otherwise make a residence in this site and climate so desirable, cannot atone for them. For the three days I had a Brigade on the Alta Biscar, the highest point of the Puerte Roncesvalles, one could not see a second person fifty yards from you.

The position I occupy is that whence Sir R. Hill, or rather General William Stewart, was driven on the 25th of July. Profiting from their calamity, I keep my people nearer to their fighting ground and with the addition of some field works which have been thrown up, feel perfectly at ease; but the enemy does not appear to have any intention of attacking us at present and would no doubt retire from the position they occupy were we to advance against them. We have immediately in front of us the Comte d'Erlon's corps. It should be of 18,000 men, but from its losses we suppose it may be reduced to ten or twelve. The main body are retired on a position in which it is said they have been entrenching themselves. An officer I sent in yesterday with a flag of truce says they are sanguine as to a general peace and that an Armistice with the Northern Powers for six months had already taken place.

Pamplona still holds out. That its provisions would last to the end of the month was the latest account I heard of it from anything like authority, but the Spaniards I fear have a very indifferent investment, notwithstanding they have exposed and lost a good many men in it, and have allowed the French to cut and carry in corn from a disgraceful distance.

The batteries against San Sebastian had not reopened two days ago, nor is it probable they have yet, or we should have heard them. The delay is, strange to say, from want of ammunition; I fear the place has been thought too lightly of.

Beautiful though the view was from Maya, the recent slaughter in the pass had left unpleasant traces. Frederick Forsyth gave an account of one incident when he accompanied his Uncle Charles on an inspection of outposts in the Maya pass:

As we were riding along one day quietly, his favourite little mare 'Moll Blake' gave a great shy and pitched the General over her head on to the ground. I was astonished at the enormous swarm of large black flies that rose all around him when he touched it, which was accounted for by his having fallen on a great heap of dead bodies imperfectly buried, gallant fellows of the 92nd Regiment who had fallen there after a desperate resistance against greatly superior numbers on the 25th July. One could see here and there the hand or foot of some corpse appearing above ground which was blackened with the flies amongst which 'Moll Blake' pitched the General.

Nor, as Frederick further recounts, were reconnaissances always peaceful:

One morning immediately after breakfast, the General mounted, and taking his A.D.C. and Quarter Master General and myself with him rode up the pass where the whole of the division was encamped. When we got there I found that the General was going down to the village of Urdax to reconnoitre the enemy's line of pickets which, I believe, he thought encroached upon our position.

A company of Light Infantry was ordered out as an escort. The mountain side down which we descended was very beautiful, being rather smooth and open, with fine forest trees scattered about, as well as groups of thicket here and there, very much resembling a fine park, but without the deer. After getting a little way down, the Light Company extended and threading the thickets, and examining carefully any rough ground they met with, gave the descent of the General the appearance of a grand battue in search of game. When we arrived at the foot of the mountain, none of the enemy appearing, the escort was halted and the General and Staff proceeded towards the village.

I happened to be riding in front, and looking down off the road perceived about two hundred yards distant a picket of eight or ten men seated around a fire. I saw no sentry out, and was not perceived myself. I galloped back to the General making signs to him to halt. On explaining to him what I had seen, the escort was again ordered to the front and the French picket retired quietly.

The General moved on to a clump of trees on a rising ground near the village, a spot convenient for making observations on the surrounding country. Before we had been many minutes there the enemy opened a fire of musketry on us from the houses in the village, the balls rattling among the trees in a manner not at all conducive to repose. On the noise of the firing, a company of the 11th appeared from some part of the position not very far from the village. It was commanded by a subaltern, a very nice young fellow. I had some conversation with him whilst he was waiting for orders, his company at ordered arms, and was very much pleased with him. He was ordered to dislodge the enemy from the houses, and to my great grief was shot dead before he had advanced many paces into the village. All this time my uncle remained among the trees looking out with his field glass. Near the clump there was the hut of a French officer, very neatly constructed as they always were, and tied to his bed post was a fine poodle, which I let loose and off he ran to the village as hard as he could go, running on scent like a hound after his master.

On 31 August the city of San Sebastian was at last taken. Soult made an attempt to relieve it, but though he outnumbered the British by three to one he was defeated and lost 3,000 men. A week later the Castle also fell. On entering the city, the British troops behaved as badly as they had at Badajos and Ciudad Rodrigo, but the 6th Division took no direct part in the affair. Instead, they and Lord Dalhousie's 7th Division were ordered to divert the attention of the enemy formations in front of them by active demonstrations. Charles used his Portuguese for this purpose and Dalhousie did the same. The Portuguese Brigade of the 6th Division, after a hard fight, captured the enemy position at Urdax. Colonel Douglas, who commanded it, exceeded his instructions and lost 184 men. This was a far higher casualty rate than was thought acceptable for what was only intended to be a feint. 'I could not but bear in mind', he said, 'the strict charge you had given me not to bring on a serious affair, but as the ground had already been ours, it was too painful to us to see it lost.' On this occasion Douglas escaped censure form the Commander-in-Chief, but his rashness was not forgotten. Dalhousie's Portuguese, on Colonel Douglas's left, also showed greater zeal than was intended and suffered severely.

After the fall of San Sebastian Charles, as an observer of the scene, wrote this criticism of the operation:

With whom the plan last originated, I do not know. Major Smith, a clever young man but without much experience, was the chief engineer at the time the siege was commenced, but I know to a certainty that Lt. Colonel Burgoyne and I believe Sir Richard Fletcher, when they came up, thoroughly disapproved of it and when Sir Thomas Graham's report so nearly admits the thing, there can be the less hesitation in my mentioning the general belief that even at the last assault the place would not have been taken but for the accidental explosion that killed or wounded every individual Frenchman on the curtain. I think it was from the horn work and frightened the rest from adjoining traverses, a confusion which was quickly and spiritedly taken advantage of by our people.

Balloons have been very generally used by the French in sieges and in reconnoitring, and I believe that they were used by our Engineers in Flanders, but I think we have in general suffered most, not from the ignorance of the interior defences opposed to us, but from too little respect for those known to exist. Why this should have been the case at San Sebastian, as it appears it was, I know not, for there were no want of mortars, which at a high elevation could have dropped their heavy shells shortly before the assault, so as to have much injured the defences of the breach. But at Badajos, the case was different, for when I myself on the morning of the day we made the assault, in consequence of what I had observed going on within the breaches from a high hill on their flank, pointed out to the Chiefs of the Artillery and Engineer Departments the necessity of doing something to destroy the defences I had seen, they agreed entirely with the proposal, but the remedy was not so easily found. The only shells that Colonel Dickson said he could spare for the purpose were, I think, ten, and these shrapnel only, which of course could only, and did only, molest the workmen, whereas common shells from mortars, even of the same size, would, if well thrown in, have broken the terrific *chevaux de frise* which have been so much spoken of, their raised platforms, loop-holed barriers, etc., etc.

We have totally neglected a piece of Ordnance of ours, which might I think have been of good use in our sieges; I mean the Royal mortar which carries a $5\frac{1}{2}$ inch shell and whose small weight would have done away with the great objection of the difficulty of transport.

The piece itself with its bed is so small as to be easily moved by a couple of men. The French have a little mortar of this kind still lighter than ours which they call Napoleons. I am sure that at Ciudad Rodrigo they killed and wounded with them six times the number they did from their 16 inch Spanish mortars, the great shells from which seldom burst in more than two or three pieces.

Sir T. Graham is going home. His successor is to be Sir John Hope, than whom there cannot be one more fit for the situation. Sir Thomas will however be much regretted and is, to be sure, a wonderful man for his time of life.

Charles's comments on the employment of artillery in sieges must be set against Wellington's consistent objection to the use of mortars because of the damage they caused to houses and the civilian inhabitants. In the siege of San Sebastian he did, however, allow eight ten-inch mortars to be brought into action.

Pampeluna held out, and Wellington was in no hurry to enter France, especially as Marshal Suchet still commanded 30,000 men in Catalonia and had proved more than a match for the two English generals in that province, Sir John Murray and Lord William Bentinck. However, political pressure and public opinion at home would brook no delay. So on 7 October he made a surprise attack with Sir Thomas Graham's corps across the river Bidassoa, near its mouth, and at the end of the day his men stood firmly on French soil. It was Graham's last engagement. Once across the Bidassoa, he handed over his command to Sir John Hope and, replete with glory, sailed for home.

D'Erlon's corps of three divisions stood strongly entrenched along a line of heights facing the 6th Division, for it was from the Maya front and not at the mouth of the Bidassoa that Soult expected the attack to be delivered. Indeed he went in person to review d'Erlon's troops on the day before the British crossed the river. Charles asked leave to attack d'Erlon with the 6th and 3rd Divisions, but Wellington replied that it was not his intention to move the centre of the line further forward although he was glad to authorise a probe by the 6th Division to examine the communications leading forward to the River Nive.

Charles's account of the proceedings was as follows;

I had hoped to give you the first news of the move into France but Lord W. takes care that his own information shall always be that, and I understand that Lord March has already sailed with his despatches, giving an account of all the operations he proposes to attempt until the fall of Pamplona.

An intercepted letter from the Governor to Soult says he

cannot hold out to some day in November which Soult had named to him (the particular one not ascertained, being in cypher), but that he can to the 25th inst. As Lord W. has however sent him word that to entitle the garrison even to the retention of their knapsacks they must have a few days provisions left, we suppose surrender may take place on the 20th.

Lord W.'s movements were confined, as you will observe by the Despatches, to the bringing forward his left and securing the mountain of Rhune as an advanced work from whence at his pleasure to undertake further operations, I had here again nothing more to do but in the way of demonstration, in which however I had the honour to occupy the attention, with the 6th Division alone, of no less a person than the Emperor's Lieutenant himself, at least we have been told that he was the great personage who reviewed them in their position the evening before.

Our Portuguese Brigade was the only one that became engaged. They behaved with great gallantry, losing about 150 men I am sorry to say, though revenged by the destruction of certainly more of the enemy. Demonstration, difficult as it is to make in front of an enemy in force without bringing on fire, is an object too indefinite to admit of one's being satisfied to lose men upon it. We took advantage of their force being subsequently reduced in our front, to strengthen their right, to move forward our posts, and we retained them so, keeping a very menacing attitude that annoys them much.

This time the dashing Colonel Douglas did get into trouble. Being successful in an initial attack by his enthusiastic Portuguese brigade, he assaulted an enemy position overlooking the River Nivelle, brought strong enemy reinforcements into action and caused Charles to summon a reserve battalion to support him. The intended probe became a heated engagement and the casualties were proportionately high. Charles felt obliged to inform Wellington of what had happened, adding, 'I am indeed led to hope that His Excellency will be pleased to overlook the exceeding of orders in favour of the gallantry displayed, and that the loss of men will merit his regret rather than cause any feeling of dissatisfaction.'

However, the noble Marquess was far from satisfied. From his quarters at Vera he sent this stinging reproach on 10 October:

My dear General,

    I have read your report of the 8th to General Murray and

I shall be obliged to you if you will tell Col. Douglas that I am concerned again to be obliged to disapprove of his conduct. He has just lost 150 men for nothing, and in disobedience of your orders. I could also observe that if the enemy's troops were ten times worse and more disheartened than they are, the conduct of Col. Douglas in getting his Brigade into unnecessary scrapes would make them soldiers again, and if the Portuguese troops were better soldiers than even they are, they would become worse from the same conduct.

I am sorry to be obliged to express my disapprobation of the conduct of an officer of whom I have always entertained a good opinion, but I must say that it is unworthy of one of his reputation to get his Brigade into scrapes for the sake of the little gloriole of driving in a few pickets, knowing as he must do that it is not intended he should engage in a serious affair, and that when once he comes engaged with a body of any strength, to retreat with honour is difficult and without loss is impossible. I hope that Col. Douglas will reflect upon what has passed, and observe in future that what he can do best is to obey the orders and execute strictly the design of his Commander.

Ever my dear General
Yours most sincerely,
WELLINGTON

Colonel Douglas was so upset by this reprimand that he felt nothing but sea air would restore his self-confidence. This was his letter to Charles:

Sir,

I have read with due mortification Lord Wellington's letter and I appeal to yourself if I have deserved so severe a rebuke.

On a former occasion when the Brigade suffered by exceeding its orders, operations were in the dark and the troops not easily kept together, and I was myself hurt in endeavouring to remedy the evil. You yourself were an eye witness of the present affair, and the ground you recommended us to gain was carried with trifling loss. I retired when ordered, but not before the enemy's reinforcements had brought on a serious engagement.

Lord Wellington taxes me with flat disobedience and childish rashness, and I am sure you must feel, Sir, that I am not guilty of either.

I trust you will endeavour to soften his Lordship's displeasure against me, which has so distressed me that I must request five days permission to go to the seashore for quiet and change of scene, or the wound in my head will again break out.

I have the honour to be Sir, etc.,

(signed) J. DOUGLAS

commanding 7th Portuguese Brig.

It is comforting to reflect that the Colonel's military career was not adversely affected. He rose to be a full general and a G.C.B., and Wellington later described him as 'one of the best and most intelligent officers that he had seen'.

Ten days after the crossing of the Bidassoa, Napoleon fought and lost the three-day battle of Leipzig, the so-called 'Battle of the Nations' in which the combined armies of Prussia, Austria and Russia drove him back across the Rhine into France. If it was the death knell of the Empire, Napoleon was not prepared to admit it. Nor was Soult. Between the Bidassoa and Bayonne there were good defensive positions and two fast-flowing rivers, the Nivelle, running from south of the Maya pass to enter the sea at St. Jean de Luz, and the Nive, a tributary of the River Adour, flowing from St. Jean Pied de Port to join the Adour at Bayonne. As winter approached there were still severe obstacles ahead of the victorious Peninsular Army, as fine a body of fighting men as Britain has ever put into the field.

While the British prepared themselves for the advance, the brave and obstinate French defenders of Pampeluna were at last driven by hunger to capitulate. They had been living on rats and roots, some of the soldiers inadvertently meeting a Socratic death when in their ignorance they devoured hemlock. Others contracted scurvy. Cassan, the French commander, offered to surrender if he and his men were allowed to return to France in return for a promise not to fight for a year and a day. Wellington refused, whereupon Cassan said he would blow the place up and order his men to break through the blockade. Wellington then instructed Carlos d'Espana, in command of the blockade, to put Cassan, all his officers and one tenth of his troops to death if this threat was carried out. It must be the last recorded proposal to employ the ancient Roman practice of 'decimation'. It may be doubted whether Wellington was serious in his intention; but it had its effect, for after a four months' siege the garrison capitulated on 31 October. Except for the small harbour of Santona, near Santander, the whole of central and north-western Spain was now liberated.

9

Into France

Safely across the Bidassoa, Lord Wellington's army faced a massive double line of defences which Soult had spent the best part of three months in preparing. Bristling with redoubts, abbattis constructed from felled trees, and every known kind of deterrent, it ran from St. Jean de Luz at the mouth of the River Nivelle, crossed and recrossed the river where it looped northwards, and stretched as far eastwards as St. Jean Pied de Port so as to withstand any invasion from Spain through the Maya and Roncevalles passes. At the centre of the river's great northward loop is the village of St. Pé and, where the landward arm of the loop turns east again into a straight-flowing river, there is a bridge at the hamlet of Amotz. It was at Amotz that the main French line of defence crossed from the left to the right bank of the river, and it was here, too, that the boundary lay between the army corps of General Clausel, responsible for the French centre, and that of the Comte d'Erlon, covering Soult's left.

Wellington waited until Pampeluna had fallen and until he was sure that Soult was unable to join forces with Marshal Suchet's army of Catalonia. By the time he was ready for an assault on the Nivelle line, Sir Thomas Picton had again fallen sick so that early in November Charles, who had just begun to feel at home in command of the 6th Division, was transferred back to the 3rd Division as its commanding officer. It was, he felt, his own division and this time it really did seem that Picton had retired from the scene for good.

He found the 3rd Division quartered in Zagaramurdi, a Basque village at the foot of the great Mount Atchubia, from which at dawn on 10 November three guns were fired in rapid succession to give the signal for the advance of 90,000 men and 95 pieces of artillery. It was a day of cloudless sunshine and it was one, rare in military annals, in which everything went according to plan. Near the sea, a realistic demonstration by Sir John Hope's corps kept Soult and 25,000 French veterans engaged. They were thus prevented from moving to the support of the centre, on the right of which a hard-fought battle, distinguished by the feats of the Light Division and Longa's dashing Spaniards, forced the French back from their first to their second line of defence and finally over the river itself.

Meanwhile Wellington launched 40,000 men towards the bridge of Amotz, at the junction of Clausel's and d'Erlon's corps. Soult had every reason to expect a strong attack at this point, for his men had captured a British sergeant-major carrying informative documents; but, like Wellington south of the Pyrenees, Soult had a long front to defend. It fell to the 3rd Division to enfilade the bridge of Amotz, while the 4th and 7th Divisions made a frontal attack and the 6th fought its way, abreast of the 3rd, along the right bank of the Nivelle.

Charles sent his brother-in-law, the Rev. Roger Frankland, a brief account of events:

The day was one of the luckiest that ever came out of the heaven. The whole army moved forward from their respective points almost at the same moment at daybreak, and from the mountains behind, where many must have been beholders of the whole line of operations in one coup d'oeil, it must have been the grandest sight possible.

Success was so general and everything went on so swimmingly, that I think it was altogether the most animating and (shall I say it to a parson?) agreeable day of the kind I was ever engaged in: the loss not being in any comparison to the difficulties overcome, and the killed bearing a small proportion to the wounded; in my British brigade being only 50 out of 400.

About noon next day the 3rd Division moved forward, as did some others, just as a heavy rain commenced on horrid roads, and which lasted the whole night; we luckily got up our tents.

On the 12th it was fair, and we closed up to Ustaritz and Arrauntz on the Nive with our advance guard on the Sugarloaf Hill of St. Barbe, from which we have a fine view of Bayonne and of the whole of what interests about us. It rained the whole of yesterday and during the night, as it does now on this morning of the 14th.

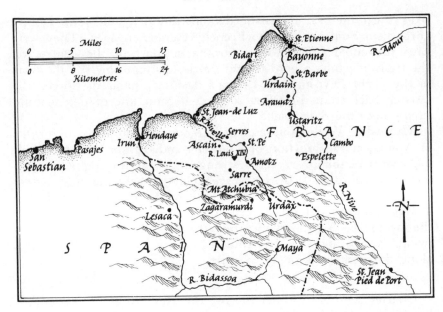

For myself, I have been under cover, my family of five pigging together, but in a room with a comfortable fireplace. Today, I believe, I shall move my quarters a little further forward, to the house of a French lady whose age she hoped would command respect while, hearing the injurious reports spread of us by the French troops, she had thought it prudent to send off her niece 'une jeune personne très amiable', and whose society, as we have told her, it would be a great satisfaction to us to have. She has promised to send to Bordeaux for her, finding we are not the savages represented. The same reports had influenced the country people, who had fled, but they are returning fast.

With this letter he enclosed a copy of his detailed report to Marshal Beresford. Wellington himself commanded the attack on the bridge of Amotz, but Charles explained that the report had to be addressed formally to Beresford 'under whose superintendence (a kind of *façon de parler*, meant perhaps to get him a peerage) the centre of the army had been placed nominally on that day'.

This is the gist of what befell the 3rd Division. On Charles's left the 4th and 7th Divisions attacked and carried two formidable redoubts and occupied the tactically important village of Sarre. On his right the 6th Division forded the Nivelle and advanced along its right bank towards d'Erlon's main line of defence, a chain of strong redoubts crowning a ridge and fronted by a ravine. Meanwhile Charles made straight for the bridge of Amotz, helping to drive the enemy from the half-completed new redoubt called 'Louis XIV' and vigorously assailing the older fortifications in front of the bridge itself. Conroux, the general confronting him, fell mortally wounded, and by 11 a.m. Charles's men were in possession of the bridge. They did not cross the river but seized the hill lying between the bridge and the Louis XIV redoubt. The line of communication between d'Erlon and Clausel was thus severed, but one of Clausel's divisions had held tenaciously to the unfinished redoubt and opened fire with eight large cannon. The 4th and 7th Divisions made a frontal assault and Charles attacked the brave but heavily outnumbered defenders on their flank. Many of the French garrison were bayoneted and others were flung into the ravines behind.

By two o'clock Charles's advanced skirmishers had crossed the river and entered St. Pé. The French fled through the village along the road to Bayonne, and once Wellington was assured that all was well on his left, he sent the 3rd and 7th Divisions in hot pursuit. There was a final contest, for the French made a temporary stand at a fortified position on the Bayonne road from which they inflicted many casualties on their pursuers. Then, as darkness fell, the weary conquerors encamped for the night while a blazing heath and forest fire illuminated the hills. Soult had lost 3,000 men killed and wounded, against 2,600 of the Allies, as well as fifty-one pieces of cannon, six tumbrils of ammunition and 1,400 prisoners. St. Jean de Luz was in British hands; and the French were obliged to fall back to their next river line, that of the Nive, with a siege of Bayonne imminent and their army suffering from an accumulation of casualties as damaging as its declining self-confidence. Even the loyalest of Napoleon's veterans could scarcely be expected to regard such a series of catastrophes with equanimity, and the Emperor's defeat at Leipzig was beginning to cast its shadow as far as the Bay of Biscay and the Pyrenees.

Charles's formal report to Beresford was largely concerned with detail, 'the more important of the operations of the 3rd Division on the 10th inst. having been under the observation of His Excellency the Commander of the Forces as well as of your own'. He described how two of his three brigades had seized the height commanding the bridge and how they had carried their objective— 'I trust it will be admitted in a style most highly creditable to them, driving the enemy assembled in force upon the summit of the height from the whole of their adjoining positions, though supported by four pieces of artillery, the two redoubts, a long breastwork and numerous strong abattis garnished with musketry'. He also reported how the two brigades had reformed and 'pursued the enemy across the bridge near to St. Pé and later in the evening followed them up with the most persevering gallantry on the heights beyond that village, when I thought it advisable to take up a position for the night'.

He spoke with feeling of the loss of two of his officers. Colonel Thomas Lloyd, a hero of Vitoria, received a most painful wound while scaling a height 'at the head of his small but gallant regiment'. He was, Charles continued, 'in the most animating manner prosecuting the combined attack when he received his mortal wound. Severe as his sufferings must have been, he seems not to have permitted them to come in competition with his anxiety for the success of the troops and in his attempt to gratify which, his last remaining strength was exhausted.' Fifty years later such a recommendation would doubtless have resulted in a posthumous Victoria Cross, but at least those who read Napier's *History of the War in the Peninsula* will find Colonel Lloyd, of 'a graceful symmetry combined with Herculean strength', and famous for his 'mirth and wit', among the handful of men to whom Napier devoted a whole paragraph of praise.

Another Vitoria hero, Colonel Hugh Gough, commanding the 87 Regiment, was also severely wounded; but Charles's hope for his recovery was fulfilled and he lived to become a field-marshal, a viscount and the conqueror in India of both the Mahrattas and the rebellious Sikhs.

On the following day, 11 November, the British advanced slowly, giving Soult time to occupy a semicircular line of fortification in front of Bayonne, with his right wing on the coast, less than five miles south of the city, and his left on the River Nive at Ustaritz. General Foy's army which had not been included in the rout on the Nivelle, marched up the right bank of the Nive and joined forces with three of d'Erlon's shattered divisions to defend a potential river-crossing at Cambo. The clear skies gave way to pouring rain and before many hours had passed the heavy clay soil made further advance impossible, especially for the artillery and cavalry. However, some of the British outposts were inconveniently—indeed dangerously—situated so that, however soggy the ground and inclement the weather, Wellington authorised two attacks in order to adjust the line. One of these fell to the lot of the 3rd Division which was required to seize the junction at a village called Urdains of the roads leading to Bayonne from Ustaritz and St. Pé. Charles used his excellent Portuguese brigade for the purpose, and they drove the French out of the woods bordering a small tributary of the River Nive which flows into the main stream half a mile from Urdains. Several counter-attacks were repelled and Charles was able to establish his headquarters in the Château of Herroritz overlooking the Nive. Here Frederick Frankland visited his uncle and wrote:

> The proprietor, a fine old French gentleman, had wisely remained in his house and gave us the use of his kitchen garden, which abounded in vegetables of all sorts. He was very sociable and dined sometimes with the General and his staff, and once or twice he gave us a dinner. I, indeed, lived in clover here, having a nice bedroom and a good French bed to myself.

This was the kind of relationship Wellington wished to establish with the local French inhabitants, both to quench the fear of British ferocity so assiduously propagated by Soult's army, and to remove the threat, on which Soult also counted, of a French guerilla movement against the invaders. Wellington's adjutant-general, Pakenham, hanged a few British and Portuguese predators, but the main danger to friendly Anglo-French relations in the occupied zone came from the Spaniards.

Charles and his brother officers consistently criticised them, but even if their own historians have exaggerated their contribution to winning the war, it was unquestionably a large one and Wellington, at least, gave them due credit for courage and energy. Having suffered for years from the rapacity of Napoleon's armies in their own country, it is scarcely surprising that they were thirsting for revenge. Unchristian perhaps, but certainly not unnatural. So Mina's fierce guerillas on the right, Longa's gallant soldiers in the centre and Freyre's Galician troops further to the left gave vent to their full fury in orgies of murder, rape, looting and wanton destruction. Wellington took immediate action. Within forty-eight hours of the Nivelle victory, he hanged all the Spanish marauders caught red-handed and set Giron's Andalusians, Freyre's Galicians and Longa's Biscayans and Navarrese packing over the frontier into their own territory. He disarmed Mina's battalions, which had mutinied in the excitement of victory, and kept with his own Anglo-Portuguese army only General Morillo's weak brigade which was believed to be comparatively well-behaved. As for the British, they received urgent instructions to fraternise with the local inhabitants, and though a subsequent raid by Mina's men into the French Basque country gave rise to local partisan warfare, the attitude of the French to their invaders did, on the whole, become increasingly well disposed.

During the days of downpour the army moved into temporary cantonments and Charles awaited instructions in his comfortable château. Wellington established general headquarters at St. Jean-de-Luz, but before he moved there spent three days of incessant rain in the house of the Curé of St. Pé. The Curé, he said, was a sensible man. 'I sent for him and talked with him of the internal state of France. By God I had him with me every day for three days and all his reports strengthened my Conviction as to the insecure state of Bonaparte's Power, and moreover he convinced me that there was a feeling for the Bourbons and that if they chose to try they might succeed . . . .' Wellington subsequently advocated a Bourbon restoration to his own Government, which at one time toyed with the idea of a regency for Napoleon's son, the King of Rome; and when at Wellington's suggestion the Duc d'Angoulème, married to the surviving child of Louis

XVI and Marie Antoinette, was allowed to go to France, there was in due course a royalist explosion at Bordeaux. So, said Wellington, the Bourbons owed their restoration to him, and perhaps indirectly to those three wet days at St. Pé after the victory on the Nivelle.

At the end of the first week of December the skies cleared. It was possible to bring up some heavy artillery and plans were made to cross the Nive at the two French strong points of Cambo and Ustaritz. At first all went well. Charles handed over the outpost duties on his front to a brigade of the 7th Division and on the morning of 9 December led his men over the Nive at Ustaritz, using a new pontoon bridge constructed to replace one which the French had destroyed. The 6th Division also went across, and further down the river other Allied formations crossed at Cambo. So did Morillo, with his 'well-behaved' Spaniards, but unfortunately they found it irresistible to kill fifteen peasants, including several women and children, in one of the villages they occupied. No doubt, back in Spain, their own wives and children had suffered a comparable fate, whereas John Bull, as Charles collectively called his countrymen, knew nothing of such horrors behind the impenetrable barrier of the English Channel.

The nature of the ground was such that even though the French outnumbered the Allies on the narrow front between the Rivers Nive and Adour, they found it impossible to attack in extended formation; and the British, for their part, were hampered by narrow sunk lanes and thick woods. So although the French fell back, and there was much skirmishing, darkness fell without any major engagement. But at least the British were across the Nive.

The next day Soult, by a brilliant strategy, took Wellington by surprise and came near to defeating him. Under cover of darkness he had transferred more than half his troops from the front where Charles's division stood to the other side of Bayonne. He united them with those defending the coastal road running southwards to St. Jean de Luz and sent 60,000 men and forty guns against an unprepared Anglo-Portuguese force of only half the size. He nearly broke through. Wellington himself was on the left bank of the Nive, ordering General Hill to occupy the positions so mysteriously vacated in the night, when he heard a loud cannonade across the river and in due course led four divisions back to the rescue across the pontoon bridges. Charles was ordered to hold Urdains, whence he had set forth the previous day, and he did so against a superior force. The ground provided thick cover. His regiments were well concealed and he reported that every internal movement of his troops was a source of alarm to the French, who, believing themselves outnumbered, called for reinforcements.

Frederick Frankland, on his extended visit, had remained in the château with the kind old French proprietor, watching events through his field-glass from a garret window. But he did accompany Charles when, on 13 December, the division recrossed the Nive and took part, albeit most of the time in reserve, in a fierce battle during which General Hill turned disaster into a belated triumph. Soult had again switched his striking force from one side of Bayonne to the other, and as a storm had swept away the pontoon bridges over the Nive, much needed support was delayed until late in the day when the bridges were partly rebuilt. Almost all the senior British officers in action were killed or wounded. At one point an officer of Wellington's staff, finding nobody to whom he could deliver a message from headquarters, himself assumed command of a battalion and led a charge. In the Peninsular War there was no safety to be found at any level on the staff.

Charles's own description of those strenuous battles on the Nive, which lasted four days, has not survived; but Frederick left this account of his somewhat inglorious personal activities on the hard-fought 13th, when the 2nd Division bore the brunt and the 3rd Division was only called upon to take a belated part in the fighting.

This was the first time I ever saw a pontoon bridge laid, and thought it a splendid sight. The gallant manner in which the drivers dashed into the river with the pontoon carriages, up to the pommels of their saddles in water, was delightful to see. After marching a few miles on the other side of the river, a staff officer of the French surrendered himself as a prisoner, and my uncle gave him into my charge to take to the Provost Marshal in the rear. Fortunately I had not far to go, so having delivered him over I turned back, and as the General had that day mounted me on a powerful charger of his own, I soon overtook him.

Our Division did not come into action until late in the day, and then only partially, when a laughable thing happened to me. Our skirmishers were ordered to dislodge the enemy from an extensive wood in front of us, and Jackson, my uncle's A.D.C., and myself both rode into it after them; but we had not got in very far when my horse took fright at the rattling of the musket balls against the trees and wheeling round suddenly dashed out of the wood as hard as he could lay his legs to the ground, and all the strength I could lay on his bridle did not enable me to stop him. The 5th Regt. was halted in column just outside and the frightened animal carried me past them at full speed to their great astonishment. I certainly made a most ridiculous figure, but they all saw I was doing my best to stop the brute. He had been wounded under the General at the battle of Vitoria and this occasioned his alarm, poor creature.

It was late in the day at this time, and the action soon ceased. My uncle and his staff made for the Château of Villefranque, where we passed the night.

Soult's imaginative manoeuvres had failed, but not before Wellington felt obliged to recall the brave, if unruly, Spanish divisions on to French territory to reinforce his hard-pressed army. Then, perhaps as an indication of the way the European wind was blowing, three Nassau regiments arrived in the Allied lines bearing white flags. They announced that their Prince had deserted Napoleon and so they proposed to do the same. Their adherence was not an unqualified benefit. Eighteen months later, on the field of Waterloo, it was these same regiments that panicked at a crucial moment and fired on Wellington personally when he made an attempt to rally them.

The battles of the Nive bear some comparison with the great German counter-offensive in the Ardennes at Christmas 1944: they were a desperate thrust, they were brilliantly conceived, and they came near to success. But by 14 December Soult was obliged to accept the fact that his counter-offensive, aimed at repulsing the Allies from the soil of France, could not be renewed. He retired across the River Adour, leaving a strong garrison to hold Bayonne, and both armies were trammelled for nearly two months by glutinous mud.

Two personal misfortunes now befell Charles. Picton returned from England with the offer of taking command of the British army in Catalonia where Marshal Suchet was still unbeaten. On reaching St. Jean-de-Luz he discussed matters with Wellington and decided that he would prefer to resume command of his old 3rd Division. Wellington's respect for Picton's professional qualities was such that he felt unable to say no. It was, contrary to what Charles supposed, Picton's choice and not Wellington's. So, as Lord Dalhousie was going home on leave, Charles was offered the 7th Division (which included, among others, that admirable letter-writer, Private Wheeler). However, before this change could be affected, command of the 5th Division fell vacant and Wellington gave it to Charles on a permanent basis, 'both in consequence of the Major General's seniority and his unremitted meritorious services'. All the same, leaving his much-loved 3rd Division, his very own as he regarded it, was cause for sorrow.

His second affliction was physical. He had hardly succeeded to the 5th Division when he was struck again by his old enemy, rheumatism. It was this, a year ago, that had caused him to be carried by sedan chair to the quayside at Portsmouth. Now he was obliged to ask for leave at St. Jean de Luz, whence after a whole month's misery he wrote this letter to one of his relations:

I have been here since this day month, endeavouring to rid myself of a rheumatic attack which had previously confined me for six days to my bed. I had, in the constant wettings I had to encounter so frequently in course of the season, cause enough to account for it, but my former experience of the disease has not made me bear this with better spirits, for it makes me set it down as constitutional, and now for the rest of my life to be as regularly expected as gout is by others.

I have here persevered for a month in the use of a hot salt water bath every night, which I have in my room, and have succeeded in pretty well getting rid of my original disease, but perhaps from want of my customary exercise have latterly been very much disorganised in my stomach and bowels, and although Vitoria, the Pyrenees, the storming of the heights of St. Pé and the passages of the Nivelle and Nive may in my future recollection make the year 1813 a satisfactory one of my life, it has been that in which I have encountered more ill health than any other.

That you have not seen my name mentioned in the despatches is of course, principally, from my not having had anything very important to do, and also from the acts of the Commander of a Division being sunk in those of a column or corps. Since leaving the Pyrenees my Division (though little more than nominally) has been under the orders of Marshal Beresford, and there has been in my own case more than one omission of the nature you allude to, but the most provoking instance was of a more serious nature, when owing to some misconception either of his, or error in making up his report of the 3rd Division, the Portuguese Brigade was extolled in the despatches of the 10th Nov. to the exclusion of my own old Brigade under Colonel

Keane, although the former, the stronger of the two by a couple of 100, lost only 91 men and the other 401. In the conduct of the two, as far as they were engaged, so well officered is that Portuguese Brigade, I do not know that there was anything to prefer in the one above the other. It is but justice to the Marshal to say that he has subsequently done everything that candour and liberality could dictate to remedy the evil he had occasioned, but unluckily the explanation will probably be made to the Marquis alone, and the merits of the Brigade and its leader on that day remained unknown to the public.

Sir Thomas Picton's second unexpected return has again removed me from the 3rd Division. Picton was sent out by Lord Bathurst and the Duke of York for that command which it is a pity he had not from the first, but Lord Wellington's pleas were different. I am now, as a permanent command, appointed to the 5th Division in the room of Sir James Leith who goes to the West Indies. They are reduced at present as low as 3,600 firelocks having been very much under fire this campaign, but they have the debris of some good regiments who are likely to recruit well from the Militia and I suppose Lord W. will, before recommencing active operations, equalise the Divisions from the British part of the army which is probably by this time on their march from Catalonia.

I shall myself be delighted to hear that there is not an Englishman left in Spain, even if Suchet with his 30,000 men should remain there to do them all the mischief he can. Every day shows more and more of the jealousy and base ingratitude of the high-minded nation they call themselves, but not to do them an injustice, this is I believe pretty well confined to the Government and Military.

We entered France for the double purpose of winter quarters and making a diversion in favour of the Allies, against whom Soult could have detached a great part of his force had we receded from the Pyrenees which we otherwise must have done. I believe it is not from want of his being urged to do it by Ministers that Lord W. has not yet advanced further, but independent of the drawback of weather, transport and roads, and the requisite re-equipment of the troops at this season, his strength has hitherto been insufficient for the measure. If Holland had not drawn to it some of the troops he had looked to, in addition to our present force, and better hopes were entertained from the turning out of the Militia than had been realised, his Lordship talked of taking the field with 80,000 British and

Portuguese. I do not know what he has now exactly to look for; some Militia volunteers, five or six regiments from the South and East of Spain, two from the Cape of Good Hope, and from seven to ten thousand Portuguese in good condition from the depot under General Blount at Mafra, and who have been several months waiting for transport from Lisbon. The only Spaniards on this side of the Bidassoa are the divisions of Morillo and Don Carlos d'Espana, the two not exceeding 7,000 bayonets. With these, the measure has been lately adopted of feeding them with British full rations by the British commissariat, and paying them from our Military chest. This is to prevent their plundering, as they were wont in their own country as well as this, and a continuance here would have totally defeated Lord W's purpose of conciliating the inhabitants.

Meanwhile Charles's brother and constant correspondent, John, Captain Lord Colville of Culross, R.N., had been having a trying time. Poor John was always in trouble. He first went to sea at the age of twelve and was only fourteen in 1782 when he took part in Rodney's victorious action against the French fleet under De Grasse at the Battle of the Saints. In 1804, however, he lost his ship off Texel, for which he was surprisingly exonerated and was even given another command. His wife was something of a hypochondriac and a lady of many discontents. She was also childless. Some of his officers in H.M.S. *Queen* conspired against him and H.M.S. *Queen* herself, a seventy-four-gun ship of the line of which he was doubtless lucky to be left in command, was slow, leaky and difficult to handle. He felt, too, he had no influence in the right quarter, though to Charles's embarrassment he wrote to the Duke of York to ask that his brother be given the colonelcy of a line regiment. As commissions in the Army were obtained by purchase, it was profitable to be the titular colonel of a regiment, but officious initiatives are apt to be the more resented when they are unsuccessful. Finally, John was much disturbed by the problem of 'the bastards'.

The late admiral, Lord Colville, saviour of Quebec, had produced two illegitimate sons, to whom he left much of the fortune in prize money he had won during his long naval service. He made no provision for his brother and successor, John, the veteran of Fontenoy and Culloden, nor for his impecunious nephews. When he died, moreover, his childless but well-endowed and well-connected widow, whom he had married late in life, felt a responsibility for the two bastards and did her best to launch them on a naval career. They were both extravagant wastrels and died young, leaving penniless children who persisted in plaguing the head of the family. John's letters from the *Queen* are full of references to their importunities.

On 2 July 1813 he wrote to Charles about 'a new left-handed cousin that, to my great annoyance, came to light when I was last in the Downs'. This young man 'stated a wish that I would extricate him from a situation so low (he is before the mast) by procuring his discharge'. It seemed that having lost his patrimony by speculation, he had made a voyage to India and had been forcible conscripted by a press-gang. John made inquiries of Admiral Foley and the captain of the young man's ship, H.M.S. *Monmouth*, receiving the reply that 'he is a well-looking man, younger than he says, has been bred a carver and gilder, in which he has shewn considerable ingenuity and has by his art been very useful to Lady Lucy in fitting up a little whimsical Chinese room'. While John was wondering what to do, the young man overstayed his shore-leave and was found to have enlisted as a Marine. Realising that he was in an awkward predicament, he disappeared and then gave himself up to the authorities as a deserter from the Coldstream Guards, which (as he informed John) was a scheme for getting out of the Navy. He asked for John's help in order to become a master's mate or midshipman in H.M.S. *Monmouth*, provided nobody expected him to go to sea again. 'He has the effrontery', wrote John, '(to prove his identity I suppose) to seal his last letter with a seal which (as I have told him), it is a punishable offence for any other than myself to use, were it worth while to notice it.'

John thought that 'he has the sort of learning which always does such characters more harm than good, that he is shrewd enough, and would be presumptuous and troublesome in his expectations of assistance if at all encouraged'; so he decided not to give the young man an interview. Fearing, no doubt, that this might be thought callous, faint-hearted and a neglect of family responsibility, however 'left-handed', he wrote urgently to Charles saying: 'I would give much to know your opinion of the conduct that I should pursue in regard to this unexpected claimant for aid, of which I have so little to grant to others who have legitimate and fair grounds to hope for it.'

While he awaited Charles's reply, John felt obliged to write again about this new encumbrance, 'calling himself the son of the elder bastard (Lieut. in the Navy) of our uncle of unjust and unfeeling memory'. He had just received an urgent letter from the barrack guardroom at Deal 'acquainting me that he was lodged there as a deserter from the Coldstream and intreating my interference to save him from the punishment that hangs over him'. But he concluded sadly, 'However much inclined, the mode to adopt in his favour I know not.' Finally, however, he managed to exert enough influence to have the boy returned to the Navy and placed in a seagoing ship.

Though it was difficult for Charles to concentrate on such problems during the battles of the Pyrenees, he did worry about John, to whom he was deeply devoted. In one of his letters home he wrote:

My brother's persevering ill-luck in his profession, exemplified on almost every possible occasion, as fast as one can follow the other, is indeed a source of infinite vexation to me. The fatality seems such that I should long since have recommended him to quit the navy, had he the means of living out of it. I only wonder how his weakly constitution and rather irritable habits have been able to withstand such a succession of evils as have molested him in one way or the other. I hope in God that he will sooner or later receive the reward of that superior worth of private character which I know is truly his . . .'

Poor John soon suffered further misery. In November, while Charles was fighting on the Nivelle, he was given command of a vast convoy, bound for Barbados. There was war with the United States of America and supplies were urgently required. On 2 December John wrote:

My fleet was wholly dispersed in the most violent tempest I ever knew that lasted 48 hours without intermission. Of 190 Sail I have now only 27 with me, and not one man-of-war, but we have a fair wind and are proceeding to Madeira where I hope we shall meet again. Our sufferings have been great, and our privation, but Providence has carried us well through all. My cabin has been filled by a sea, and I have had everything wet, nor has anyone in the ship had better luck than myself. One of my quarter galleries was beat in by the sea when I was in it: I escaped by a miracle. I shall think little of these things if I succeed in collecting my convoy and find the other men-of-war safe, of which I have some fears.

On 14 December H.M.S. *Columbia* and eighty-six sail were collected off Madeira and Lord Colville finally reached Barbados on 10 January with 102 ships in company. Eighty-eight had strayed or foundered.

Meanwhile, on the River Adour, Soult was ordered to send a large contingent to reinforce his troubled Emperor. His field army, already weakened by casualties and the loss of many prisoners of war, was soon reduced to some 35,000 seasoned veterans and an intake of young conscripts with no military experience or staying power and a notable enthusiasm for desertion. With these Soult resolved to contest control of the upper Adour and the series of river barriers, stretching as far as Toulouse, that flow south-eastwards towards the Pyrenees. Wellington, for his part, decided to leave a strong force, under the command of the physically gigantic Sir John Hope, to invest Bayonne, while he himself prepared to set off with 40,000 men in pursuit of Soult. Thus matters stood early in February 1814, when Charles was sufficiently recovered to assume active command of the 5th Division.

10

The First Fall of Bonaparte

During the wet January days of 1814, while Charles nursed his rheumatism at St. Jean de Luz, neither army could move. There was plenty of time both for planning and for politics. Napoleon, defeated at Leipzig but refusing to accept defeat, manoeuvred successfully in eastern France and played havoc with the Prussians under Blucher, whose renown in German history is greater than his achievements. It seemed that Napoleon might yet succeed in saving his throne by a compromise peace, even if his dominion were confined to France itself and he must forego his foreign conquests and the colonial empire of his predecessors. It would, no doubt, have been a temporary arrangement: his ambitions were unquenchable, as was his dedication to political intrigue. Even while the Allied delegates assembled at Chatillon to negotiate with French emissaries, the Emperor was deploying all his wiles to embroil Spain and Great Britain so that the Peninsular army might be conveniently stabbed in the back.

Wellington kept his own counsel, leaving his divisional commanders to guess what his plans might be. Charles concluded his letter of 24 January with these sentences:

> Colonel Bunbury, Under Secretary of State, War Department, arrived here from England yesterday. Curiosity is on tiptoe to know the purpose of his trip, but it will most likely for the present be a secret between him and the Lord. It was said some days ago that the French had sent away three divisions and, whether from that cause or another, they two days since drew back their outposts on this side, so that Lord W. rode yesterday with only a very small escort to the very shore of the Adour close to its mouth.

> I do not see any preparations for the immediate siege of Bayonne, and I rather think it is his Lordship's intention to

leave it behind, pushing on for Bordeaux, but on account of the supplies which he must continue to look to the sea for, more tranquil weather should take place than we expect at this time of year in the Bay of Biscay. There is however said to be somewhere between this and Bordeaux a good anchorage well known to some of our navy, to which it is meant we should look perhaps to the furnishing of our supplies and opening our communications with the Channel fleet.

When the Allies advance by the Northward and Eastward, Buonaparte, so I have always called him, will be in a pretty scrape.

O'Donnell's army would be sufficient for the investment of Bayonne should Lord W. on any account feel inclined to bring a Spanish force forward, but there is so much intrigue and ill disposition among that people that it is the common talk that we shall have to thrash them into a proper sense of their insignificance before we embark.

What Wellington had decided to do was to divide his army into two parts. In order to invest and eventually to storm Bayonne, it was necessary to detach some 30,000 men, for although there were only 14,000 French defenders, the city was so placed, at the confluence of the Nive and the Adour, that the besieging force was bound to be divided by fast-flowing streams. It was therefore essential to have enough men available in each sector to resist a sortie in force by the garrison. Sir John Hope, commanding this army of investment, was a general whom Charles respected and admired. Charles himself was second in seniority. Hope's force consisted of the 1st and 5th Divisions, two Spanish Divisions under Carlos d'España, a brigade of cavalry, three independent brigades of infantry and twenty field-guns. With the remainder of his army Wellington intended to dispose of Soult, to cross the Adour, to march through the Landes and to capture Bordeaux.

Apart from the difficulty of finally defeating Napoleon in battle, heavily outnumbered though his troops now were, the Allied statesmen were by no means certain that a restoration of the Bourbons in France would be the wisest policy to pursue. The French Empress was, after all, the daughter of the Austrian Emperor and her son, being half a Hapsburg, might be considered a respectable heir to the French throne. Moreover, although there were enthusiastic supporters of the Bourbon claim, especially in Brittany and the west of France, there was no deep loyalty to the dynasty among the people as a whole. The *Tricolore*, the Eagles and the Legion of Honour had become an integral part of the nation's life: the last twenty years meant more to the French people than the previous two hundred. The British historical analogy was of dubious value. The Stuarts had indeed been welcomed back to the throne with enthusiasm after eleven years of Cromwellian puritanism; but even though Cromwell had a nobler character than Napoleon, and takes a distinguished place among the founders of Britain's greatness, he never won the hearts of the people nor dazzled them with the flame of imperial glory and conquest as Napoleon did the French.

The British Cabinet was hesitant, but the Prince Regent had no doubts at all. To the indignation of the Whigs who frequented Holland House, he drove through London in an open carriage with the Comte de Provence beside him and the postillions wearing white cockades in their caps. Wellington was less flamboyant and he knew that he must make no overt move until his Government reached a decision; but the Curé at Saint Pé had done his work well and nothing had happened since those three rainy days on the Nivelle to dissuade Wellington from his view that a Bourbon restoration would be best for Britain, for France and for Europe. Therefore when the Duc d'Angoulême arrived at his headquarters at the beginning of February he was received with courtesy and without the slightest embarrassment.

Angoulême, son of the Comte d'Artois, who was the younger brother of Louis XVI and of the Comte de Provence, was fourteen when the French Revolution broke out. He had no great presence, nor remarkable gifts, but his marriage to the only survivor of Louis XVI's unhappy family endowed him with greater interest than he would otherwise have offered. Moreover, he had excellent manners. It was his fate, ten years later, to become the last Dauphin of France, but never to be her King.

On this occasion Angoulême brought to St. Jean de Luz news of Charles's host on that first visit to Versailles, the Marquis de Bombelles. He had lost his attractive wife and had forsaken the Army for the Church. Temporarily a monk, he had now assumed less cloistered clerical duties. Though Angoulême did not know it, he was about to become an Austrian bishop. Charles had originally been entrusted to Bombelles's care through the good offices of his cousin, Alexander Blair, a London friend of the Marquis in the early '80s. So he now wrote to Blair:

Although I wrote to you by the last mail, I know you will be glad to learn what has taken, or what is likely to take place

here in the fast approaching fate of French affairs, and in consequence of the arrival of the Duc d'Angoulême. I had the honour
of sitting next him at dinner at Lord Wellington's yesterday,
and found him very amiable and communicative. He gave me
an account of our worthy and long lost sight-of friend the Marquis
de Bombelles, which Mrs Blair and yourself will agree with
me in thinking infinitely more satisfactory than the monastic
immurement to which it was said he had sacrificed himself.

He is a Curé in Silicia, the duties of which situation he
has long discharged with all the devotion and zeal for the welfare
of his parishioners which we would expect of him. His second
son, a particularly fine boy when I knew him, has fallen in
battle. His other sons are in the service, domestic and military,
of Austria. His Highness's memory in regard to persons seems
to rival that of any of our Royal family. He made particular
enquiries after my brother, whom he had known when commanding a brig of war in Leith Roads in '96, but had never seen
since, and was now aware of his disastrous voyage to the West
Indies. He of course prepares himself for such civil things by
references to the Army List, and enquiries as to who he is
likely to meet.

His coming out was either entirely of his own act, or it was
so much meant to have that appearance, that embarking with
the Comte de Damas alone and one servant between both, he
was not even known to the master of the packet. The Pactolus
frigate had, however, orders (secret) to keep a lookout after
her. 'Pour ne pas compremettre les pauvres gens du pays' by
any show of their attachment, he remains as it were incognito,
but the Comte de Damas, who has this instant left my room,
assured me he is 'parfaitement enchanté' with what he has
learnt of the disposition of the people and that, as we can
readily believe, he has not for five and twenty years known
such a shower of happiness as that produced by the prospect
before him.

The Comte d'Artois they suppose, is arrived by this time
in Switzerland. The Duc de Berry, when they last heard of
him was in Jersey watching what may be done on the coast
of Brittany.

From today's accounts from Bayonne it appears that the French
on the 27th ultimo burnt their fleet at Antwerp, which upon
the whole is perhaps the best thing for England that could
have been done with it.

I learn that Suchet has at length evacuated Catalonia, of course leaving a garrison in Barcelona, but I have not heard what other places he has retained possession of. I think this movement of his is rather to be lamented; the diversion of so great a body of his best troops was a measure we had wondered Bonaparte had so long admitted of. He may now be of material use to him on the side of Lyons, whereas the acquisition we shall now obtain in British troops, rendered thereby disposable, will be, as I mentioned in my last, but inconsiderable. Lord W. will not, I conclude, think of bringing Sicilians or Calabrians forward.

Our stationary condition here, however much to be lamented, promises to continue for some time longer unavoidable. The full moon brought two fine days, but today it rains again as hard as ever and we have now no hope before the new moon of the 20th of any change. Fourteen large pontoons in addition to five or six already on the Nive passed through this two days ago. They are to be thrown across the Adour, but I can hardly conceive when they will arrive at their destination, considering the state the roads and country are in on both sides of the Nive.

I rode two days since to pay my compliments to my new Divn. but how I got to their cantonments, or managed to return without injury to myself or horse, is more than I can account for.

Although Charles did not overstress the fact, he was deeply disappointed to be left behind at Bayonne when, on 16 February, Wellington set forth in pursuit of Soult across the numerous small rivers that run south to the Pyrenees. It was, of course, gratifying to command the 5th Division. Its record was a proud one, even though its strength had been seriously depleted and the replacements awaited from the Militia at home had in large part been diverted to Holland. But the place for an active soldier was with 'the Lord', and all his friends were now eastwards bound with the practical certainty of great battles ahead. He missed the 3rd Division, especially his own old brigade in it, now commanded by Colonel John Keane, and he had just learned to know and respect the 6th Division, which he commanded for three months, when he was transferred back to temporary command of the 3rd. It was clear that he was highly regarded at G.H.Q., and that Wellington personally had faith in him, but it had been his fate to be denied permanence of command.

Now there were new faces, an unfamiliar staff, brigade and

regimental commanders who were only acquaintances, and the boredom of sitting out a long siege and investment. As Colonel Keane wrote to him 'I am not surprised at your detestation of stone walls. God knows, you as well as your Division have had a very fair share of sieges'.

He was a spectator rather than a participant in the feat of building a wide bridge of boats across the Adour below Bayonne. This was achieved in the face of enemy troops holding the northern bank. It was a combined operation, for the Navy, with considerable loss, sailed boats through the surging waters of the bar at the mouth of the River Adour, the artillery drove the French gunboats upstream, the engineers produced a marvel in the way of bridge construction, and sixty men of the brigade of Guards crossed the river in small boats to attack the enemy outposts and secure the far end of the bridge. Sir John Hope was among the first across and Wellington, temporarily leaving his advancing army, rode many miles back to spend two days on the scene.

This exciting enterprise fell to the lot of the 1st Division which was able to cross the river on the 25 February and complete the investment of Bayonne. The northern suburb of St. Etienne was taken by storm and the French garrison was thenceforward effectively besieged in the citadel of Bayonne itself. Charles, who had been holding that ground between the Nive and the Adour where General Hill had fought so gallantly against superior odds on 13 December, now crossed the Nive and occupied an arc south of Bayonne from the Nive to the sea. Carlos d'Espana filled the gap left by the 5th Division and on 3 March Charles sent this letter home:

> The *désagrément* has occured to me of being with the 5th Division, forming part of the left column devoted to the invest-ment and probably a place in the siege of Bayonne, instead of the more animated service of the field. For a week I occupied the ground between the Nive and Adour and now being relieved by Don Carlos D'Espana's Spanish Division (not a desirable exchange for the unfortunate inhabitants) do occupy that, with the addition of Lord Aylmer's weak Brigade, from the Nive to the sea, a long line for so small a force, (not above 4,000 duty men), were the strength or energies of the enemy calculated for vigorous sorties.
>
> After the nine days of fine weather which our noble chief knew so well how to take advantage of, we must not grumble for some time at the reverse, but for the three last days it

has been as bad as bad can be, with snow, hail, rain, wind, thunder and lightning. It is severely felt by the troops on duty, and the state of the clay soil is much against the operations of the siege.

It sometimes happens in war that objects considered of the greatest difficulty are from contingent causes accomplished with the greatest comparative facility; thus it has been with the passage of the river below Bayonne by the troops under Sir John Hope. The idea was worthy of Lord Wellington's great mind, and the preparations were suited to its magnificence, but difficulties of roads by land and of the bar by sea might have delayed and thus wholly endangered its accomplishment, had not Sir John Hope fortunately had the headiness to resist the objections started, and the enterprise to commence his embarcation with six boats carrying six men each, instead of the rafts of pontoons which were to have thrown over 600 men at a time. The total want of opposition to the measure by the enemy would go to prove a thorough want of information of the preparations for the passage that had been going on for some time at St. Jean de Luz and Passages. The sea battery which commanded the entrance to the river and which was to have been stormed by a small corps thrown over for the purpose was evacuated a few days ago.

The bridge is a chef d'oeuvre of its kind, and although it has been assisted by the best possible aids of locality, the greater credit is due to the quickly discerning eye that could catch at and profit by them. The boom for its protection is made fast on the enemy's side to a mooring ring in the pier. The ends of the cables on which the bridge rests are secured on one side by means of five old 18 pdr guns thrown over the pier for the purpose, while on the other side they are tightened by the pressure of sand bags and a windlass.

Everything passes this bridge without unloading, carriage or beast or burden, and lands upon the stone pier, five or six hundred yards in length, instead of wading, as is generally the case in such situations, through deep sand or mud to the infinite destruction or delay of the means of transport. The cables rest on the decks of 26 two masted vessels of about 60 tons burthen, and the cutting of the cables separately, as well as of the apparatus of the bridge laying on them, in case of the approach of fire vessels, or other danger, would not occasion much injury to the whole.

When I passed the bridge yesterday, tho' blowing at the time a hard gale of wind from the sea, it rode very easy, the bar serving as its break water. The sea-going people of the place, however, expressed their apprehensions for its safety last night when, as they anticipated, the gale increased. Not having heard anything to the contrary today, I trust all is safe with it.

Sir John Hope, tho' by no means recovered from the wound received in his leg in Decr., crossed with nearly the first of the troops I believe, and superintended the driving the enemy into their works two days after.

He is now nursing himself again and will, I hope, prove not to have suffered materially from his premature exercise.

Meanwhile Wellington's pursuit of Soult had been successful despite that Marshal's determined resistance. After crossing numerous rivers, almost always contested, the British army brought Soult to bay at Orthez on 27 February. It was not a battle easily won and over 2,000 British soldiers fell. It seemed at one moment that the French would triumph; but Wellington's attack, with the 3rd and 6th Divisions, on the flank of the advancing French turned potential defeat into overwhelming victory. Wellington himself was hit and temporarily incapacitated by a spent musket-ball, an event which delayed the pursuit of the retreating enemy and may even have saved their army from final disintegration.

Charles's old colleagues of the 3rd Division, realising how grieved he must be to miss this auspicious day, sent him detailed accounts of the battle. On 12 March Picton wrote him a long letter from his new headquarters at Barcellone, north of the Adour. This was followed by two from John Keane, commanding Charles's old brigade, who idiosyncratically referred to the French as 'toads' (Crapaud) instead of the more usual 'frogs'. He wrote on 17 March:

I beg you will believe that I never allowed many hours to pass after the glorious 27th, without giving you a line detailing hastily the several points which occurred in the arrondissement of my view.

The morning of the 27th set in fine, but very few thought the enemy would stand. The Lord had reconnoitred and each corps was in its place by nine o'clock and moved forward as follows; 3rd on the right, Light in the centre and 4th on the left. The 6th supported the right, the 7th the left. The enemy's position was well chosen for defence, keeping also a good eye to retreat as each ridge they occupied was connected with the great Bordeaux road. Once in motion we were soon in fire, and for two hours it was furious. The ground certainly was well contested. Crapaud truly fought to endeavour to restore his lost honour. At last the three old Divisions started them, and then the 6th and 7th were laid in and soon turned a retreat into a rout, and I'll promise you gave the morning's work a very neat polish. Their loss was great, but still I conceive they got off cheap, report says between 5 and 6,000, added to which 4,000 have deserted since.

Heath was our only shelter and we got well pounded, the 45th, 83rd and 87th particularly, as also the 88th, on the other side. Poor Parker was cut in two by a cannon shot close to the God of War. Taylor was wounded in the neck but is up again. Greenwell severely, Carr ditto—ball entered the chin and lodged in the roots of his tongue. It has been cut out and he is doing well. Elliott severely in the belly, but also doing well. Poor Nugent dangerously in two places, but there are some hopes. Baldwin severely, right arm broken. Capt. McDermot, 88th, only joined the day before, with his Vitoria wound open, was killed.

On the morning of the 24th, the Lord manoeuvred with the 2nd and 6th Divisions to the right in order to turn the gentleman, desiring Sir Thomas to make a demonstration to occupy their attention to the front. In the play, the village of Murien was my allotted berth, which was close under the enemy's position and guns, and received with a very jealous eye. A bad and dangerous ford was here discovered and Stovin arrived with orders for me to cross. I could not say no, but dreaded the consequences. Accordingly with the four light companies I made the attempt assisted by a Captain and six Hussars, and countenanced by a squadron. On reaching the enemy's bank without any opposition, we lined the hedges etc. when I found Sir Stapleton withdrawing the cavalry. Crapaud instantly perceived it, and finding our men not supported, came down with three strong battalions and knocked the poor Bobs headlong into the river under a tremendous fire, the 5th Regt. returning it from the flank of the village.

Reassembling on friendly ground, I found the four companies had lost five officers and 70 men killed, wounded, drowned and taken; a very bad business; added to which my poor pony was badly wounded and Campbell's horse killed. Golby was wounded in this affair, but from his known zeal Sir Thos allowed me to recommend his name together with Desterre's and Campbell's to the Lord's consideration for the battle of Orthez.

On reaching the second river on the morning of the 26th the bridge was no more. A deep but safe ford was found near it and stripped up to . . . —upon my modesty I can't say what, the old Corps dashed into it headed by the Grande Lord. Strange it was unwatched. Fifty Jagers would have rendered it impassable. Safely landed the Lord quickly learnt that the Marshal, by two fords lower down, had escaped the 4th and 7th with Vivian's horse. Orders were immediately sent to the 6th and Light to move on our ford, and in the afternoon and night they crossed; out of which force grew the spectacle by Orthez next morning. After such a severe lesson one can hardly believe that the very same Soult is now seeking a second addition.

March 24th, 1814

I hope my last letter dated on or about Saint Paddy's Day has reached you. In it I spoke of fighting and I really thought so, as crafty Soult was before us in force, avowedly for the purpose of falling on Sir Roland, not knowing he had support, but the moment he learnt the old 'stuff' was come up, he decamped, taking the road to Lembeye. No time was lost, we advanced on the 18th and on the 19th, at noon ran into them in a large mead on the Tarbes road, two miles short of Vic de Bigorre. Lord Wellington was up, and reconnoitred; found them strong and the country stronger, for both sides of the road produced nothing but nearly impenetrable vineyards. The enemy's whole force was there, and Count d'Erlon with two divisions was charged with the defence of the road. The 3rd, supported by the 6th, was the leading column, my Brigade forming the advanced guard. From 12 to 2 a greal deal of cannon and spitting on both sides. Sir Thos then looked vexed and decided on attack, tho' positively contrary to Lord W's directions. Accordingly we were at them and ably countenanced on the right by my friend Power the road was ours in 15 minutes and in the 10 following they were driven from a number of scattered houses by a brilliant charge of the 83rd, 87th and 94th in two columns, one headed by the knight and the other by your humble servant. Here Arbuthnot was wounded (arm) and I hope not dangerously; and here two thousand *tirailleurs* flew before our little band. The old 5th, headed by its Marshal, panted for employ but could not find it. There now only remained the vineyards, which certainly presented divers obstacles. However we walked at them and what between firing, roaring and bugling we chased Drouet and his frogs from one to the other into the town, then charged them through it, making a few prisoners. The rascals would not stand or they all would have been taken. Our great Lord had a very commanding view and honoured us by saying that he never saw a more gallant attack in his life, and the execution spoke for itself. Our loss was very trifling considering the nature of the affair. I had 5 officers wounded, 12 men killed and 71 wounded, Power's 100, Total in the Division 220.

We bivouac'd that night one mile in front of Vic. and next morning started for Tarbes in the same order, only Brisbane joining the advance. On nearing the town Sir Thos gave me a squadron and two guns with the Brigade to turn it. No opposition was offered, and we met and formed in the great square, as Emperors and Kings did at Leipsic.

The town was beautiful, equal to any in England, and the ladies and gentlemen in numbers making a magnificent appearance, received us with ' Vivent les Anglais ' and every other mark of seeming delight.

Here Dalmatie's Duke took leave of the Adour, on which he has faithfully done his duty, and placed his army, 30,000 strong, in position two miles from the town on the ridge covering the great Toulouse road. Having married a Tarbes lady, there was some interest expected, and the day proving particularly fine, the bridge gardens soon were crowded with spectators and certainly the scene was grand; something in the way of a grand review in Hyde Park on a Sunday.

At two o'clock our flank columns were placed, 2rd right, 6th left, 3rd and Light in contiguous columns of Brigades forming the centre. In this state we moved across the plain but on nearing the hill Johnny's heart failed, and he descended, continuing such a quick pace until dark that we never neared him. There was great manoeuvring on both sides; indeed the Lord's dispositions were monstrous fine. I feel satisfied of having received a capital military lesson.

We shall be in the neighbourhood of Toulouse tomorrow afternoon. The occurences there must form food for another epistle. The inhabitants *partout* are favourable to the Bourbons. The Duc de Berri seems the favourite.

After the Battle of Orthez, Marshal Beresford set out for Bordeaux. Accompanied by the Duc d'Angoulême, he entered the city on 12 March. The royalist ' explosion ', as Wellington called it, duly occurred: the Mayor dramatically pulled off his *tricolore*

sash, white cockades sprouted like mushrooms. However, Angoulême went too far. He not only proclaimed his uncle, the Comte
de Provence, king (as Louis XVIII), but appointed royalist *préfets*
in districts far removed from Bordeaux. This was embarrassing
to Wellington, inclined though he was to promote the white cockade,
for the Allied Governments were still not committed to a Bourbon
restoration. He felt obliged to send Angoulême a long remonstrance.

Nevertheless, Napoleon's star was close to setting. Vastly outnumbered, his troops fell back before the advancing Austrians, Russians
and Prussians, and on 31 March the Czar and the King of Prussia
rose side by side down the Champs Elysées. The French Senate
deposed Napoleon, who was at Fontainebleau, at one minute
resolved to abdicate, at another to commit suicide and at yet
another to collect his veterans and fight to a finish. On 4 April
he signed his Abdication, but then withdrew it and shilly-shallied
for a further week. Effectively, however, his reign was over when
Paris fell and the Senate's decision to depose him was endorsed
by the lower House.

To the French soldiers still in arms, it was such a cataclysmic
event that they could scarcely credit the news. And that news,
lacking certainty while the Emperor himself delayed his decision,
travelled slowly. It travelled so slowly that two blood-stained engagements took place after the war was in reality over.

The first was the Battle of Toulouse, a desperate assault on
Soult's army in that city made by Wellington on 10 April. Wellington for once made an understatement when he called it 'a very
severe affair'. It cost the lives of 8,000 men, approximately half
on each side, and it was, as events proved, totally unnecessary.
Picton, ordered to make a feint with the 3rd Division, turned
it into a real attack and lost 500 men to no good purpose. Frederick
Frankland, who fought with the 4th Division, sent his uncle a
detailed account of the battle and the grave losses. His description
of the aftermath, written from La Bastide, was as follows:

Nothing was done the next day and on the morning of the
12th, before daybreak, as General Anson and myself were visiting
the posts we found that the enemy's picquets were gone, and
on finding that some men whom we took to be French were
the Cacadores of the 6th Division, we pushed on into the town
and rode smack through it over the main bridge, where we
found General Byng on the march to take it by storm. Lord
Wellington, having heard that they intended to blow it up,
the General was not sorry to find that General Anson had taken

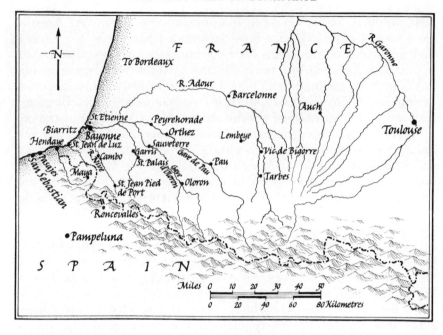

possession so quietly. We found the Garde Urbaine all at their posts who paid the proper compliments and who were desired to continue their functions. The people soon crowded out of their houses and showed the greatest joy. They threw the bust of the Emperor out of the window of the Capitoleum and hoisted a white flag.

The town is very pretty. I went in yesterday with General Anson. This place is three leagues from it. We marched to this place immediately on finding it evacuated by the French, but the news of the abdication of Buonaparte has stopped us and we only wait for Soult's determination to march to Bordeaux to embark. This sudden change of things is almost incredible. It appears to me like a dream. We all wear the white cockade; Lord W. set the example.

The second unnecessary shedding of blood did affect Charles Colville personally. At 3 a.m. on 14 April the French garrison, despite the fact that rumours of events in Paris had reached both besiegers and besieged, made a desperate and, in the circumstances, inexcusable sortie from Bayonne. Shortly before they did so, a French deserter sought to give warning to General Hay who commanded the British outposts, which on that night were taken from a brigade of Charles's 5th Division, from the King's German Legion and from the Guards. Unfortunately General Hay spoke no French and did not grasp the warning. Moreover, reports that the war was over lulled the British into a false sense of security.

Three thousand French soldiers crept from the Citadel, surprised the British pickets and with a wild rush seized the village of St. Etienne with the exception of a single fortified house defended by a gallant captain of the 38th Regiment. General Hay was killed and in the darkness and confusion nobody quite knew who was fighting whom. The King's German Legion, under the leadership of a sensible Hanoverian, General Hinuber, together with elements of the 5th Division and a battalion of Portuguese, eventually counter-attacked and drove the French back with heavy casualties.

While the tumult was at its height, Sir John Hope advanced with reinforcements. He rode along a narrow, sunken lane towards St. Etienne straight into a French ambush. He was hit in the arm and his horse, falling under a hail of bullets, fell on his leg. The men Hope was leading turned to escape, and only two officers, seeing his predicament, stayed to defend him. They were both badly wounded and were carried off with Sir John as prisoners.

It now fell to Charles to take command. He did so with energy so that by 7 a.m. all the ground lost had been recovered, and the French were back in the Citadel. This final act of bravado caused over 800 casualties on each side. It is scarcely surprising that many years later Wellington still 'spoke with indignation of the wanton sortie from Bayonne' and thought he would have been justified in hanging 'its author, Colonel Taupin'. Wellington's memory seems to have failed him, for Taupin was commanding a division under Soult at Toulouse and the sortie from Bayonne was directed by the Governor of that fortress, Baron Thouvenot. It was with him that Charles must now negotiate the surrender of the still recalcitrant garrison.

11

Winding Up

In Paris, while fierce battles still raged in the south of France, Prince Talleyrand, with his customary facility in changing sides, deserted Napoleon and persuaded the Czar, who had had serious doubts in the matter, that the best solution for the future of France was a constitutional monarchy under the Bourbons. The Czar even accepted an invitation to dine with the bewitching renegade on the very day he entered the French capital. Within a fortnight Napoleon was pensioned off (handsomely by twentieth-century standards) with the kingdom of Elba, a substantial pension for himself, a large capital sum for his family and three Italian duchies for his wife and child. He was offered Corfu and Corsica, but he preferred Elba.

So the white cockade became not merely permissible, but obligatory. It was worn with sincere enthusiasm in Bordeaux; Wellington himself displayed it at Toulouse; but by and large it was with resignation and regret rather than with elation that the *tricolore* flags were lowered. Louis XVIII himself had such bad gout that he could not leave London till May. He had to be content with the Prince Regent's suitably bedecked postillions and a great deal of adulation at Grillion's Hotel in Albemarle Street where the Mayor and Corporation of Westminster ('their fair round bellies with fat capons lined', as Lady Crewe remarked to Fanny Burney) headed a large throng that assembled to salute him. However, Louis' brother, the Comte d'Artois, escorted the Duchesse d'Angoulême to the Tuileries in April. Artois exercised to great effect the considerable charm which camouflaged his reactionary intentions. A beautiful, smiling Princess at his side might have won the hearts of the people of Paris; but Marie-Thérèse d'Angoulême had never recovered from the three hideous years in the Conciergerie and the Temple during which she saw the intestines of the beautiful Princesse de Lamballe held up to the window, her father, her aunt and then her mother dragged to the guillotine, and her little brother separated from his family and condemned to a scrofulous, tubercular death in solitary misery. Now plain, devout and reactionary, she had little appeal for the citizens of Paris.

The white cockade was not to be seen in Bayonne. On the day after the bloody sortie from the citadel, Charles sent a messenger with a flag of truce to tell Baron Thouvenot of the Senate's decree deposing Napoleon, and to confirm it with formal letters and copies of the Paris newspapers. Wellington, he wrote, was already in Toulouse and 'I rejoice in the opportunity of offering these proofs of the total revolution in the Government of France which, if received by your Excellency at an earlier period, might have saved that unnecessary effusion of blood of both nations which took place yesterday'.

Thouvenot was not impressed. He agreed to receive the letters, but not the officer who brought them. He sent a message to say that he would be grieved by the events of the previous day if arrangements between the belligerents had put an end to the war, but that he had no knowledge of such arrangements.

Charles tried again. He received a letter from Wellington telling him of the cease-fire agreements and enclosing a letter for the Governor of Bayonne. Charles sent it into the fortress on 18 April, but Thouvenot paid no attention to the contents on the grounds that nothing of an official nature had reached him.

By now Bayonne was the only city in all France which had not capitulated. The Governor was himself prepared to negotiate, but there were in his garrison officers so fiercely loyal to Napoleon that even though the former Emperor was on the point of departing for Elba, they were still unwilling to admit or accept the painful truth. The garrison continued to fire at the British troops investing them.

Charles decided to see what effect hoisting the white flag of the Bourbons, with its pattern of fleur-de-lys, might have. On 19th April he wrote to express regret at the Governor's attitude and ended his letter thus:

As however it becomes incumbent on me no longer to delay that mark of respect to the Government and Nation with which we are entering into friendship, I beg leave to acquaint you that it is my intention to hoist the white flag tomorrow at 12 o'clock under a royal salute of artillery unshotted.

I had hoped for the satisfaction of doing this in concert with your Excellency, but the fire of musketry and wall pieces that is allowed to continue on our sentries, etc., from your entrenched camp, and that of Artillery this evening, has lessened that expectation.

In a letter to Wellington on the following day, he described the result:

The hoisting of the white flag under royal salute of artillery from four different points in the circle of investment had no other effect than that of making the enemy, as I must still call them, shew their *tricolore* flag in all directions and rather, if anything, increase the fire which they now only occasionally give us, and as seemingly with a good deal of caprice.

A few days later, however, Charles was able to send Thouvenot a copy of the convention for the ceasing of hostilities signed by the Marquess of Wellington and Marshal Soult, Duke of Dalmatia. The Bonapartist officers began to waver, but Thouvenot still declined to surrender until a French officer should arrive bearing a copy authenticated by Soult. He would order his men to stop firing on the British outposts; but he still forbade any communication between the opposing troops.

Sir John Hope remained a prisoner, but his A.D.C. was allowed to cross the lines. He reported that the people of Bayonne were so exasperated by the intransigence of the army that their hostility prevented the French troops from patrolling the streets of the city.

Finally, on 26 April, more than a fortnight after the war had ended, Thouvenot condescended to write to Charles, in the third person, to the effect that since 'la place de Bayonne' was apparently included in the convention signed by Soult and Wellington, he was willing to appoint a delegate to discuss a suspension of arms. The negotiations were rapidly concluded and the volatile Governor wrote this to Charles on the 27th:

Too long has the roar of the nation's cannon resounded in Europe for the destruction of the people. I shall be well pleased when to-morrow, at noon, the sound of the Allies' cannon and those of this fortress are heard together in salutation of a flag which has always been revered by the French.

It is understandable that Wellington regretted not having hanged him. However, Charles took a more charitable view. Arrangements were made to place Sir John Hope on a ship in the Adour and to exchange prisoners; and Charles wrote this to Wellington about Baron Thouvenot:

> He appears to me to be a most gentleman-like, well intentioned man, having a difficult post with a garrison, great part of which cannot be supposed to be in a moment reconciled to a revolution so extraordinary.

The Baron, for his part, became enthusiastic about the new order and on 7 May he invited 'His Excellency the Commander-in-Chief of the Allied Forces in front of Bayonne' (by which he meant Charles) to accompany him to a Te Deum in celebration of Louis XVIII's accession and to dine with him afterwards. He also thought it would be pleasant to invite the Spanish and Portuguese commanders, always provided they left their troops behind. Indeed he inquired anxiously about the proposed date of departure of the Spaniards and Portuguese.

There followed a long and amiable correspondence about every kind of administrative matter. By the middle of May Charles and Thouvenot, lately determined enemies, were on the friendliest of terms. At that point, Wellington having returned home and been created a Duke, Charles was entrusted with the repatriation and dispersal of the Allied armies in the south-west of France while Lord Dalhousie was given a similar commission for those in the neighbourhood of Bordeaux.

The brave though indisciplined Spaniards marched to the frontier along the coast road. The Portuguese followed on their longer journey home through Viscaya, Salamanca and Ciudad Rodrigo. The British cavalry and the Horse Artillery rode across France to the Channel ports. On 18 May Wellington sent word that he would pass through Bayonne on his way to Madrid where he hoped to act as an honest broker between the newly returned, reactionary King Ferdinand and the Spanish Cortez. He would, he wrote to Charles, hold an inspection of the British troops; and could Charles, please, send six artillery horses for his carriage.

Administrative problems at Bayonne were constant but seldom grave. Thouvenot reported a row at the theatre between a French and a Portuguese officer over 'une mauvaise fille', a consequent duel and the death of the Portuguese participant. There was also Charles's request that the home-bound Spaniards should be allowed to march through Bayonne, and Thouvenot's anxious insistence that they should only march *through* and not be quartered, even

179

for a night, in the town. Then there was a Monsieur Moulis who said that he had suffered every possible loss in his property, his woods and his investments, and now a whole British division, with its animals and camp-followers, had settled on his land. The regiments of the division were, he said, constantly changing their positions, 'but always from one bit of cultivated land to another'.

There was a shortage of troop-transports, both at Bordeaux and the port of Pasajes (which the British called 'Passages') whence the troops from Bayonne and St. Jean de Luz were to sail for home. So weeks passed before Dalhousie at Bordeaux and Charles at Bayonne were able to embark the majority of their men. Wellington, before leaving for England, issued final embarkation orders from Bordeaux in the middle of June. Dalhousie, who was senior to Charles, was placed in command of the remaining troops. He hoped to have them away as soon as possible and wrote to Charles on 30 June:

> My dear Colville,
> A messenger passing to Madrid tempts me to drop you a line without any news to give you.
> We are hanging on here in the utmost ignorance of any arrangements at home to remove us, without a transport here of any description; a state of idleness and suspense most tedious and unpleasant.
> I desired Murray yesterday to write you that I consider you as chief manager at Bayonne, just as I am here. Direct everything with Admiral Penrose with the view of bringing away your part of the Army in a military style, embarking first your sick and lumber, and then marching your troops clean on board when a sufficiency of transport is arrived for you. I mean that sufficiency of force that will command the respect and quiet behaviour of our affectionate Allies in your neighbourhood.
> Here they are very tired of us and we of them, but I have little hope of getting way before the end of July.

John Colville, safely returned to European waters—with a convoy of 336 ships—after his tempestuous voyage to Barbados, arrived in the Gironde with H.M.S. *Queen*, ready to squeeze 800 troops into his ship which already contained a large naval complement. On 15 July he sent his brother a letter from the Hôtel des Ambassadeurs in Bordeaux:

> We sailed from Portsmouth on the 6th, having calm and foul winds. The passage was so tedious that I was glad Lady

C. did not accompany me as I had proposed; though now I am snug here, and the difficulties of getting up 60 miles from the ship over, I long that she could have seen this fine city which the Admiral and the other ladies are come so far for. It is really superb and I am handsomely and comfortably lodged. I fancy that should you, as I conclude you will, come here, I may recommend it as the best. I find that the Duc D'Angoulême is here, but on the eve of departing, so I fear I shall not be able to pay him my devoirs.

My time here will be short as our troops, 800 Germans, are to embark on Tuesday 19th and we shall sail immediately after. So you see the impossibility of paying you the visit I should have been so glad to have done. A German General, whose name I forget, is to go with us. Of course I wish it had been an English one, but we shall pay every attention to any of the heroes of your late glorious band, as they are so well entitled to them. Fortunately I go to Portsmouth, where I hope to be paid off, but the English troops now here all go to Ireland, except the Guards, who remain till the last. So I must take my Germans at the price of my destination.

Sunday

I have called today on Lord Dalhousie and am to dine with him. I have also attended the levée of the Prince, who enquired immediately about you, and to my great surprise recollected our slight acquaintance at Edinburgh. He seems to have as good a memory as our own Princes and a more agreeable manner. He knew all about my ship and spoke of the terrible storm we had on the passage out to the West Indies. I am quite pleased to think that he sets out for Bayonne tomorrow.

Charles moved to Biarritz and John was informed by General Howard, commanding the Guards Brigade, that the gaiety in that resort, including Charles's expansive birthday dinner and a series of weekly balls, showed his brother to be 'agreeably situated'. Charles was much more disposed that his elder brother to enjoy social diversions and, it may be deduced, female company. The Duc d'Angoulême duly arrived at Bayonne, reviewed the Garde Nationale and the garrison, visited the scenes of the recent siege and battle and then asked Charles both to give him permission to review 'l'armée de Sa Majesté Britannique' and to dine with him afterwards.

In due course the troop transports arrived, the frivolities ceased and Charles, whose old wound in the leg had been giving him severe pain, obtained leave to spend a month at Cauterets in the French Pyrenees to try the effect of 'the baths and douches'. While he was there the Adjutant-General wrote on Wellington's behalf to express the Duke's satisfaction with the good conduct of the troops under Charles's command, his opinion of the 'assiduity and intelligence' with which he had accomplished the embarkation, and concluding with an offer of an appointment to the staff in Scotland. This, wrote Charles, 'I felt obliged to decline'.

The cure at Cauterets was remarkably efficacious (though Charles had an insular feeling that Bath or Buxton would have done just as well). On leaving the resort, he made a short stay at the Hôtel des Ambassadeurs in Bordeaux, recommended so highly by John, and wrote to say 'I took yesterday a lesson in wine-making at the estate of Haut-Brion'. He reported that Margaux, La Tour and Lafite had small but excellent vintages which had been bought lock, stock and barrel by an English speculator called Bractonbury, at unusually high prices, to the fury of the Bordeaux merchants and shippers. He sent his brother a hogshead of 1807 Médoc, *deuxième cru*.

At the beginning of November he reached Paris. Louis XVIII was now installed in the Tuileries and, by a strange turn of fate, the lately defeated Marshal Soult was Minister for War in a Bourbon Government. Charles sought out his old friend, the Marquis de Bombelles, newly consecrated Bishop of Oberglogau, and presented him to the Duke of Wellington. The Bishop lamented that after so long an absence in foreign lands his sons had now lost their affection for France.* So, too, must the children of many of the French *émigrés*.

The weather was deplorable; 'owing to the reduced finances of the better sort of French families but little is to be seen of good society'; and although Paris was crowded with inquisitive British visitors, Charles could, he said, see them in London. He looked forward to returning home, though for him home could only mean lodgings in London or long visits to his relations in the West Country.

Amenities in London were less easily discovered in 1814 than they are today. After so many years abroad, Charles wrote to John from Paris to ask him to recommend an hotel, a tailor and a bootmaker. As regards the hotel, he said, 'To Blake's in Jermyn Street, besides the objection of being very gloomy, it has what

---

* The Bishop's descendants in fact became prominent in Austria-Hungary. One was implicated with Crown Prince Rudolf and the tragedy at Mayerling; another became a landowner in Croatia and an agent of King Alexander of Yugoslavia among the Croat nationalists.

I think a great one when you have not a large dining acquaintance, that of not having a coffee-room.' John replied: 'Blake's has the objections you mention, but there are many good dining-shops near and I am not aware of any coffee-house which is comfortable but what are too much infested by bucks. Ibbotson's, one of the best, you would find too distant, so are all in Covent Garden, but for a few days you can hardly be wrong in going to any of the hotels west or north of Charing X.' As for a tailor, he explained that Davies of Cork Street was fashionable, civil but expensive, or there was Thompson and Son at 11 Frith Street, much employed by military men. He was not too sure about bootmakers, but there was one called Taylor and Bowley at the corner of Spring Garden, Charing Cross, who was civil and punctual and, he believed, 'getting into great business.' With this useful information Charles set off for England in November, almost on the anniversary of his departure from Paris at the end of his last visit in 1785 and from precisely the same spot in the Place Vendôme. The façade of the houses was still as he remembered it, but in the middle of the *place* stood the tall new column which Napoleon had had constructed from the metal of the Austrian guns captured at Austerlitz.

During these months an army, which was perhaps the most effective and experienced that Britain has ever possessed, was inopportunely dispersed. Had it stood united on the field of Waterloo in the following June, there can be little doubt that Wellington would never have had to describe that famous event as a 'damned nice thing'. Indeed he subsequently asserted that with the army he had had in the South of France he would have attacked Napoleon at Waterloo instead of himself waiting to be attacked. The French, he declared, would not have stood for three minutes against them. At the head of his Peninsular army he would not have had to look anxiously for Blücher's arrival on the scene, and it must have been in large part due to the leavening of raw troops by a good sprinkling of Peninsular veterans that he did in the event triumph against all odds.

Now, in November 1814, the unbeaten army was scattered. Some had been sent to Ireland, some to the Cape of Good Hope, and many had been discharged with much gratitude but little means of subsistence. Thousands of the best had crossed, or were still crossing, the Atlantic to take part in a war with America which was one of the most unnecessary ever fought.

The blame, without any doubt, lay with the Americans, or rather with an aggressive minority among them, for the New England states had been opposed to the war and the sentiments of many of their inhabitants were frankly on the British side. They even supplied the British army fighting in Canada and went so far as to consider seceding from the Union. The Americans had declared war in 1812 nominally because the British Orders in Council denied the European ports to their trade, because their ships had been searched on the high seas and because a few of their seamen had been illegally impressed by the Royal Navy. The real reason was that a handful of southern hotheads with influence at Washington saw Britain's preoccupation with Napoleon, whom they greatly admired, as a golden opportunity to seize Canada.

So Peninsular veterans were shipped to Canada, Virginia and the Mississipi. Because the American invaders of Canada had burned villages and homesteads in Ontario, the new British arrivals retaliated by burning Washington—including the White House, from which President Madison was obliged to fly in a hurry, leaving his breakfast on the dining-room table. At the end of 1814 common sense finally prevailed, but just as the slowness of communication had cost the lives of 8,000 men at Toulouse and 1,600 at Bayonne in the previous April, so Ned Pakenham, Wellington's brother-in-law, was killed leading his men in an unsuccessful and expensive attack near New Orleans on 8 January 1815, a fortnight after the official end of hostilities.

Pakenham was gallant and charming, with a touch of romance in his Irish recklessness; but good as he had been as Wellington's Adjutant-General, he is by no means the only example of an excellent staff officer whose talents did not extend to command in the field. His frontal attack on the American lines at New Orleans has been described by Winston Churchill as 'one of the most unintelligent manoeuvres in the history of British warfare'.

After the Battle of Vitoria Pakenham had been made a Knight of the Bath, although he was junior to Charles in the Army List. If Charles felt any resentment, and there is some evidence of it in his correspondence with both Picton and Wellington, it was entirely dissipated by a letter he received after the battles of the Pyrenees. 'It would', wrote Pakenham, 'have afforded me peculiar satisfaction that we had entered together an Order to which you must soon belong. My insulated Staff situation has given this start on you which I neither expected nor desired, for you are one of the few in this army to whose pretensions I would give way at the post, could it but serve your views.' Charles was entirely mollified and when a Grand Cross of the Order of the Bath, available by Pakenham's death at New Orleans, was given to him in March 1815, he wrote to Wellington saying 'I would to God it had not been upon such a vacancy'; for he regarded Pakenham as his 'most gallant and liberal-minded friend'.

Now that the great enemy of peace was safely isolated in Elba, there seemed to be a prospect of quiet years ahead. Returning to England to be reunited with his family for the Christmas of 1814, Charles could expect to lead a much changed life. He might hope to be given the lucrative colonelcy of a regiment and, with luck, a still more lucrative colonial governorship or command. He could look back with satisfaction on years of honourable achievement. Fate had seldom placed him in a sector of the battle-line where particular distinction crowned a successful commander. He had arrived in Portugal a month too late for Busaco. He had been posted a little too far to the right at Sorauren and a little too far to the left on the Nive. He had missed Orthez and Toulouse altogether. His wound at Badajos, and the failure of his effort to persuade the medical board that he was fit to soldier on, had deprived him of almost certain command of the 3rd Division at Salamanca when, in Picton's temporary absence, Wellington gave it to Pakenham and used it for the decisive stroke that won the battle.

All the same, he had won signal honour at Sabugal, at Fuentes d'Onoro, at Vitoria and on the Nivelle. Perhaps his finest achievement had been when he was primarily responsible for that brilliant retreat of the columns and squares across six miles of open plain during the 'Affair at El Bodon' and his brigade of the 3rd Division fought off attacks of the French Cavalry in overwhelmingly superior force. Wellington had then felt justified in including in a general order to the entire army his opinion that 'it is impossible that any troops can at any time be exposed to the attack of numbers relatively greater than those which attacked the troops under Major General Colville'. It afforded, Wellington wrote, 'a memorable example of what may be effected by steadiness, discipline and confidence'.

Thus Charles could look to the future with only a shadow of regret for the past and, as his brother John had delicately hinted in several letters, he could do worse than consider some suitable domestic arrangement which might provide continuity for his family name. Such must have been his thoughts as the New Year of 1815 was rung in at his brother's house near Bristol. It has been the first peaceful Christmas and New Year for more than twenty years, and, as later generations have discovered, it is when peace breaks out that troubles start.

12

The Waterloo Campaign

Trouble was not slow to start. On 25 February 1815 Napoleon sailed secretly from Elba and on 1 March he landed at Fréjus, near St. Raphael. By the 10th he was at Lyons and by the night of the 20th, after a ride from the Mediterranean coast during which not a drop of blood was shed, he was in Paris. Louis XVIII remained at the Tuileries until dangerously late in the belief that Marshal Ney, who had set out from Paris vowing to bring Napoleon back in an iron cage, would be as good as his word. He was not: coming face to face with the Emperor, Ney was overcome with emotion and deserted to his former master's side.

Louis fled to Ghent. All over France the white cockades were discarded and the *Tricolore* flew once more. Most of the marshals, who had accepted the Bourbon king, changed their coats for a hundred days, only to change them back again in due course. Soult was the preeminent opportunist. In 1814 he avowed himself a royalist and was appointed Minister of War; in March 1815 he declared himself a Bonapartist; and he was Napoleon's Chief of Staff at the Battle of Waterloo. After that he became a royalist again as soon as he decently could, an active Orleanist after 1830 and a republican in 1848. His death in 1851 prevented him from announcing, as he would surely have done when Louis Napoleon became Emperor of the French, that he had always been a Bonapartist at heart. He ran Talleyrand to a close finish in the Vicar of Bray Stakes. Indeed, it may be argued that he won.

Of the other Marshals and Generals against whom Charles had campaigned in the Peninsular, d'Erlon, Roy, Clausel and Reille fought with Napoleon at Waterloo; Jourdan became one of Napoleon's new House of Peers; Suchet, too, rallied to the Emperor. Marmont, criticised for having treated with the Allies in March 1814, remained quiescent. Junot had already thrown himself out of a window; and Masséna, appointed Commander-in-Chief at Marseilles by Napoleon, a position in which Louis XVIII had confirmed him, sat cannily on the fence during the Hundred Days, awaiting the outcome of events.

Toulouse kept the loyalist flag flying for a few days, but perhaps the most courageous stand against Napoleon's lightning *coup d'état* was made by the Duchesse d'Angoulême. For ten days she held Bordeaux for her uncle, riding from garrison to garrison and calling on the troops to maintain their loyalty. Her effort was finally in vain, for Clausel advanced on Bordeaux and the garrison declared in his favour; but all, including Napoleon, respected her brave determination and no serious effort was made to prevent her escape to England when, despite the undoubted royalism of the city's inhabitants, the white flag was at last replaced by the *Tricolore*. This reactionary and inflexible Princess, sad relic of revolutionary excesses long ago, lived to see her family again restored and again deposed, the House of Orléans rise and fall and the government of France in the hands of a Prince-President, Louis Napoleon. Like Soult, she died in 1851, spared by a few months the ultimate bitterness of seeing the Usurper's nephew (if, indeed, he was his nephew, for many believed him to be the son of a handsome Dutch admiral) proclaimed as Napoleon III. At least her endeavours at Bordeaux did much to encourage a royalist revolt in la Vendée two months later and thus diverted 10,000 of Napoleon's best troops from the battlefield of Waterloo.

In England the flight from Elba caused astonishment; but it was at first believed that Napoleon's aim was to establish himself in Italy, and it was a few days before the full implications of the event were realised. Charles, writing from Bath on 13 March to his cousin Alexander Blair, devoted most of his letter to family news and only at the end expressed the hope that 'Bonaparte will not succeed in insurging France, whatever he may do in Italy'. He was, like everybody else, worried about the internal economic situation, commenting that 'the Government must be sadly puzzled and circumstances suit most unfavourably for the recovery everywhere felt so necessary'. John went further, saying that 'no coalition will prove serviceable to Great Britain if she, as usual, is still to pay the piper; and I fancy we have some in power who are conscientious and wise enough not to plunge the country headlong into another war.' However Charles, in thanking Wellington for the part he must have played in securing him a Grand Cross of the Bath, added on 25 March: 'Permit me now, My Lord, to say that in the prospects opened by the late unfortunate events in France, I hope it will not be long before I have the honour of again serving under Your Grace's immediate command.'

So indeed it was to be. At the end of March Charles was given the local rank of lieutenant-general and ordered to join the British Army, sadly depleted by the absentees in America, that Wellington now set out to assemble in the Netherlands. Not all the Peninsular generals went too, but Clinton, Hill, Kempt, Pack, Byng and Cole were among those who did, and late in the day, on 11 June, Picton also crossed the Channel to command his old 3rd Division, now redesignated the 5th.

Before he sailed, Charles received distressing news of a pipe of vintage port which he had arranged to have shipped home from Portugal as a gift to his brother. John forwarded the following communication: 'As I know not how to direct to Sir Charles, I must request you to convey to him the unwelcome information of the ship *Thomas* having been taken by an American privateer. I hope the pipe of port was insured or, if not, that the capture was made after the time allowed by the treaty of peace, in which case he may sooner or later recover his wine.' John added: 'This is sad news, and I little thought the Yankees had so sharply paid me home for my opinions of them. As to insurance, I dare say you never thought of that . . . but rest assured that your intentions in regard to it are as highly prized as if they had been gratified'. Luckily, some time after Charles had crossed the Channel, news came that the *Thomas* had been recaptured, but this was accompanied by John's warning that he feared 'the recapture charges will come very heavy'. Prize money was, after all, important to the solvency of the officers and men of the Royal Navy.

By contrast, Charles received two gratifying pieces of information. He had long been hoping for the colonelcy of a regiment. This was a lucrative reward for distinguished service, especially if it was a regiment with two battalions. He had hoped for the 72nd, which did have two battalions; but that was given to an elderly retired general and Charles had to be content with the 94th. They had formed part of his brigade in the 3rd Division, when they were known as the Scots Regiment; and now they were called the Edinburgh Regiment, wearing an elephant as their badge in commemoration of their service in India. Unfortunately, in spite of their name, they were now on the Irish Establishment 'which is somehow the less profitable of the two, but not in so great a proportion since the income tax in Great Britain has become a set-off against loss by exchange'. At least it provided what John called 'a respectable and easy competence'.

The other piece of good news was that the Prince Regent of Portugal had conferred on him the Order of the Tower and Sword 'for the great ability and determined intrepidity exhibited in various engagements in the late war in the Peninsula'. Whether Charles was so wholly gratified as he should have been may be doubtful, for he persisted in calling it 'The Tower and Spade'. However that may be, he always wore it.*

Before he was informed of these honours Charles had arrived in Belgium, taking Frederick Frankland with him as A.D.C. He wrote to John from Ostend on Monday, 24 April to announce his safe, if stormy, arrival.

The bad weather will have made you anxious about us, so I lose no time in saying that we commenced our disembarkation five hours ago, having anchored about midnight, and I am happy to say that with the exception of some few blemishes on the latter, men and horses are all safe, which is most surprising considering the ill fitted state of the cutter we all came out in. For in the gale we experienced the night we sailed upon (Saturday) the midship pole was obliged to be cut away to disembarrass some animals that had got on top and some underneath it, and the consequence was that when got on their legs again, this was effected at the risk of the lives of my man James and Capt. Streenivitz (the latter young partisan you must have read of occasionally in the Peninsula), and who were almost the only persons on board who were of any use besides, I must acknowledge, the master, an active young fellow who also certainly exerted himself. Our early hour was perhaps the occasion of it, but finding no assistance ready for us, I was obliged to stay on the beach in a heavy rain until every horse of three and twenty were disembarked.

Poor Frederick was terribly sea sick; I myself escaped, keeping snug in a midship berth and with no other annoyance than the cascading of others and the abominable tumult and kicking of the horses, which led me to suppose I should not have one left fit for service.

Finding no orders for me here or any information of where my Divn. is, I shall proceed this afternoon on my way to Head

---

*When the Portuguese monarchy fell in 1910, it was the only order of chivalry that the new republican government continued to recognise and award.

Quarters. I leave Frederick to see the horses off tomorrow, and proceed with Darling, Lord James Hay, and our baggage to Bruges by the canal, proposing to continue the same conveyance tomorrow to Ghent, and from thence follow the plan we may then find most adviseable.

The 4th Divn. will I presume be mine, being at present under the command of Genl. Hinuber, who I am happy to have with me from what I saw of him at Bayonne. The two Brigades of British are commanded, the one by Genl. Johnstone late of the 93rd, and the other for the time by Col. Mitchell of the 51st, which Regt., as well as the 23rd, 54th and 91st are in the Divn. and must be good and strong Regts. The circumstances of the others I am ignorant of, but must hope they are respectable.

It was with the 4th Division that Charles had stormed Badajos, but the numbers of the divisions had been changed and the new 4th Division was the old 2nd, containing little to remind him of the officers and units he had known so well in the Peninsula. It was included in the Army Corps entrusted by Wellington to Lord Hill who, as Sir Rowland Hill, had earned rapid promotion by his consistent excellence in almost all the Peninsular battles and had recently been created a peer. On 1 May Charles received from Hill the first indication of enemy movements. It seemed that the Imperial Guard had marched from Paris to Beauvais and since it was reported (quite wrongly) that the Emperor was about to visit the northern frontier, 'His Grace has given directions that the cantonments of the troops should be concentrated in order to their being ready to act as may be required.' His Grace had also, it seemed, deduced that the attack would either be made on the eastward side, between the Rivers Scheldt and Lys, or between the Scheldt and the Sambre; or, Lord Hill added, by both these lines. The 4th Division was to assemble thirty-five miles west of Brussels, at Audenarde, better known in the history books as Oudenarde, where Marlborough and Prince Eugene had defeated the French in 1708. The country there was to be inundated, as was that round Ghent, and both those towns were to be held at all costs.

These orders were followed on 2 May by a personal letter from Hill who said: 'You will find your troops very much scattered at present, and having had no Head I have scarcely been able to get a correct return of them. I do, however, hope that in the course of a few days we shall be better arranged in every respect than we are at this moment. I dine at six and when you come to Grammont you will find accommodation for yourself and staff.' Everybody was doing their best, but as in the early stages of most British military operations, disorganisation was rampant.

Once settled in a deserted château at Poteghen near Audenarde, Charles found time to send John an account of his journey. It was 5 May and there was as yet no sense of urgency or more than rumours of impending action.

After writing to you on the 24th, I proceeded by the canal to Bruges, and by the same conveyance reached Ghent at an early hour the next day, a most convenient mode of travelling, not only carrying all your baggage with you, but getting a very good dinner chemin faisant, and all at so moderate a price that I believe I paid more for a single dinner at Ramsgate than my expenses from Ostend to Ghent amounted to. I immediately after however found that when there was a greater array of English, English prices also came nearly into play.

His Grace was absent on my arrival at Bruxelles on the 26th, and matters there having no appearance of any hurry of martial preparations, I accepted the invitation given me by his staff to await the dinner and ball at the Investiture of the Commanders of the Bath in this country on the 28th. Heard Madame Catalini in most charming voice at a concert in the interim, and at which by particular request of the Queen of the Netherlands she gave us 'Rule Britannia' in a style of most superior effect. Was introduced to the King at his levée on the 29th, but declining the honour of an invitation to dine with His Majesty on the 30th, returned to Ghent that day, and the next morning reached Audenarde where I found two British Regts. of my Divn.

I had no very particular conversation with His Grace further than about the composition of my Divn., and his desire to accommodate me as soon as he could with such officers of the staff as I had before had with me, but had otherwise every reason to be pleased with my reception by him as well as by the Prince of Orange and Lord Hill, in whose Corps I am, as I had wished for, placed.

Jackson has joined me, and the Duke not having a situation to immediately give Lord Jas. Hay he stays with me for the present as extra A.D.C., and which with Darling and a Captain Brereton as D.Asst. Q.M.G., acting till the appointment of a senior of his department, makes my family already consist of six.

The Duke had promised me that my Divn. (the 4th), being very much scattered, should be brought closer together, and the Hanoverian Brigade were ordered up from Ostend and Nieuport to this place, but the day of their arrival, without my even having time to see them, were sent off to Bruxelles. One British Brigade, at present under the command of Col. Mitchell of the 51st and which I have not yet seen, closes to me this day from Grammont, and the other, Major Genl. Johnstone's, have one Regt. at Courtrai, one in Audenarde, and the third in advance upon the Tournai road. I lost no time in visiting my outposts, going to Courtrai the day after my arrival, making a circuit of between forty and fifty miles, more to the fatigue of my horse than myself, as the effect of that ruinous mode of transport is still severe upon them all in a greater or less degree. Your favourite, Nell, seems the freshest among them but has lost the skin off both her hips; two of them I fear are seriously lame, but a few days rest and quiet may bring them about, and for this I have sacrificed the greater convenience of the town to come to a Château with hardly any furniture and only two old servants, but where I have capital stabling, and myself and animals are out of the way of the continued din and uproar which night and day prevails in all the towns and stages I have visited from the passage of troops, stores, and passengers.

I was pursuaded to treat myself at Bruxelles to a second hand *barouchette*, and which cost me £70 British without harness, so that I should have done better to have brought an English second hand post-chaise with me. My draft horses are in the best trim of the whole, so that I propose putting one pair into the carriage, another into a cart, and keep the third disposeable to help the others out of the mire or to use with pack saddles when nearer the enemy. General Officers are exempt against the restrictions in the use of the conveniences of cart and carriage, as they well ought to be, encumbered as those of Divisions are with family.

In regard of housekeeping, being backward as yet in preparations, although I brought a cook at 50 louis a year from Bruxelles with me, I have hitherto been obliged to make use of a neighbouring *petite auberge*, a convenience which being to be found here at the distance of every three or four miles makes a striking contrast. I have thus far dwelt upon subjects which will not be without interest to you, but others will wonder that I should have time or thought for such information. The fact is that so backward even yet is the state of preparation for a forward movement, that no one seems to think that immediately interesting, and while that of the enemy is no more advanced, I have reason to believe our ideas have been hitherto mostly confined to the study of the defensive measures that have been pointed out for us on the information that the National Guards had left Paris, and that Buonaparte was to leave it to visit the frontier on this side.

There has been firing heard towards Valenciennes, which seems to strengthen the report of his having arrived there. His troops have been kept in a constant state of movement, and to meet which perhaps has been the occasion of the same on our side. There has been a good deal of desertion from the French outposts, I believe, principally among their cavalry, and which opposite to us has occasioned their being relieved by infantry latterly.

The Duke of Wellington is this day, I understand, to give the meeting to old Blücher, who has an excellently organised force of 152,000 men. The Duke I believe can, the Prussians of course included, move forward with 223,000, but he is very anxious for a greater proportion of British, and I suppose he judges it prudent that the Austrians and Russians should be well up before he undertakes anything.

We had very raw, disagreeable weather for the first week, and to which succeeded very close and warm with thunder and lightning and heavy rain, and it is yet by no means settled or pleasant. My Château and its garden have their beauties for this part of the world, but I hope to move off before the mosquitoes get in or out of the moats around it. One side of it is so ingeniously contrived as by its straight, high bank and avenue of aspen trees to completely hide from the view of the house, and even nearly so from the grounds, the Scheldt itself, which passes within 100 yards, meandering in a style of elegant sweep.

Whatever the appearances, Wellington was in fact giving deep thought to the strategic probabilities in the forthcoming campaign. Late in the previous summer, on his way from London to Paris, he had made a close personal inspection of the ground, noting in particular, that in front of the village of Waterloo 'Hougoumont and La Haye were like two bastions to the ridge between, and made the position very strong'. Now, after his arrival at Brussels early in April, he made a number of reconnoitring rides. Like all good generals Wellington was a keen student of battles fought long ago, and he was well versed in the details of Marlborough's campaigns in the Netherlands. He told Lord Ellesmere many years later that he had inspected the position once occupied by Marlborough in front of Hal. The reason why he posted Colville and Prince Frederick of Orange in force in that position was because he thought then, as he thought now, that Napoleon ought, after Quatre Bras, to have manoeuvred in that direction in order to draw away the British from the Prussians with the ulterior chance of acting between them. 'For this purpose he should have moved along the Nivelles road by which we had advanced from our right.'

It was a compliment to Charles that Wellington should place the 4th Division where he expected the initial attack to come; but Napoleon did not have the same strategic thoughts as the Duke and so, in the event, Charles took no personal part in the Battle of Waterloo—his division, all but one brigade, was too far away on the right flank. Thus Wellington lost the invaluable use of 17,000 men in a battle in which his French opponents were not only, one and all, battle-trained but also outnumbered him.

However, throughout the month of May and early June, while Napoleon consolidated his administration and collected his veteran soldiers, all was quiet in the Netherlands. The headquarters of the 4th Division, scattered though its units continued to be, remained at Audenarde. There was time for writing and even for sightseeing and courtesy visits. In a letter of 17 May, Charles described a visit to the Bourbon Court in exile at Ghent.

I returned here this morning from Tournay, about 20 miles off, having taken that place in my way home yesterday from Grammont, Lord Hill's Head Quarters, where I had gone to spend the day with him and see the greater part of my Divn., who are at present either with or near him, my Hanoverians (one field Regt. and three of the Landwehr), fine young men, but badly officered, having now taken up their cantonments in their proper situation between the two British Brigades.

I had just before gone over for a day to Ghent to make my bow to Louis 18, and who asked me in consequence to dine with him. Monsieur was however the only royal personage at table, His Majesty being at present kept under regime by the Père Elisée, a circumstance he speaks of with apparent feeling, having particularly among the people here who see him at his dinner from the streets the character of a great gourmand. The company of fifteen or sixteen were all of the *ancien régime*, the greater part Dukes, and among them a member or two of the Voltigeurs de Louis Quatorze, as are called at our Head Quarters a veteran groupe who generally attend the Prince de Condé, and who, including His Highness, have it is said but two pairs of eyes among the five; but as none of them require to be led, I suppose they may have one or two more. At all events their appearance is very grotesque, and certainly, like that of very many of those His Majesty has given high military rank to, not calculated to inspire with much respect the French armies of the present day. The Duke of Gramont, Duvas and two or three others are of a modern school and, as was Monsieur himself, were all very civil, and took care that I like themselves should make a very good dinner.

Among recent desertions from the other frontier were seven of His Majesty's cooks, who I hear have made a material change for the better in his cuisine. Until his late illness, he has always made one, since he has been at Ghent, of such a party as the one I attended. When we broke up from table, we were ushered in separately to an audience of His Majesty. I found him sitting at the end of a long table with his legs, which are swollen, upon stools underneath. He was troubled with a rheum, I suppose, but not as an Englishman would in that case, or the West Indians at their smoking clubs, have a bason or a goat skin along side of him, he had a silver bason on the table, and which, as I had to go up close to him to say my phrases, had not the most pleasing appearance. He was however, poor man, very civil, and I hope to see him once more at the Tuileries, but certainly, as must be his own feelings, much less on his individual account than for the good he makes his return and firm possession of the throne do to others. This is an event which every thing we hear out of France, as well as the magnitude of the preparations of the Allies to ensure it, tends to make appear most probable.

Great as is the stake, one cannot but approve the prudence, which unmindful of the clamour against delay, awaits the fulfilment of every combination originally calculated upon. Such is I conceive the present rule of the Duke of Wellington's conduct, but as, unfortunately, equal prudence is not to be found everywhere else, some bad consequences may, as well as good, attend the protracted invasion of France. I allude here to the Prussian Government, who by their folly, to call it no worse, have lost us the cooperation of 16,000 Saxons, and who were to be reckoned perhaps the finest troops of the confederation. The consequences are bad enough in its being found necessary to send them across the Rhine, and it is well that they showed their well grounded dissatisfaction so soon, for had they repressed it, they might have taken the opportunity for augmenting the force of the enemy at the same time they diminished ours. You have of course read of the mutiny at Liège. The French, as was to be expected, made the worst of it, but it was in reality so serious that old Blücher, who at the time had no Prussians with him, was, with his staff, obliged to make his escape by a back door, or some say a window. What a change from the circumstances you saw him in not twelve months since. The complaint of the Saxons was that, from the force which was to have been sent to act immediately under our Duke, the Prussians wanted to pick out the natives of the Provinces lately made over to them, and which separation from their comrades was certainly very grievous to them, and a most imprudent measure to be attempted at such a moment.

The Duke seems to have believed in the report, at more than one time, of Boney's having left Paris for this frontier, and which, along with the concentration of the French force between Valenciennes and Maubeuge, made countermovements on our side necessary. I believe they have been as much felt by the 4th Divn. as any, and which has been the occasion of my not writing by the last post or two. We are now again perfectly quiet, and think of no other than offensive measures when the proper moment shall arrive, and which I should suppose would not be later than the first or second week of next month.

My stomach is in much better state than it was, and hitherto I have not found the *Rhenish* or second quality French wine which we get, to disagree with me.

At this stage of the war letters to and from Audenarde took less time than in the second half of the twentieth century, so John was able to reply within a few days with all the home news and a few admonitions on keeping healthy. 'Should Ward's paste not do its duty,' he suggested, 'let me remind you of the great advantage I derived from sulphur and honey: should the latter not be within reach, the former can be taken in milk. I should be cautious in the use of light wines, tho' perhaps few may be worse after all than port for your complaints.'

There was little to report in a letter written on 25 May except that 'I have at last the Secretary of War's information of the

Regent having granted me a military pension of £350 a year in consideration of my having been severely wounded', and that 'you may be sure I have not omitted to thank Lord Palmerston for his obliging reception at the interview which led to the further surgical examination of my case'. He begged John not to disseminate this information as it 'might call from others the observation it did form my A.D.C., Frederick, that he now supposed I did not care how soon I lost another finger'. He added that nothing indicated an early move and he was therefore contemplating a trip to Antwerp.

Since everything was so quiet, and British intelligence about Napoleon's activities was remarkably lacking, Charles duly went to Antwerp for a six days' excursion with his Quartermaster-General, Colonel Woodford, and Lord James Hay. So on 11 June, only one week before the Battle of Waterloo, he sent home this account. He was still at Audenarde, almost forty miles from the coming scene of action.

Breakfasting at Ghent, we passed the Scheldt in the ferry boat at the Tête de Flandres, and had time enough to see the noble cathedral of Antwerp and other buildings that evening. The greater part of the next day was but indifferently spent at a race meeting set agoing by two weak British Regts. in service in the Citadel. We dined on the course in tents, the party being joined by several *boss* ladies and gentlemen (such among the military at least is the general name of all animals, two or four footed, with what propriety I know not, of this country). Our people and those of the town seem to be on very good terms; and to give the latter a greater zest for this kind of amusement, there was a sweepstake for boss horses. Flanders horses you have before heard of, so may suppose much fleetness was not exhibited by them, though their owners prize their breed much.

In the evening General K. McKenzie, who commands there, gave us horses to visit the Citadel and remains of the Arsenal. Of this last, all that remains is the superb rope-making house of immense length, and some forges; the ships are all taken up, and the timber sold, and the intrenched camp in advance of the Citadel, and which was meant for the protection of the Arsenal, will all be levelled in the course of this week.

Early in the next morning, the General again mounted us, when we visited the basin, which is below the town, while the Arsenal and Citadel are above it on the same side of the water. There is no intention of destroying it on account of its commercial advantages, and Antwerp indeed promises, if the Netherlands remain attached to Holland, to be no loser by the change of masters, notwithstanding what Bonaparte did for it, and must materially injure Amsterdam. In the basin there were only two two-deckers, one frigate, and a brig. Two two-deckers were yet in sight between the town and Batz, having only left the basin a day or two before, and there were ten in the basin when Louis first retreated out of France, and when it was so much expected Boney would have followed him that Genl. McKenzie had made his arrangements in his own mind for burning the ships. It was indeed an error of Boney's not following up his first success by entering this country that I hope he will ever have to regret.

The walls round the town of Antwerp itself are in general very respectable, but were so faulty and out of repair immediately about the basin that Carnot began new works to cover them, and which we are yet employed upon.

After a detailed description of the fortifications and their recent history, Charles continued:

We returned the next day to Antwerp to dinner, and the next ascended two thirds of the beautiful tower of the cathedral (which is I think 466 feet high) for the sake of the view. Visited a private house of one of his descendants, saw the celebrated *Chapeau de Paille* of Reubens [sic], his tomb, on which is a picture of his own done for the place, and a couple of private collections. Dined, and taking the road by Malines, arrived at Bruxelles late in the evening.

I saw the Duke the next morning, and was asked to dine that day and go to the ball the ensuing night, but was anxious to get home, hearing that Lord Hill wanted to assemble the Divn. for a grand field day, which has however been prevented by a continuance of rainy weather.

Knowing ones say we shall not move before the 20th. Boney is said to have been at Arras on the 7th, and was expected at Lille on the 9th, but strange to say we have nothing yet positive about him.

On 12 June Napoleon, so often rumoured to have set off from Paris, actually did so. With nearly 130,000 experienced troops and 366 guns he crossed the French frontier and the River Sambre, driving the Prussian defenders before him. Wellington did not receive the news of the French advance till the evening of the 15 June. As for Charles, he was halfway through another of his letters home when he was suddenly given good cause to stop writing.

On 16th June the two battles of Ligny and Quatre Bras were fought, Ligny ending in a modified victory for the French, who lost 11,000 men against 20,000 Prussian casualties, and Quatre Bras in an indecisive success for the British who checked Marshal Ney and dislocated Napoleon's plans, but lost 4,300 men in the process. It may seem, with hindsight, that on the following day, while Wellington was establishing his line on the ridge of Mont St. Jean near the village of Waterloo, he ought to have called in towards his centre all the troops under Charles and Prince Frederick of Orange. However, the Allies had a line 100 miles long to defend, while Napoleon could concentrate wherever he wished, and Wellington still believed that part of the attack would be a left hook from Mons through Braine le Comte and Hal along the road to Brussels. Nor, indeed, was he wrong to make this assumption, for an attack further to the westward would have denied the outnumbered British forces, with their high proportion of untrained Dutch-Belgian levies, any chance of help from the slow-moving Prussians.

As things were, Wellington's army, with only 24,000 British troops (of which but 7,000 were Peninsular veterans), 5,800 of the excellent King's German Legion, and an uncertain balance of Hanoverians, Nassauers, Brunswickers and Dutch-Belgian recruits, was assaulted by 74,000 of Napoleon's hardiest soldiers. By the time Wellington was convinced that there was no danger of an attack along the Mons-Brussels road, it was too late for any but one brigade of the 4th Division, under Colonel Mitchell, to reach the scene of action. The Divisional Commander, with a British and a Hanoverian brigade, as well as Prince Frederick's Division of 11,000 men, moved long after an active and invaluable contribution could have been made to 'the nearest run thing you ever saw in your life'.

The day after the battle, Charles, disappointed by his inability to take part, wrote from Seneffe, south of Nivelles to which he had been ordered to move.

The knowledge of the previous partial affairs will I am certain have occasioned my kind friends some uneasiness about me, but the official accounts of the great victory of the 18th in front of Waterloo, will I hope, be the first that will have reached

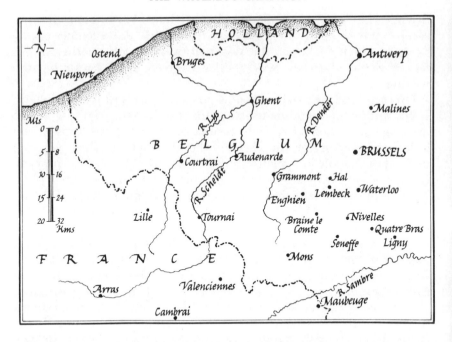

The Waterloo Campaign

England, and thus assure them that nothing amiss has occurred to me, if they do not further state, as they perhaps may (in explanation of the arrangements of the army) that I was not in the battle.

I am not such a fire eater as to think it necessary to say that I have fretted myself at having been unavoidably absent from it, but at the same time am aware that I should have felt a proud satisfaction in being able to inform you of my having shared in the efforts of a day which must be recorded as perhaps the most important in modern history.

The case is that being on the extreme right of the line of cantonments when the order of march arrived at six in the morning of the 16th, Major Genl. Johnstone's and the Hanoverian Brigade of my Divn, on account of the retrograde movement of the army, could never get up in time to join the remainder of Lord Hill's Corps before the evening of the day on which the battle was fought.

On the 17th the two Brigades reached Braine le Compte, and I myself having ridden on to Nivelles, then Lord Hill's Head Quarters, found the army in march to the rear, taking my Brigade under Col. Mitchell, which had moved from Grammont with Lord Hill, along with them, and for the time attached to Sir H. Clinton's Divn.

Having the artillery with my two other Brigades, they of course became my regular command, and rejoining them at Braine le Compte, I got an order early in the morning of the 18th to march upon Halle. In that neighbourhood I found the Prince Frederick of the Netherlands with his Corps of 11,000 Dutch troops (9,000 bayonets), who had orders on my arrival to take up a position with his left upon Halle and right extending towards Enghien, and which he was to hold to the last. I placed myself on his left, reaching from Lembeck to Braine le Compte, and sent off my Quarter Master Genl. to seek for Lord Hill and get his further orders, but he did not return, being detained by his Lordship during the battle, till after I was in march again the next morning at 6 o'clock, a quarter of an hour after receipt of a message from the Duke to notify the victory and direct my march upon Nivelles. There I fell in with the main body of the army, all moving in this direction. I have at present the advance, but tomorrow morning we all move again upon the Mons road, and will incline towards Maubeuge.

Col. Mitchell's Brigade shared in the latter operations of the day. I hear a good account of the very young 3rd Battn. of the 14th, and the 23rd and 51st conducted themselves as well as was to be expected from corps of their established character, their loss not very heavy did it not include Col. Sir Henry Ellis, who, if not already dead, is by what I learn and very much regret, mortally wounded.

I shall not attempt to say more of the battle than that our infantry and artillery on no occasion ever behaved better. As much is not said of the cavalry, especially the Light, and which opinion their gallant Chief, Lord Uxbridge, is said to have given a much stronger expression of before he received his wound. This last paragraph is entre nous or cautious friends only.

The French cavalry, especially the Imperial Guards, are most highly spoken of, but the expressions of surprise their subsequent conduct seemed to evince on their reception by our squares, showed they had never before had to do with British troops.

Such a victory could not be obtained but by most heavy loss on the side of the victors, and without entering into the melancholy list of names, which will be much more fully learnt by the Gazette than I even know of, suffice it to say that every moment brings fresh cause to bewail the wanton sacrifice occasioned by the folly of the Emperors and Kings in the divan of last year in turning the *tigre* loose and un-muzzled.

In respect of his ruffians, ample provision has been found for those whom unluckily Louis has not an Egypt, a St. Domingo, or a Botany Bay for. In this direction I can only hear of about 1,000 men retreating in any way connected on the Charleroi road. Stragglers have passed hereabouts who say that the army is ruined, and they themselves selling every thing military, and purchasing peasants' clothing. This is of consequence when it is considered that the troops now employed had few, if any, conscripts among them, but were formed of his oldest and best.

Even those soldiers with the most hardened emotions, even Wellington himself, were shattered by the slaughter. When Charles wrote home on the 19th he did not yet know that his friend Picton had died leading the 5th Division in a destructive charge against D'Erlon's massed columns. In all the French had lost 30,000 killed and wounded and over 250 guns; but 7,000 men, more than a quarter of Wellington's British troops, had also fallen, and there were another 6,000 casualties among his foreign allies. There was at least some comfort in a letter Charles received from a friend, Dr Collier, who wrote from Brussels on 23 June:

> I arrived here on the very night the wounded came pouring in, and I have been almost constantly employed since in the saddest exercise of a sad profession. I trust not unusefully although from the hurried state less successfully than our brethren in private life. So far as the affair goes however, I never saw such comforts for wounded, never that with so few deaths from wounds, never so gratified from the results of operations, and never, never witnessed such devotedness and goodness as are exemplified in the conduct of these good people of Bruxelles. As they are Catholics, I would certainly, were I Pope, issue my bulls for canonising the whole of the females; they work more miracles than the Relics of the most devotional anchorite that ever obtained the honours of Sainthood.

The decisive battle had been won, but there had been nearly 300,000 French troops in arms when Napoleon crossed the Sambre on 15 June and there were in addition 135,000 National Guards as well as the navy, the gendarmes and thousands of armed *fédérés*. Only some 130,000 men had entered the Netherlands with the Emperor and of these 33,000, under Grouchy, had escaped unscathed. So although Napoleon had been utterly defeated, France, fearing the vengeance of the angry Allies, might well continue to resist. The French, whose enthusiasm for the Bourbons was both regional and spasmodic, might also feel entitled to choose their own form of government. Therefore Wellington counselled Louis XVIII, who was mercifully not suffering from gout at the critical moment, to follow close behind him as he marched into France and to establish himself at Cambrai. Unfortunately the citadel and town of Cambrai were held by a French Governor and troops who showed no sign of wishing to surrender. It looked as if it might be Bayonne all over again.

13

The Occupation of France

When Wellington crossed the Pyrenees in 1813 he won the confidence of the French population by taking rigorous steps to discourage his troops from the excesses in which conquerors are prone to indulge. It was still more important now to convince the people that he came as a friend and liberator, even though the Prussians and perhaps, when they arrived on the scene, the Russians might emulate the unsatisfactory example set by the Spaniards in the south-west of France. Two days after the battle he therefore issued a proclamation to his troops of which this is an extract:

> As the army is about to enter the French territory, the troops of the nations which are at present under the command of Field Marshal the Duke of Wellington are desired to recollect that their respective Sovereigns are the Allies of His Majesty the King of France and that France ought therefore to be treated as a friendly country. It is then required that nothing should be taken by the Officers or Soldiers for which payment be not made.

If requisitions were necessary, those who made them would be held responsible to 'the inhabitants of France in the same manner in which they would be esteemed accountable for purchases made for their own Governments in the several dominions to which they belong'.

Charles was sensitive to these instructions when he was ordered by Wellington to lead his division to the investment and, if necessary, the storming of Cambrai. His account of the affair is given in letters written from Montdidier and Clermont on 29 and 30 June.

> The Duke overtook us on the 22nd as we were marching into Le Cateau. He spoke with much enthusiasm of the battle

of the 18th, which he says, and all other accounts agree, was one of the most determined ever fought. In respect to individuals lost upon the occasion, we spoke only of Sir Thos. Picton and Col. Ellis, but he said that when he considered the valuable lives that had been closed, and that the sacrifice was not attended with all the results expected, it would break his heart. I told him that I myself felt so much the same way, that disappointed as I was in being absent from the battle, I never could form a wish for any personal further success at the expense of one drop more of British blood, and in the present context it does not appear that there will be much.

Our rapid advance must much disconcert the Provisional Government in Paris, and make them inclined for the King, though I perceive his family and ministers, especially Blacas and D'Aubray, are held in great abhorrence.

The Divisions are by this hour on their march to Clermont, where I expect to rejoin Lord Hill, from whom I have been absent since the 23rd.

On that day the Duke, hearing that there was but a small force left in the town and citadel of Cambrai, and which it was of great consequence to get possession, sent me with one Brigade of cavalry and its troop of artillery, one of my own Brigades of infantry, and my 9 pdrs. against it. My orders were to summon the Governor and in case of his refusal to fire a few shells into the citadel (the town being supposed loyal was not if possible to be hurt) but not to risk any serious measure, and in case of want of success, I was to retire the troops in the evening to the neighbouring villages. The Duke's written summons the Governor would not receive, and he gave himself as usual some foolish airs, upon which I treated the citadel to six and twenty howitzer shells and about a dozen round shot, and moved the troops off with but the casualty of two men wounded.

The Duke came up the next morning, and thinking it of most material consequence that so important a place should early be obtained as a place d'armes for the King, gave me the rest of my Divn. and two additional Brigades of artillery, to assist me in taking the town. The citadel, upon a close reconnaissance, he thought too strong and fully manned to fall by any thing but regular siege, and upon having given me my general instructions, left me to myself.

I had made all my arrangements, and the attack was to have commenced at six in the evening, when about a quarter of an hour before that time, two French officers came out to meet me, one from Douay, the general camp in the Department du Nord, with proposals to the Duke of Wellington for an armistice on account of the abdication of Napoleon: the other was immediately addressed to myself, but including the additional act of the Provisional Government in favour of Napoleon 2nd. It was now my turn to ride the high horse, so sent him back word I knew no such person as Napoleon 2nd, and that if in an hour he did not surrender both the town and the citadel for the King of France, I must do my best to force him. The escalade of the north of the town by three small columns accordingly took place at 8 o'clock, while the fire of my eighteen pieces of artillery kept down theirs in the citadel excepting three flank guns that couldn't be got at, and two small ones in the town ramparts, which annoyed the troops as they debouched from the cover they had been placed in.

In about half an hour I had full possession of the town, and then my greatest difficulty was to be encountered in preventing it from the plunder which the troops couldn't be persuaded but that they had a right to. In this however, by sending the greater part out of the place, I succeeded much better than was to have been expected.

The Duke wrote the next morning that he congratulated and was much obliged to me for my success, and desired that I would continue my endeavours to get the citadel (which I had shut up) by treaty, or if not, by force. A suspension of hostilities, which the Governor now asked for, gave us good opportunity of looking about us, and the cover which the works of the town gave us for our operations would, I think, notwithstanding its tremendous ditches of 70 feet, have facilitated them so much, that I thought we should have succeeded in taking it in a day or two, had not the Governor at last surrendered it for Louis 18, to one of whose Generals I gave it up in the evening, and leaving him one Hanoverian Battn. for its garrison, I marched the rest of the Divn. the next morning to Omiecourt, and yesterday through Peronne (a trifling place, but withstood a slight attack by the first Divn.) to this town, in the neighbourhood of which the troops were encamped.

Clermont, June 30th

The 2nd Divn, the right of Lord Hill's Corps, march today for Chantilly, while we, the 4th, halt a little way short of it. The public despatches will point out the distribution of the rest of the troops and state of affairs in Paris better than vague rumours here allow of our hearing of.

I overtook a gentleman coming with despatches for the Duke and King the other day from Paris. He assured me that Fouché is working hard for the King, and has been so ever since Bonaparte's return, so that I expect the proclaiming of Napoleon 2nd has been a deception meant to keep other claimants or proposed kinds of Government at a distance until the arrival of the Allies, who they know would never hear of the Bambino's claim.

I fear you will have much difficulty in making out what I have last written, but you will I am sure make allowance for my being generally ten and twelve hours on horseback a day, now in a broiling sun and clouds, or rather seas you may suppose, of white dust. This has come upon us with a sharp wind, and in the course of three days only, for it was then only that the rains ceased which made the other part of our march so distressing. You perceive we have advanced by forced marches, and the troops are much fatigued.

Ever your most affectionate brother,

C.C.

P.S. I had one officer killed and about 40 rank and file killed and wounded at Cambray, more than we had bargained for, but their loss was partly owing to their own imprudence. I slept in this town the morning I left Paris in Novr. last.

Although Wellington did not interfere with Charles's handling of the military operation required to reduce Cambrai, he wrote him letters at hourly intervals on 25 June about the diplomatic approach to the Governor of the fortress, saying that he would not consent to suspend hostilities for a moment in case the Governor seized the occasion to communicate with Paris. After the surrender of the garrison, Charles sent Wellington an official dispatch commending his officers and men. Conscious of the Duke's proclamation about plunder, he wrote that 'some depredations were committed, but of no consequence when the circumstances the place was entered by are considered.' On the Duke's instruction he then left behind two Hanoverian battalions to strengthen the royalist French troops under the Duc de Berri, which were soon expected, and set off to join the rest of the army on its march to Paris.

The entire British nation wallowed in the luxury of reflected glory as the story of Waterloo was told; but there were a few questions asked which were then, and are still now, a little hard to answer. One of them reached Charles in a letter, dated 27 June, from his brother-in-law, the Rev. Roger Frankland:

It appears rather queer to us ignorant country folk that our Duke should not have had better intelligence of the advance and preparations of Napoleon, so as to have had his cavalry and artillery at hand to support his infantry, for from this separation the chief slaughter seems to have arisen. The resistance of the troops under such unfavourable circumstances covers them with glory, but it also covers them with wounds and death. Napoleon can now hardly escape the fosse at Vincennes and the fate of the duc d'Enghien.*

John, too, was surprised by the failure of the Intelligence Service. He wrote, with due tact:

In the blaze of glory achieved nothing like a suspicion of want of anything desirable in the illustrious Commander's arrangements, seems ever to have been even hinted at, *but* I shall be anxious to know whether his information of the enemy's forward movement ought not to have been better. Could he have guessed it, the D. of Richmond's ball would not have been so well attended and your trip to Antwerp would not have taken place.

In the House of Commons, Castlereagh felt called upon to answer another question that was being widely asked. He said: 'The position of the Allied army was a very peculiar one, and without meaning to impute blame, or to suppose any neglect of security, I must say that the circumstances of the armies not being actually engaged in hostilities necessarily led to a distribution of force for the more convenient obtainment of subsistence . . . if Marshal Blücher and the Duke of Wellington had concentrated their forces, they must have left open a long line of country at the mercy of the enemy. It must be evident that the attacking army would have the advantage.' True though this certainly was, the lack of concentration and the poverty of military intelligence almost led to disaster. The latter, as in the case of the British Desert Army when Rommel appeared unexpectedly on the scene in 1941, is hard to explain.

* In 1804 Napoleon, despite pleas for mercy by the Empress Josephine, had the Duc d'Enghien, last of the House of Conde, shot in the moat at Vincennes.

These were matters for the historians. The immediate consideration was that a glorious victory had been won and Napoleon must be eliminated before he could contrive some remedial act of mischief.

The defeated Emperor ordered the remnants of his army to reform at Laon and himself made haste for Paris. There the unscrupulous Fouché, Duke of Otranto and Minister of Police, who had once voted enthusiastically for the execution of Louis XVI but was now working secretly for the Bourbons, assured Napoleon that the Senate and Chamber of Representatives were on his side. Napoleon thought of calling on the people to rally behind his standard and fight to defend Paris; but Fouché was deceiving him. The Chambers made their antagonism plain and on 25 June Napoleon retired to his house at Malmaison, having abdicated in favour of his child, the so-called King of Rome.

The Allies advanced as quickly as they could, meeting resistance from the French troops at Laon, and from Grouchy's unbroken corps as they fell back on Paris. Indeed the Prussian advance guard was put to flight as it approached Versailles. The story of Charles's division is told in this letter written to John from Neuilly on 9 July.

My last must have been I think of the 28th from Clermont (Deptnt. Oise). We continued our forced marches till, speaking of the 4th Divn., we reached a village called Dugny, abreast of Bourget on the Senlis road, and having St. Denis on our right. We here fell in with the Prussians, but who having commenced crossing the Seine, I was ordered by the Duke to relieve a post they held at Abbervilliers, a village in front of their fortified canal, which reaches from St. Denis to La Villette, where it joins the canal de l'Oise, and from which it receives its water. It had cost the Prussians 250 men to take the day before, and 20 men had that day been killed in maintaining it.

The French still held two or three houses at the end of it under cover of their artillery on the canal, and were still firing when I entered the village to reconnoitre. We had judged however that the Prussians had erred in keeping too large a force in the place, which gave the suspicion that further operations on that side were intended when they were not. We therefore sent in only 400 men with strong supports outside, and as I have always found the French perfectly soldierlike in that respect, I particularly constrained my people to avoid unnecessary fire, and when I expected they would equally cease theirs, it turned out as I expected, one sentry being killed by the *méchanceté* of an individual, most probably, being my only casualty during the three days I occupied the village.

On the evening of the 4th I occupied St. Denis in consequence of the convention, and on the 7th removed to this village, about three miles from the Tuileries, the Divn., as well as the rest of the 1st and 2nd Corps, being encamped in the Bois de Boulogne, on which this touches. The wood is as ugly a thing as a wood can be, and the encampment has neither appearance nor convenience, so that those who are in it must wish themselves soon removed. Those in houses are not much more comfortably off, for though some like myself are in what were the most celebrated villas of the environs, their frequent change of masters, the apprehensions of their present owners which have induced them to send their furniture into Paris, and the wanton depredations of first their own troops, and then of the Prussians, makes their appearance in general most deplorable.

The state I found the very pretty villa I was in at Dugny exactly resembled that of the three or four houses the flames had left unconsumed at Leiria in Portugal on Masséna's retreat; the debris of the wantonly destroyed, beautiful furniture and glasses, as well as of the contents of the library, ladies' working tables, fans, letters, etc., etc., etc., showed them to have been the property of most respectable people. The father was a Comte Maret, a *conseiller d'état* and who to this had just before suffered the misfortune of having his son, a General Officer, killed at the Battle of Waterloo.

I am happy to say that I have seen or heard of hardly any injury done by the British, but all our allies are so mischievous, as well as intent upon plunder, that Louis will be under the necessity of requesting their departure as soon as the measure can possibly be deemed safe: when this however may be, it is hard to guess, for we know nothing of the refractory army, and I have no doubt it was owing to the entry into Paris of the Prussians alone that the change of the national flag and cockades was so quietly effected and the garrulous members of their soi-disant Chambre de Representatives so speedily silenced. The King's proclamation however on the subject of the colour was a good one, and has been followed up by some good essays in the journals, which cannot fail to reconcile to the resumption of the white flag.

The Prussians behave with great regularity and decorum when

on duty, and I do not hear that they have extended their devastation to their quarters and bivouac in Paris.

I have not heard our Duke's reasons for not giving to his troops a share of the internal duties, or quartering them in town. At present we hold only the Bossiers on the right bank, but there is a report of barracks clearing out for at least some part of our force, perhaps the Guards.

I invited myself to be of His Grace's cortège on his entrance into the capital, which he made in just his usual blue riding dress. Five minutes before he mounted, he was standing in his stable yard giving directions to his coachman with his handkerchief thrown over his head instead of a hat. On our way in, a carriage passed with a lady in it, who saluting him as if she knew him, he leapt his horse over a small drain to go to speak to her, to the great astonishment of some of the Parisian lookers on who suspected who he was; but these were few, and I had the mortification to hear an old Bavarian with scarlet uniform and tawdry star taken for him. I took care Sir Sidney Smith in all his decorations should not pass unknown, and half aloud told those about me, as I was riding by him, that it was he who had first beaten their Emperor. I think my attention was not thrown away upon him, as no two heroes can certainly be more unlike than our Chief and he.

An Aide de Camp of Masséna's met the Duke with a message to know whether he would have a salute of artillery, which he declined, and without waiting to be met by anyone, cut across the end of the Champs Elysées, and rode to the house taken for him at the corner of the rue Louis 15.

The next day, happening to be in town at all events, I took my station on horseback in the Cour des Tuileries, and not only witnessed the entrée of the King, but heard the only words of his address from the balcony which the acclamations of those around would admit of being heard; these were:- 'Bon jour mes amis' with a very good natured and appropriate look and gesture, as much as to say 'you have been bad boys, but I trust you have seen your errors, and be assured I heartily forgive and shall endeavour to forget it.' The trait of the slobbering grenadier of the National Guard is not correctly given, for instead of pressing him to his bosom, the King seemed a good deal annoyed at him, and the fellow himself seemed ashamed of himself when he fell back to his place. He would have cut His Majesty's throat for five francs a week ago. The acclamations were no doubt loud, but the spectators were mostly National

Guards and boys who joined in it. The Maison du Roi behaved with becoming reserve. Spanish like, I doubt not the nation will be shortly browbeat generally into the most respectful acknowledgements of the propriety of this last change, on which let me not omit to wish you joy, for a most happy event it truly promises to be for Europe.

I break off to dress for dinner with the Duke at Vary's, the restaurant near the Tuileries where he has invited all General Officers, etc., to meet old Blücher. I wish you were of the party, but as that cannot be, I must be satisfied with the hope that you will not be long absent from such amusement as is to be had here. By the bye, pray bring with you my dress sword from Tiffanies, and get from Sir G. Naylor my decorations of the Tower and Spade, and write a note to Sir H. Torrens to ask for my clasp for Martinique, and get from Rundle and Bridges, which they will send you by the twopenny post, three yards of the Peninsular medal ribband.

Napoleon had vanished. He left Malmaison on 29 June, a few hours before a Prussian detachment arrived to seize him. Had he been taken it would indeed have been for him what the Rev. Roger Frankland called 'the fosse at Vincennes'; for Blücher had every intention of shooting him as an outlaw.

Napoleon's characteristics included refusal to admit either defeat or error. The first was estimable: the second was not. He was so persuasive that he has cast a spell on posterity as well as on his own generation, and on English liberals, such as Lord Rosebery and Winston Churchill, as strongly as on his compatriots. Thus the Napoleonic legend took root even in the aftermath of Waterloo, and it so captivated France that a second Empire, under a well-meaning but less gifted Bonaparte, was established thirty-five years later.

There were in those weeks after Waterloo two examples of Napoleon's refusal to admit guilt and his total rejection of humility. First, in a declaration to the French people on 23 June, he announced that he had only renewed the war to preserve national independence (which, as he well knew, nobody at all had threatened). He offered himself, he said, as a sacrifice to the hatred of the enemies of France (of whom, in view of all that he had done, there were surprisingly few). He then formally proclaimed his son as Napoleon II and evidently expected his wishes to be dutifully met.

A second example of his inflexible self-esteem is found in his behaviour on 15 July when, thwarted in his plan to sail to America, he boarded H.M.S. *Bellerophon*. He so mesmerised her captain, Maitland, that he was almost immediately taken on board *Superb* to have breakfast with the admiral, to whom Maitland formally presented him as 'The Emperor'. His treatment of the admiral on his own flagship was thus described by an eyewitness:

Napoleon bowed to the Admiral, without further ceremony walked into his cabin, and sent him compliments that he would be glad to speak with him. Nothing escapes his notice; his eyes are in every place and on every object, from the greatest to the most minute. He immediately asked an explanation of the ropes, blocks, masts and yards, and all the machinery of the ship. He sent for the boatswain to question him. He requested the marines to pass in review before him, examined the arms, evolutions, dress etc. and expressed himself highly pleased. He inquired into the situation of the seamen, their pay, prize-money, clothes, food, tobacco, etc.

Neither the Admiral nor Captain Maitland made the slightest remonstrance to the man who less than a month before had declared that he would eat the English for breakfast.

Sir Hudson Lowe has long been execrated, both in France and England, for his unsympathetic handling of Napoleon in exile at St. Helena. The fact that, but for his insatiable lust for personal power, Napoleon could have stayed in comfortable retirement on the agreeable island of Elba, and thus not been directly responsible for the unnecessary deaths of thousands of young men at Waterloo, is largely ignored by Lowe's detractors. The victors in the twentieth century, who thought about hanging the Kaiser and did hang the Nazis, would certainly have treated Napoleon less kindly than did Captain Maitland or Sir Hudson Lowe, even though he had maintained no concentration camps and had never even contemplated genocide. He had, however, killed the flower of a generation in almost every European country merely because he aspired to be the dictator of Europe.

With Napoleon safely on board *Bellerophon* and the Allied armies in occupation of Paris, Talleyrand and Fouché spared no pains to ingratiate themselves with both the victors and the returning Bourbons, whose popularity, however, was even less than a year before. Wellington and the curé of St. Pé had misjudged the sentiments of the French people, and Castlereagh observed that 'if the Allied troops were withdrawn, His Majesty would not be on his throne a week'. Indeed the Bourbons were never reestablished in the hearts of the people. Thanks to the common sense of Louis XVIII and the moderating influence of two of his ministers, Richelieu and Decazes, they survived for fifteen years; but such loyalty as the dynasty once inspired, under Louis XIV, *le dieu-donné*, and Louis XV, *le bien-aimé*, had evaporated and could never be revived. Nineteenth-century France, intoxicated by the stimulants of romanticism and liberalism, looked back with elation to the Revolution, the American Declaration of Independence and the magic of the Empire, not to the palace of Versailles. Eighteenth-century traditions and conventions lingered on under artificial respiration, but in 1830, together with the Bourbons and George IV, they finally expired.

There was no more fighting; indeed although in the years ahead savage clashes took place between nations, it was a hundred years before Europe was again plunged into full-scale war. Every consideration was shown to the French, who were in due course given frontiers slightly wider than they had held in 1792. The British, as a friendly gesture, restored Martinique and Guadeloupe which they had conquered with such pains and bloodshed. France was required to pay an indemnity and sentenced to five years occupation by an Allied force not exceeding 150,000 men.

The French strongly resented the order to return the artistic loot which Napoleon had brought to Paris from Italy and Germany. Despite their vociferous opposition to what they thought an outrageous demand, the golden horses of St. Mark were sent back to Venice and cartloads of pictures and statuary were removed from the Louvre for restoration to their owners. This, perhaps even more than Wellington's refusal to make an effort to prevent the trial and execution of Marshal Ney, induced several of Napoleon's generals, now conveniently rallied once again to the Bourbons, to turn their backs on the Duke at a reception given by Louis XVIII in the Tuileries, Wellington pertinently remarked that he believed they had long become accustomed to doing so. If further twentieth-century comparisons can be tolerated, it is noteworthy that the Germans for their part made no protest at all when, in 1945, Goering's artistic loot was impounded for return to the museums and private collections whence it had been stolen.

There was a rumour that the 4th Division was to be moved to cantonments in Normandy. Charles had invited John and his wife to visit him in Paris and so the thought perturbed him. However, as he wrote from Neuilly on 26 July, Paris had its drawbacks:

As for myself, excepting in the proud feeling excited by having a British Army so situated, I would as lief be in country cantonments, so horrid and comparatively out of condition and uncomfortable does every thing appear at present here. I could not, however, as the troops passed by the Emperor of Russia on the Place Louis 15 at our review on the very spot where Louis 16 was beheaded, but think of the triumph we have obtained, and how Carnot, Barrière, St. Jean d'Angely, and others of their kidney, some of them still in Paris, must have grinned in horror at the sight.

The statements you see in the newspapers are in general pretty correct, but I cannot but remark on the malevolence towards the British with which the editors ascribe every measure of lenity and forbearance to the magnanimous Alexander, but I hope they will find he has not the power of doing as much harm as he had last year. Louis' denunciation of the three classes of traitors you will with me think ridiculously late, when he knows the worst of them to have already escaped out of his hands.

Our Duke have his Generals etc. a dinner at Vary's to introduce us to old Blücher, and we gave him one on the anniversary of the Battle of Salamanca. Those and our public introductions to Emperor and Kings, seeing sights, and some little interchanging of dinners among military friends, have been the chief of my occupations or amusements since I last wrote.

It was by no means only the return of the looted works of art that antagonised the French. They objected to being occupied no less than the Germans objected to the occupation of the Rhineland after the First World War. In both cases it seemed obvious to the victors that steps must be taken to prevent a renewal of aggression, and bearing in mind the expensive episode of the Hundred Days, the Allied attitude in 1815 was not unreasonable. But the French felt they were being treated as a conquered nation and that their undoubted contribution to European civilisation was insufficiently recognised. They thought the English almost as bad as the Prussians, which was unfair in view of the stringent measures Wellington took to restrain his troops; and the credit for the liberal treatment they did in fact receive was given to the Czar Alexander who had long posed as a champion of freedom and enlightenment. So the lot of an Allied general was less happy than might have been expected in a Parisian summer. Indeed the hostility to the British soldiers was such that at one moment

Wellington thought of concentrating his entire force on the Franco-Belgian frontier; for however effective a thin red line might be on the field of Waterloo, it was by no means a safe device for occupying an ill-disposed country.

There was intensive activity for the politicians and diplomats throughout the summer of 1815. There was none at all for the soldiers who had so long been used to nothing else. John paid Charles a visit and had hardly reached Southampton on his return, after an unpleasant forty-eight-hour crossing from Havre, when the importunities of his unpredictable wife, who had declined to accompany him on the first visit, obliged him to put to sea again. Charles must have groaned when early in September he received a letter headed 'Havre again'. It began:

> Perhaps you will not be surprized to hear of my being here again,—you will judge not quite *alone*. After a week's suspence at Southn. Lady C. joined me, but I confess she had given me so little reason to think she was up to a Paris trip that I was a little annoyed at embarking again at an hour's notice, but I clearly saw it was best to do so. So here I am after a passage of 52 hours, with Ly. C. and maid under convoy.

They stayed for six weeks and had a disagreeable return journey over roads which were not paved, staying in inns where the accommodation left much to be desired.

Deep in the regimental archives of the 5th Regiment of Foot there may be a reference to the crime that Private James O'Shaugnessy committed. Perhaps he drank too much and struck an officer or an N.C.O.; perhaps he deserted; perhaps he stole French property and thereby exacerbated the anti-British feeling that seemed to be growing month by month. Wellington had made his views on plunder crystal-clear.

Whatever the offence, it seems that Charles thought greater leniency was permissible in peacetime than when the army was on active service. As this letter shows, Wellington did not share his views.

Cambray, Sept. 25th, 1816

My dear General,

Upon perusal of the proceedings of the General Court Martial with trial of James O'Shaugnessy of the 5th Regt. it occurred to me that you had not the power to revise the sentence, and that it could be touched legally only by myself, and having referred it for the opinion of the Judge Advocate General, I enclose his report.

I don't know why you disapproved of the sentence of 800 lashes, as it is strictly legal, and in my opinion a punishment much more likely to operate as an example than that of transportation. I dislike the punishment of flogging as much as others, but I dislike crime still more, and I must say that our squeamishness about corporal punishment of late years, and our substitutes for it such as, transportation, general service, marking with the letter D., etc., are an encouragement rather than an example to prevent crime with the majority of our drunken soldiers, who are indifferent about every thing excepting drink and vanity.

If therefore you have not some particular reason for preferring in this instance the sentence of transportation, I would confirm that of corporal punishment, and in this case it would be necessary to send back the proceedings of the Court in order that they may expunge all that follows the first sentence.

Ever yours etc. etc.
WELLINGTON

The report from the Judge Advocate General has not been preserved.

On the day after Wellington signed this letter, the Holy Alliance was proclaimed, its signatories pledging themselves that all their acts would be founded on the sacred principles of the Gospel of our Lord and Saviour Jesus Christ. Britain was not a signatory, but the Prince Regent wrote to express his whole-hearted approval of the principles. It is improbable that Private O'Shaughnessy was ever invited to comment.

The French Chambers, whatever the attitudes of the people they represented, passed the financial and other measures required by the Allies. As a reward the size of the Army of Occupation was reduced at the end of November, and its term was shortened from five years to three. Wellington therefore retained only three divisions in France and the officers he selected to command them were three of his Peninsular generals, Cole, Clinton and Colville.

14

Calm Waters

Charles remained a divisional commander in France during the whole period of Allied occupation that ended on 30 November 1818. After twenty years of action in the sands of Egypt, the Caribbean islands and the rugged Iberian Peninsula, he had now to adjust himself to the routine of a peacetime military establishment. Those who have participated in the great events of history do not easily find satisfaction in less heroic activities, however comfortable their situation and senior their rank.

In January 1816 he was given command of his old and favourite division, the 3rd, which moved from Paris to Valenciennes, near the frontier with the Netherlands. As brigade commanders he had two of his closest Peninsular comrades, Sir Manley Power and Sir John Keane. The latter, destined to win fame and a peerage in Afghanistan, had succeeded Charles in command of the 3rd Division brigade which he had led in Spain and Portugal. Charles was appointed Governor of Valenciennes as well as divisional commander and he settled down to a life quieter than he had ever known, with plenty of spare time for hunting and shooting, and with no shortage of interesting local tours and social frivolity. His reputation as a sportsman may be judged from a letter his son wrote to him in 1841 after shooting in Scotland with Colonel Charles Hay of the Coldstream Guards, a former member of his father's staff: 'Hay says I am a chip of the old block to a certain degree, so far as shooting is concerned, for one day I shot a grey-hen and a partridge before the season'.

Charles did not hesitate to decline an offer of the Governorship of Grenada, where he had spent six dismal months in 1810, for it was pleasant to be within easy reach of England, even though he had no home of his own. Moreover, while governorships were being provided for all the superannuated generals whom the Government could accommodate, it was as financially rewarding and far more distinguished to command one of the three remaining British divisions on the continent of Europe.

At this period most of Charles's own letters are missing; but John was a regular correspondent and since the career of his brother and heir was now his principal interest in life, the sequence of events can be followed without difficulty. The situation at home, in the aftermath of the war, grew more disturbing month by month. In July 1816 John wrote:

> The weather, which has already caused many things to rise, and which if it does not soon improve will raise alarm for the corn harvest, adds to the gloom in this country which from various causes seems to be very great; and I think we shall not have much to cheer us on the next meeting of Parliament, for plans must be hatching to make up for present deficiencies.

For several years John had been hinting that Charles should give thought to matrimony. In November 1816 he congratulated him on the way his investments in the Funds were prospering and added that he could 'see nothing to prevent your looking out for an agreeable helpmate to propagate on, as our uncle Alexander expressed his desire of doing when contemplating his retirement from the service'. Charles had doubtless been thinking on the same lines himself and so early in 1817, newly decorated with the Grand Cross of the White Horse of Hanover ('the Guelphic Honors' as John somewhat disparagingly described it), he went home on leave. He met Jane, the eldest of the ten children of Mr William Mure of Caldwell, who owned estates in Ayrshire and Renfrew and was suitably connected with a number of leading Scottish Lowland families. Jane was twenty-five, young enough to be Charles's daughter, but after a short acquaintance he proposed to her and they were married at Caldwell on 13 February 1818 by 'the Episcopalian Clergyman of Glasgow'.

In celebration of the marriage, the Mures had their daughter and son-in-law painted by the sixty-one-year-old artist Sir Henry Raeburn, recently elected to the Royal Academy. The marriage settlement was drawn up and Charles, writing from Caldwell, explained to John that the arrangements were different from those in England. 'In addition to the ten thousand pounds, I settle one thousand, as is the custom in Scotland, in lieu of furniture, etc., and notice is made of the thousand pounds I receive with the lady'. John had also offered to place a sum on bond, but the Mures apparently escaped with a solitary £1,000, which was just as well in view of their nine other children.

After a honeymoon in Scotland, Charles went back to Valenciennes with Jane, who immediately became pregnant. He found, on his return, that Keane had been offered the Governorship of St. Lucia, worth £3,700 a year, that Kempt, who had fought gallantly at Badajos, at Vitoria and at Waterloo, had been given Nova Scotia, and that Cole, former commander of the 4th Division, was to be Governor of Gravesend, a post providing a salary but demanding no government. It was a little galling to learn that the shrinking of the army included the disbanding of the 94th Regiment and thus the determination of his colonelcy. All the same, the full pay of a lieutenant-general was, while it lasted, sufficient to ensure the comfort even of a married man. Unfortunately it was unlikely to last long, for the end of the three-years' occupation of France was approaching.

Jane took her sister Catherine to Valenciennes. At the end of July Wellington wrote from Cambrai to say that he would make a farewell inspection of the 3rd Division. He sent in advance a letter giving instructions how the troops were to be formed on parade and proposing himself to dine 'or make a luncheon' at two o'clock precisely. He announced that he would order on the spot any movements he might wish the troops to make and he desired to see 'all your carts, carriages etc. formed in the rear of the cavalry'.

Catherine Mure, who like most young ladies of her generation kept a journal, wrote this description of the Duke:

At first I was rather disappointed at his appearance. He is no dandy in dress and looks older than I had expected. His hair is grey and his teeth not good. His looks improve much when you know him better. He has the most animated, intelligent and expressive countenance I ever saw. He is like the pictures one sees of him, but not so tall as they lead one to suppose. He is stout made, with broad shoulders: his figure is best on horseback, his bust being fine. He is fair, eyes a fine greyish blue: this does not sound fine, but they are so animated and keen. They quite look through you and are the beauty of his face. He handed Jane to dinner.

The Duke was in great spirits. He is very lively, talked and laughed a great deal and told us all the gossip of Cambray, which he seems to enjoy as much as the young men on his staff. It seems odd to see so great a man, with so many important concerns to transact, amusing himself with such trifles, but they say he has the most extraordinary powers during his hours of recreation to banish from his mind all serious matters and that during the most awfully important periods of the war he could at any time, when he had a spare hour, amuse himself like a schoolboy. He seems much liked by those about him and on such a pleasant footing with them. What a pity, with such talents and powers of pleasing, he should not be equally estimable in private life.*

In the same month John, to his delight, was elected a Scottish Representative Peer, having long been canvassing for votes. There were, until the 1960s, sixteen such representatives, elected at the beginning of a new Parliament by all the Scottish Peers with no United Kingdom peerage entitling them to a seat in the Lords. Unlike Charles, who coveted honours but not money, John hoped that his election might bring pecuniary advantages, and he was in due course gravely disappointed that it did not. It was, however, gratifying to receive forty-seven votes from his fellow Scottish noblemen, Lord Lothian heading the list with fifty-seven.

Still more exciting was an offer to Charles, as soon as the occupation should end in the following November, of the Commandership-in-Chief at Bombay. He immediately consulted Wellington, who replied that he was flattered by the confidence Charles reposed in his opinion. Charles must, he advised, insist on being a member of the Bombay Council of Government too, 'not only because the salary of the Commdr. in Chief alone would scarcely be sufficient to defray your expense, but because you could not have the power and dignity to enable you to perform your duties'. Subject to that, however, Wellington recommended acceptance.

The climate is by no means bad and I think that if Lady Colville were once arrived there she would like the place more than otherwise. You must consider that there is at present but little prospect of employment in Europe; that you must go abroad to the Colonies, and probably to a tropical climate, to seek it; and if this is the case you cannot be in a more respectable situation than that offered to your acceptance.

So Charles accepted. In November a son, Charles John, to be known as Charly, was born at Caldwell. His parents decided

---

* Catherine Mure had evidently been listening to tales about Wellington by the courtesan Harriette Wilson, and others, which circulated freely in society.

that he must be left behind there rather than face the long voyage to Bombay. They finally embarked at the end of April 1818, and after five months of storms alternating with flat calms reached Bombay just in time for Jane to give birth to her second child, a daughter, on dry land. Their first letters home, written as soon as they landed, also took five months on the journey. Thus in those days of travelling under sail round the Cape of Good Hope an exchange of letters between India and the British Isles took almost a year, though occasionally, when the winds were favourable and consistent, a single voyage might be made in four months.

In Bombay there was also a new Governor, Mountstuart Elphinstone. After a series of sharp conflicts with the Mahrattas, a period of comparative peace had ensued. In this quiet interlude Elphinstone introduced a programme of sound administrative reform. Charles was called upon to mount one campaign against Scinde, which was accomplished to his satisfaction, but during the five years he was Commander-in-Chief the main interest is to be found in John's letters to him describing events in England. The best commentary on his own letters is in John's reply to that announcing his daughter's birth:

The familiar name of that dear little Lady I cannot make out, for indeed your hand is getting more difficult from the hurry which you evidently always write in. I shall no longer, I fear, be able to execute the task of family decipherer . . .

He could at least decipher that it was a girl, and he comforted Charles by the reflection that 'they on the whole generally prove the least expensive pets'.

On the death of George III in 1820, Parliament was automatically dissolved. John reported with elation that in the new election of Representative Peers he had come equal top of the list with fifty-four votes, tying with Lord Lothian and beating Lords Rosebery, Elgin and Home by a single vote. The Duke of Roxburghe, who had deplorable radical views despite his eighty-five years, came bottom.

His pleasure at doing so well in the contest was diminished by worries about popular unrest.

He wrote from Edinburgh:

The state of public affairs here seems little mended as to the ill spirit prevailing among the lower classes though it has been kept more in check by the late decided measures. At this moment there is not a regular or yeomanry soldier hereabouts—all gone to Glasgow and its neighbourhood in consequence of a general *strike*, as it is called, among the workmen of all descriptions, accompanied by the most unequivocal determination to open acts of sedition.

Unemployment, sweated labour and actual starvation were the cause; but John, who was used to dealing with naval ratings in the fashion then prescribed, can have had no conception of the misery that racked a high proportion of the civil population. Charles would probably have been less harsh in his judgement.

Violence had erupted both in Paris and in London. In Paris the Duc de Berri, ultimate heir to the throne, was assassinated at the Opera and Charles's old friend, the Bishop of Oberglogau, formerly Marquis de Bombelles, was summoned to give spiritual comfort to the unhappy widow. In London the Cato Street conspirators were foiled in an attempt to murder the entire Cabinet.

John's High Tory views were outraged by the state of public opinion displayed at the conspirators' public execution.

This is a day which causes most melancholy sensations as to the state of things here. The five devils in human form who have this day terminated their guilty career at Newgate quitted the world in a state which it was hardly possible to contemplate, notwithstanding their characters and their conduct whilst under trial. But they are gone and their conduct and intentions, which to the last they boasted of are now of little consequence compared to the disgraceful conduct of the base multitude whose overwhelming numbers would doubtless, if the best arrangements had not been made to prevent it, have endeavoured to rescue from their punishment villains who in better days would have left the world loaded with the execrations of every Englishman. But the national character is gone and we cannot hope to see it restored in our days. The air was rent with the cheers of condolence for the culprits when they appeared, as it was with the groans and other expressions of anger when their heads were taken off.

John's mercenary instincts also led him to comment sourly as vacant colonelcy after colonelcy went to other generals. Without Charles's permission he went so far as to complain to the Duke of York, the Commander-in-Chief, who quite reasonably replied that his brother was, after all, holding an employment that was

223

well remunerated whereas a lot of other retired generals were not. John's aspirations, too, were far from satisfied by his Scottish seat in the Lords. Indeed when the new King, George IV, wished to divorce the vulgar and promiscuous Queen Caroline, the House of Lords was obliged to sit six days a week all through August 1820. He had a particular aversion to the Queen's Attorney-General, Lord Brougham, whose manner was querulous, whose logical deductions he found 'insulting', and whose oratory was prolific. He was, John thought, 'radical, troublesome and overbearing'. An added injury to their lordships was the fact that 'the House of Commons are all enjoying themselves while we are prisoners here'. John had discovered that Sir Miles Nightingall, Charles's predecessor in Bombay and now a Member of Parliament, was shooting grouse in Perthshire.

His report of the proceedings against the Queen contains these passages:

In other times the flagrant conduct of this personage, the indecency and imprudence of which no one can deny, would have at least prevented the middling classes of society, male and female, from openly espousing her cause, whatever might be their wishes in regard to it, till the investigation was over. But now, as the proofs of guilt multiply, the frenzy in her favour increases. It is no question with the people of England whether their Queen is a licentious woman who has stooped to have her passions gratified by a menial servant, and who has even taken pains to give publicity to her misconduct, or whether she is an injured and innocent woman. It is enough that she has returned to throw herself into the arms of the populace, who are resolved to support her in opposition to the higher authorities of the Kingdom and to make her cause the ground on which all those in enmity to the King personally (who certainly are very numerous), and hostile to his Government from whatever cause, are to take their position.

The ferment of this crisis brings to light daily proofs of the prevailing hostility of the populace to religion and to law. The Bishops and Judges are always insulted in that daily ordeal which those who sit in the House are exposed to on their return from it. The D. of Wellington and Ld. Anglesey are particularly unpopular and always meet a volley of hisses and imprecations. The Duke of York is always cheered: one of the numerous plans (I think) to gain over the military. His manliness in attending the House is a fine contrast to the conduct of the D. of

Sussex in pleading consanguineity. The King in all this bustle is well advised in remaining at his cottage: he would be exposed to daily insult if here.

Nothing said or sworn against the Q. has given me so bad an opinion of her as going to the House of Peers for the pretended purpose of instructing her Counsel and confronting, by her dignified presence, the witnesses. False pretences both: the former would not receive her instructions and, brazen-faced as she is, she dares not continue in the presence of the latter longer (hitherto) than to dart at them when they are sworn the looks of a Fury, looks which whilst I live I shall never think of without horror.

John, so careful himself with money, could not bear to think of his brother being extravagant. Charles, however, thought it was unfair to his employers, the East India Company, not to spend a high proportion of his salary on making a suitable impact on the community, even though his predecessor, General Nightingall, had never spent more than £2,000 a year and had thus returned to England with huge savings. John did his best to preach parsimony:

I have always known your generosity, your hospitality and laudable wish to make a respectable appearance in the situation which you fill, but am sure you have no taste for Oriental pomp and am rather inclined to think you have some people about you who have great notions of shew and expense and who may consider more the appearance you make at present than the comforts you should look to by and by.

In case this should not make sufficient impression on his younger and, as he felt, excessively hospitable brother, he wrote in another letter:

Pray let us have no more of suppers etc. to 250, which the first anniversary of the birth of your first-born must alone excuse. Your four carriage-horses, too, I have heard the distant neighing of, and am told your predecessor drove with a pair only: he is enjoying himself well now, it would appear, in consequence. I now close my lecture on oeconomy.

At long last, in November 1821, John received a command of his own and promotion to flag rank. It was the naval command at Cork and he heard that it had been highly profitable to his predecessor, Sir Josias Rowley, who had made £10,000 in prize money from the capture of American tobacco smugglers. He remarked, lugubriously, that he feared the naval measures recently taken to prevent such smuggling might seriously diminish the profits of the appointment.

So John's letters lost their metropolitan interest; but he did inform Charles, who had a warm spot for that amiable buffoon, that his nephew and former A.D.C. Frederick Forsyth had married in Paris a Miss Scarth. 'A very silly act, I suppose,' John considered, 'inasmuch as I understand that the extent of her fortune will probably be a thousand pounds.' As this was also the extent of Jane Colville's fortune, it was scarcely a tactful comment to make. He did, however, admit that the match was better than that from which Frederick had been dissuaded six months previously, 'with the Attorney's daughter at Wells'.

On 8 June 1821 the Governor of St. Helena, Sir Hudson Lowe, sent this information to Charles, because the military superintendence of that closely guarded island was the responsibility of Bombay. After a paragraph of personal compliments Lowe's letter continued:

Napoleon Bonaparte has ceased to live!

The general circumstances are mentioned in my public letter. Captain Alsager, the bearer of this letter (whom I take the liberty of recommending to your kind attention) can furnish you with full details of anything he saw or heard at the time.

On opening the body, which was done with Bonaparte's own previous desire to such effect, in order to discover if any means could be found to preserve his son from the same disorder, an ulcer was observed near the pylorus, which occasioned adhesions to the liver, and on opening the stomach the ulcer was found to have made a hole sufficiently large for a little finger to pass through: the coats of the stomach, internally, being as described in my public letter.

Count Bertrand and Montholon, in their letter to Europe, have described the cause of his death to be an ichirrus and cancer of the stomach near the pylorus, and spoke of the disease being hereditary. The blow must have reached him on the throne of France, at the head of an Empire, as well as here. He suspected the cause of his approaching dissolution, and it favored so much the bias of his own mind to predestinarianism, that he latterly refused taking any medicine, saying it could be of no use in protecting his life.

He has remembered in a very handsome manner his medical attendant, Dr. Arnot, having desired that a gold snuff-box, the last he had in use, and upon which he with his own hand cut the letter N., should be presented to him, as also the sum of £500.

Etc, Etc, Etc, Etc, Etc, Etc,

Yours most faithfully,

H. LOWE

Charles remained in Bombay till the end of 1825, working harmoniously with Elphinstone in the establishment of a civil and military administration which, fifteen years later, stood the test well when the British army was called upon to fight in Afghanistan and on the North-West Frontier. Charles's services were rewarded with the colonelcy of the 5th Foot when he and Jane reached home. They now had two daughters (another girl had been born in Bombay), and Jane produced a fourth child (and second son) in 1827, and yet a third daughter after Charles had accepted the Governorship of Mauritius. Charly was sent to school at Harrow, and the rest of the family left for that pleasant island in the Indian Ocean where they lived in muted viceregal splendour from 1828 till 1833. It had been seized from the French in 1810 and had not, like Guadeloupe and Martinique, been restored at the peace; for it lay on the vital route to India and was strongly garrisoned. The inhabitants were sugar and cotton planters of French descent and language, with a large dependent population of African slaves whom the French had imported. These were emancipated, with all the other slaves in British colonies, the year after Charles left the island.

Returning to England at the age of sixty-three for final retirement, he had the satisfaction of being promoted to the rank of full general and of seeing his elder son appointed first to the staff of the Governor of Upper Canada and then to that of the Governor-General of India. In 1839 his eighteen-year-old daughter, Emily, married Lord Newry, whose family lived by the Mountains of Mourne, and his younger son, Willy, went to Sandhurst at the early age of thirteen, prior to receiving a commission in the Rifle Brigade. Meanwhile, also in 1839, John lost his wife, whom he deeply loved despite her hypochondria and her demanding habits. Lonely and depressed, he was soon married again, this time to the middle-aged sister of Lord Ellenborough, who was about to take office as Governor-General of India. All would have been well, had not Jane gradually developed a mental instability and unpleasant forms of behaviour, the exact nature of which were, in Victorian fashion, never revealed to later generations. Suffice to say that in their letters to Charles his children expressed concern about 'poor Mama', her 'stormy and troubled life' and her 'unfortunate habits'. Her end was an appalling one.

In March 1843 Charles, full of years and honour, died peacefully a month after his silver wedding, at a house he had taken in the rural surroundings of Hampstead. It seems that he had never for a moment wavered in his tenderness to Jane and he was soothed by her presence at his deathbed. Some weeks later his daughter Catherine heard shrieks from upstairs. At first she thought her sister Georgy had been given a fright by her young brother Willy; but on rushing up to investigate, Catherine found her mother enveloped in flames. She had knocked over a candle she was using to seal letters and had set fire to her clothes. She lingered for twenty-four hours and then died, just two months after her husband.

Charles would have been gratified to know that as soon as Wellington heard of his death, he wrote to John saying that he not only wished, but considered it a duty, to look to Charly's and William's future interest in the Army. He would have been pleased, too, had he been able to look further into the future and see that every one of his twenty five great-grandsons fought, in one war or another, on active service for King and Country, eighteen in the Army, six in the Navy, and one (such was the generation gap) in the Royal Air Force.

His children all thrived. The three daughters 'married well', as was said in those days, and Willy distinguished himself in the Crimean War. His elder son, Charly, became an officer in the 11th Hussars, a regiment commanded by the gallant but insufferable Lord Cardigan, future leader of the Charge of the Light Brigade.

When Lord Ellenborough, at Charly's request, wrote to Wellington asking for his intervention to effect an exchange of regiment with another officer, Wellington felt unable to help; but in his reply to Ellenborough he said: 'I much prefer to endeavour to obtain leave of absence for Capt. Colville, though that is very unpleasant for me as I must communicate upon the subject with Lord Cardigan . . . The real truth of the whole affair is the desire to avoid getting under the command of Lord Cardigan, which desire I have no objection to gratify . . . .' Charly's father would not have approved his next step, which was to seduce Lady Cardigan, whose fiery husband then divorced her. At least it enabled him to transfer from the 11th Hussars to the Coldstream Guards.

Charly prospered. After succeeding John as Lord Colville of Culross, he was for twenty-five years Chief Conservative Whip in the House of Lords under both Derby and Disraeli, and also Master of the Buckhounds to Queen Victoria. He declined Disraeli's offer of an earldom on the grounds that he had no landed estate with which to support such a high distinction. So they waited till he was almost dead and made him a viscount. That, it seems, required no territorial backing. He was Chairman of the Great Northern Railway, and finally he, who had been born in the reign of George III, was Lord Chamberlain to Queen Alexandra at the Coronation of Edward VII.

There was one strange incident in his career which is worth recounting, for it distantly echoes his father's experiences at the Court of Versailles and the dance with Marie Antoinette. On his way home from India in 1843, Charly made the newly organised land journey from Suez to Alexandria, thus avoiding the long voyage round the Cape. One of the carriages in which the passengers were travelling across the desert broke down, but they were sufficiently unperturbed to improvise a dance. Rescued from the desert they set sail for Malta where Charly, whose talent as a painter was far greater than that of the usual amateur, painted sketches of the harbour. Then, disembarking at Gibraltar, he made his way to Granada. He painted the Alhambra, the Generalife and the terracotta landscape. Himself tall, good-looking and bronzed by the Indian sun, he fell in love with a beautiful seventeen-year-old Spanish girl called Eugenie de Montijo. It was a youthful passion, doubtless hampered by duennas and discouraged on grounds of religion. When he left for home, the passion evaporated, but the memory lasted.

Twenty-seven years later, in September 1870, Charly, who was devoted to yachting and had a house at Cowes called Culross Lodge, was ordered by Queen Victoria to receive on her behalf the fugitive Empress Eugenie. Flying from the Tuileries on the outbreak of revolution in Paris, the Empress had been sheltered by a chivalrous American dentist who spirited her and her lady-in-waiting away to Deauville. There the dentist discovered Sir John Burgoyne's forty-two-ton cutter yacht *Gazelle* which lay in the harbour sheltering from a severe storm. When the dentist insisted that the Empress was in danger, Sir John set sail in defiance of the gale and after a rough crossing, on which all but the Empress were seasick, he landed her at Ryde in the Isle of Wight. Charly, by then a grave and well-known courtier, duly received in Queen Victoria's name the beautiful Spanish lady whom he had loved in Granada so many years before. Six months later Bismarck released Napoleon III from captivity and, before retiring to die at Chislehurst, the Emperor rented a small house on the Green at Cowes close to Culross Lodge. Every morning Charly's four-year-old youngest son was taken along the sea front, and there he used to meet the Emperor on his own morning walk. Napoleon invariably stopped to talk to the little boy and they became friends.

Just as that four-year-old child can have had no rival at the end of his life in claiming that his grandfather danced with Marie Antoinette, so his own son, the author of this book, fears no contradiction in saying he is the youngest person living whose father was a friend of Napoleon III.

15

Epilogue

The General hangs on the dining-room wall, close to poor Jane from whom he had been parted so long, and within hailing distance of Charly, painted by Sir Francis Grant in the green tailcoat of the Master of the Buckhounds. The conversation to which he listens has a familiar ring, though his brother John, who is not present, might find it a little unseemly. Especially some of the expletives.

He learns that education is now universal, compulsory and mostly provided by the State; but he hopes he is not being smug in reflecting that children of fourteen no longer write as grammatically or as graphically as he did when he went to Versailles. He doubts whether even those of his great-great-grandchildren who took 'A' Levels in Latin would be capable of conversing in that tongue with an itinerant capuchin friar.

Since he lives in a house at Stratfield Saye, the name of his great leader, Wellington, often crops up, while the blue tunic of that arch-fiend, Bonaparte, now hangs in Stratfield Saye House. Sometimes he hears talk of a latter-day adventurer whose ambition for conquest and domination also set the world on fire. It is pleasing to know that when, as in 1805, the invasion of the British Isles was again threatened, a new pilot was found to weather the storm, and he is proud that his country once more inspired a Coalition which brought the tyrant down. The tyrant's successors appear to have renounced his wicked ambitions and to have worked so hard that they have become a great deal more prosperous than his own victorious countrymen.

It seems that there have been two world wars, and that after each of them a new Holy Alliance was formed with many more members than in his day, that they made a great clangour, but that in each case their intercourse was no less futile and unproductive than that of Russia, Prussia and Austria in the years after Waterloo.

He understands that on the other side of the Atlantic the Czar Alexander, well-meaning and liberal-minded, has been reincarnated at least twice, under names such as Wilson and Carter, but that he has continued to have the same second-rate abilities and ignorance of foreign lands, so that his excellent intentions have only occasionally been matched by practical achievement.

It sounds as if the present ruler of France bears no resemblance at all to Louis XVIII; but a recent French leader did, he gathers, have a number of Napoleonic characteristics, though fortunately no Grande Armée to support them.

At home the conditions which John described in his letters to Bombay and Mauritius still prevail. There are unprecedented falls of rain and snow, only equalled by drought and heat-waves such as no man can remember. The mob is still out of hand. 'All is grumbling and discontent,' John had written, and 'never was the arm of a strong and watchful government more necessary than at this moment.' The mob is evidently spurred to excesses by radicals as contemptible as Brougham, Whitbread, Sir Francis Burdett and that agitator, Leigh Hunt, whose visit to Bristol entailed four troops of yeomanry being exposed to pelting rain for twelve hours, and a regiment of Light Dragoons being summoned from Weymouth, so that, as John put it, there was 'every preparation to meet a serious rising of the demagogue's friends'. Quite a lot of visitors to the house echo John's words that 'it would certainly be too much to hope that all the mischief so long breeding, and certainly too long allowed to be encouraged by the most vicious Press that ever disgraced and endangered a country, could be put down at once.'

He hears voluble criticism of the Government's folly in withdrawing a British military presence from eastern seas and gulfs and reducing the defences of the country. It reminds him of a letter he received from John informing him that the flag appointment in Indian waters was to be abolished. 'Nothing seems now secure', John wrote, 'from the clamour for retrenchment which I fear must one day be sure to lead to great inconvenience and a ruinous exposure in re-establishing either army or navy.' The Duke, too, had told him, as early as the year after Waterloo, how he 'could already perceive that among foreigners this country has lost ground in the idea of its ascendancy . . . the money sent abroad must be severely felt and add greatly to the pressure at home.' The situation, or at any rate the assessment of it, does not seem to have altered much in a hundred and sixty years.

When Charles listens to arguments for the reduction of public expenditure, he remembers John's sensible comment that 'the cry for retrenchment has already been carried as far as I suppose is possible'. People could not, after all, have it both ways. Then, as now, 'your papers will shew you what a clamour pervades this country (in my view most unaccountably) against the Income Tax and I cannot help thinking it a most discreditable trait in the national character—the call now made is a necessary one consequent on so just and necessary a war.' This new generation argue that the clamour is by no means unaccountable and that it all depends on the rate at which the tax is levied. They certainly talk a lot about it.

They also complain endlessly about prices: how much you pay in the shops and how little you receive for your labours. That reminds him of John writing that 'the distress of the agricultural interest is undoubtedly as great as ever. Indeed prices were never so low, at least for many years, altho' to the consumers (especially here in London) the necessaries of life are kept at the same heighth as in more prosperous times'. It appears that now the distress of the agricultural interest is alleviated by the creation of 'mountains' of butter and other foods, and by 'lakes' of wine; but that is almost as mystifying to those he hears discussing it as it is to him. The one thing that is entirely clear is that there is no advantage to the consumer, for whom prices rise month after month.

Clearly the 'oeconomy', as John always spelt it, is as precarious as it was after 1815. He recalls how many banks collapsed in those days, including Davison, Noel, Templer & Co. of Pall Mall, where he and John had their accounts, and how John hesitated to transfer his own to the care of Mr Thomas Coutts because 'the present are such ticklish times that it is hard to say where safety lies'. In retrospect he would have urged his brother to be more prompt in accepting the offer, but he could not be expected to foresee that it would be thanks to Mr Coutts's bank that his dear Jane is now at his side again.

They say that until recently British foreign policy has passed through a deplorable period, being principally contrived to appease enemies and antagonise friends. People used to say that about Canning, he remembers; but he cannot help feeling that even Canning was a stalwart patriot by comparison with some of those he hears discussed, and certainly less self-righteous.

It sounds as if most of the inhabitants of the Caribbean Islands have moved to England. He wonders why. Perhaps it is the yellow fever. There are, as always, problems in the Peninsula and he hears that guerillas are still at large. They sound less estimable than the bands Mina and Longa used to lead. The Irish, too, are evidently as turbulent and murderous as he remembers them in 1798, when perhaps they had more reason for disaffection. Bombay is seldom mentioned, but apparently India, despite all Wellesley's efforts, and Mountstuart Elphinstone's and his own, has lost the unity so laboriously imposed by the East India Company. As for Mauritius, some people who came to dinner recently had been there for the sole purpose of lying semi-naked on the beautiful white sands. Even that is less surprising than what he hears about lovely rural Hampstead, where he spent the last year or two of his life. It is now said to be thickly populated, over-built and much patronised by people who write for the newspapers, paint pictures, revel in intellectual fantasies and express political views more radical than those they really hold.

There is occasional mention of 'Quangos', which are not, as at first he assumed, one of the extinct Mauritian birds, but a new form of governmental patronage. They clearly provide the same kind of gratification as, in those spacious days before the 1832 Reform Bill, Lord Liverpool was able to dispense in appointing General Cole Governor of Gravesend and giving Lord Combermere both the government of Sheerness and the colonelcy of the 3rd Dragoons. Charles realises that his descendants must be miserably poor, because no colonelcies of regiments have come their way. Doubtless that is why there is such a surprising absence of men-servants and why they even serve themselves at the sideboard above which he hangs. He can hardly be expected to realise that a Mr Cardwell abolished the purchase of commissions in the Army as long ago as 1871, but scarcely any of his descendants know that either.

It is pleasant to come home again and to see one's posterity, shabbily attired though most of them (especially the males) almost invariably are, and barbaric though the jargon of the younger generations sounds. In most respects things do not *look* quite the same, but almost everything he *hears* evokes memories and comparisons. Can it be any truer now than it was in the 1820s that the national character has deteriorated, that the virtues of the war generation have vanished and that the country is not merely going, but has actually gone to the dogs? John used often to write and say these things, but Charles wonders whether people's anxieties and ambitions, or indeed their qualities and defects, have much changed.

Biographical Index

Abercromby, Sir Ralph (1734–1801): won distinction against the French in Flanders 1794–5; captured St. Lucia and Trinidad in 1796; commanded the army in Ireland 1797–8; Commander-in-Chief British Army in the Mediterranean 1800; killed in the victory near Alexandria 1801. M.P. for Clackmannan. **15**

Alten, Count von (1764–1840): a Hanoverian general who commanded British troops at Walcheren (1809), and was also prominent in the Peninsula. In Spain succeeded Crauford as leader of the Light Division and commanded the old 5th Division (renumbered the 3rd) at Waterloo. Became a field-marshal in the Hanoverian Army. **69**

Beresford, William, Viscount (1768–1854): illegitimate son of the Marquess of Waterford. After service in many fields, including the capture of the Cape of Good Hope from the Dutch and Buenos Aires from the Spaniards, became the King of Portugal's Governor of Madeira in 1807 and Military Commandant of Lisbon in 1808. Created a marshal in the Portuguese army (in the training of which he made a major contribution to victory in the Peninsula) and a Portuguese count. In Wellington's absence led the Allied troops at the Battle of Albuera, for the conduct of which he was unjustly criticised. Fought in most of the subsequent Peninsular battles and was appointed Governor of Jersey at the end of the war. **19, 25, 34, 49, 53, 58, 149–50, 156, 173**

Byng, Sir John, later 1st Earl of Strafford (1772–1860): after service in the Irish Rebellion (1798) and at Walcheren (1809), won great esteem as a brigade commander in the Peninsula, especially in the Roncevalles pass during the battles of the Pyrenees. Commanded a brigade at Waterloo and eventually became Commander-in-Chief in Ireland. M.P. for Poole and later created Earl of Strafford and a field-marshal. **132–3, 174, 188**

Cameron, Lieutenant-Colonel Philip (killed 1812): son of General Sir Alan Cameron who had raised the Cameron Highlanders in 1794. Stood alongside Charles Colville in the village of Fuentes d'Onoro a few minutes before he was killed. Noted for his courage and military ability. **54**

Campbell, Sir James (1773–1835): as Colonel J. A. Campbell, served in the 3rd Division under Picton, commanding Charles Colville's brigade at Ciudad

Rodrigo and Salamanca. Became a major-general in 1819 and was made a K.C.B. **23, 54, 85, 102, 108, 133, 170**

Clinton, Sir Henry (1771–1829) : son of Sir Henry Clinton, who had been Commander-in-Chief in the American War of Independence in 1778 and quarrelled with Lord Cornwallis after the capitulation at Yorktown. A.D.C. to the Duke of York at the outbreak of war in 1793. Captured and held prisoner by the French in 1796, he was in due course exchanged. Adjutant-General under Sir Arthur Wellesley in India, and attached to the Russian army at the Battle of Austerlitz. Having been Adjutant-General to Sir John Moore during the retreat to Corunna in 1809, commanded the 6th Division in Portugal and Spain 1811–14, apart from periodic visits home to attend to his duties as Member of Parliament of Boroughbridge. Commanded the 2nd Division at Waterloo. **99, 134, 188, 201, 217**

Cole, Hon. Sir Galbraith Lowry (1772–1842) : son of the Earl of Inniskillen and Member of Parliament for Fermanagh 1803–23. Commanded the 4th Division through much of the Peninsular War. He had gone home to visit his constituents when the storming of Ciudad Rodrigo and Badajos took place in 1812, and Charles Colville was given his command. In July 1813 he and Picton were left without instructions : they made the tactical withdrawal from the Roncevalles pass towards Pampeluna which was criticised by Wellington, but which may well have saved the British army from a serious defeat. Commanded his old division, by then renumbered the 6th, at Waterloo. Charles Colville's predecessor as Governor of Mauritius and went on from there to govern Cape Colony. **77–8, 132–3, 188, 217, 220, 234**

Crauford, Robert (1764–1812) : fought against Tippoo Sahib in India, and against the Irish rebels in 1798; then commanded the Light Division in the Peninsula. A martinet, he was equally renowned for his courage and determination. Killed at the storming of Ciudad Rodrigo. **86–7, 98**

Dalhousie, George, 9th Earl of (1770–1838) : after service in the West Indies, Ireland, Holland and Egypt, commanded the 7th Division throughout the Peninsular War. Subsequently Governor of Canada and then Commander-in-Chief in India. His youngest son became Governor-General of India in the period immediately preceding the Indian Mutiny. **115–19, 121, 123–4, 140, 155, 179–81**

Douglas, Sir James (1785–1862) : fought at Busaco in 1810 and was then given command of the 7th Portuguese Brigade, which he led with rather too great dash (see Chapter 12). Became Lieutenant-Governor of Guernsey and ended as a full general and a G.C.B. **140, 143–5**

Erskine, Sir William (1769–1813) : having helped to save the life of the Emperor Leopold II of Austria in 1793, and become M.P. for Fifeshire, his career seemed well established, but his folly in risking the Light Division at Sabugal in 1811 and his subsequent ill success were followed by a declaration that he was insane. Cashiered from the army and committed suicide at Lisbon. **47**

Fletcher, Sir Richard (1768–1813) : Wellington's chief and most highly esteemed engineering officer. He had helped the Turks erect their defences against Napoleon's march from Egypt to Acre and after taking part in the expedition of 1807 against Copenhagen, assumed the main responsibility for building the lines of Torres Vedras. Not only fought at Busaco and Vitoria, but directed the

236

technical side of the siege operations at Ciudad Rodrigo, Badajos, San Sebastian and Pampeluna. Killed at the storming of San Sebastian. **62–3, 91, 141**

Gough, Sir Hugh, 1st Viscount (1779–1868): adjutant of the 119th Foot at fifteen. Severely wounded at the battle of Talavera and, as a lieutenant-colonel, at the Nivelle. In later life captured the Canton forts, defeated the Mahrattas, won the first and second Sikh wars in 1846 and 1849, was made a Knight of St. Patrick and a Privy Councillor, and became a field-marshal. **122, 135, 151**

Graham, Sir Thomas, later Lord Lynedoch (1748–1843): raised the Perthshire Volunteers (2nd Scottish Rifles), was M.P. for Perthshire, defended Messina, blockaded Malta and helped to capture Minorca. A.D.C. to Sir John Moore at Corunna, was principally responsible for the defeat of the French at Barossa, and thereafter served under Wellington until the British army crossed the Bidassoa into France. Given a peerage in 1814. His extra-curricular activities included playing in the first Scottish cricket match, introducing Cleveland horses and Devon cattle into Scotland and founding the United Services Club. **49, 90–1, 94, 111–12, 115–18, 123–5, 131, 141–2**

Hamilton, Sir John (1755–1835): having fought in India against Tippoo Sahib, in San Domingo and in the Kaffir War of 1800, was made Inspector-General of the Portuguese army. It was he whom Charles Colville, at Badajos, described as 'a queer fish', but Wellington evidently approved of him, for he was given a division, became a lieutenant-general in 1814, and though he did not fight at Waterloo, and was not an M.P., was made a baronet in 1815. **58, 62, 64–5**

Hay, Andrew (1762–1814): personally raised the Banffshire Fencibles. Commanded a brigade at Walcheren and then in the Peninsula, being promoted major-general in 1811. Killed in the French sortie at Bayonne, having failed, because of his ignorance of the French language, to understand the warning brought to him by a deserter. **175, 190–1, 197, 218**

Hill, Rowland, 1st Viscount (1772–1842): a lieutenant-colonel at twenty-two, commanded his regiment at Aboukir, alongside Charles Colville, and was promoted major-general in 1805 (aged thirty-three). Praised for his leadership of the 2nd Division at the battle of Talavera, defeated the French at Merida in 1811, stormed Almaraz in 1812 and commanded the right wing of the army at Vitoria the following summer. Took a prominent part in the remaining battles of the Peninsular War, and in the Waterloo campaign commanded the Army Corps in which Charles Colville's 4th Division was included. He was Wellington's Second in Command of the Army of Occupation in France and in 1825 became, for fourteen years, Commander-in-Chief of the British Army. **17, 34, 58, 90–1, 94–5, 111–12, 115, 118, 124, 132, 138, 153–4, 167, 188, 190–1, 194, 198, 200–1, 205–6**

Hope, Hon. Sir John, later 4th Earl of Hopetoun (1765–1823): an officer of huge stature who had been Abercromby's Adjutant-General and conducted the evacuation of Corunna by the British Army after Sir John Moore's death. In 1813 succeeded to Sir Thomas Graham's command and led the 1st Division at the battles of the Nivelle and the Nive. Captured in the French sortie from Bayonne. M.P. for the county of Linlithgow, and was made a full general in 1819, shortly after succeeding his brother as Earl of Hopetoun. **142, 147, 161, 163, 167–9, 175, 178–9**

much liked by Wellington and admired by Charles Colville. Having helped to recapture St. Lucia from the French in 1803, joined his brother-in-law, Wellington, in Spain. At the battle of Salamanca (1812) was given temporary command of the 3rd Division (in the absence of both Picton and Colville). Was thus Wellington's principal lieutenant in delivering the decisive stroke that won the battle. Briefly in command of the 6th Division when it marched to the rescue of the beleaguered troops at Sorauren (1813). Wellington's Chief of Staff when the Army crossed into France, and was killed leading an ill-planned and ill-advised assault on the Americans entrenched at New Orleans in January 1815. **77, 184–5**

FRENCH SOLDIERS

Foy, Maximilien Sébastian (1775–1825): like d'Erlon, served under Masséna in Switzerland and Italy, but being a staunch republican opposed Napoleon's creation of the Empire. Redeemed himself by fighting brilliantly under Junot in the early stages of the Peninsular War and was promoted to general. His republican convictions did not embrace opposition to capitalism and it seems that he speculated in the English gilt-edge market. His conduct at Salamanca and in the Pyrenees won Napoleon's approval and at Waterloo he commanded a division. Forgiven by the Bourbons and elected to the Chamber, where he stood up for liberal principles and opposed French intervention in Spain on behalf of the reactionary King Ferdinand. Wrote a history of the Peninsular War which was published after his death. **43, 151, 186**

Jourdan, Jean Baptiste, Comte (1762–1833): having fought for the Americans in the War of Independence, abandoned military life to become a draper at Limoges. The revolutionary wars brought him back into the field and he was largely responsible for winning the battles of Wattignies and Fleurus (1795). His army was famous as the 'Sambre-et-Meuse'. Took command of the Army of the Rhine but after suffering a defeat was superseded by Masséna. Elected a Député, he opposed Napoleon's *coup d'état* but was nevertheless made a Marshal and sent to support Joseph Bonaparte, first in Naples and then in Spain. After the Battle of Vitoria, where Charles Colville's brigade captured his Marshal's baton, he retired in disgrace. Later given the command at Rouen. During the Hundred Days Napoleon appointed him to his Chamber of Peers, but he accepted the Restoration with a good grace and Louis XVIII made him a Peer of France, a count and Governor of Grenoble. In 1830 switched happily from the Bourbons to the House of Orléans and was buried in the Invalides with Napoleon. **113, 118, 127, 186**

Junot, Andache, Duc d'Abrantes (1771–1813): was Napoleon's Secretary at the siege of Toulon and remained one of his favourites, especially when he married into a family to which Napoleon was devoted. Acquired the reputation of being a bold '*sabreur*' and a society favourite. In 1807 was given command of the army which invaded Portugal, but despite a spirited dash from Abrantes to Lisbon with 1,500 horsemen found the Portuguese fleet, with the royal family on board, just out of shot when he reached the fortress of S. Julian on the Tagus. Wellesley defeated him at the battle of Vimiero in 1809 and he was forced, by the Convention of Cintra, to withdraw his army. When he returned, under Masséna, he was wounded in the skirmish at Rio Maior described by Charles Colville. After taking part in the retreat from Moscow and then becoming Governor of Illyria, went mad and killed himself by jumping out of a window in 1813. His widow became famous by writing eighteen volumes of spiteful memoirs. **19, 35–6, 186–7**

Marmont, Auguste Frédéric, Duc de Raguse (1744–1852): A.D.C. to Napoleon, accompanied him to Egypt and Italy where he distinguished himself on the field of Marengo and was promoted general. Fought at the Battle of Ulm in 1805 and was then for five years a highly successful Governor of Dalmatia. When Masséna was disgraced in Spain, Marmont, by then a Marshal and a Duke, succeeded him and showed strategic ability. Badly wounded at Salamanca in 1812 he was hardly cured when, in 1814, he commanded the corps which was intended to defend Paris against the Allied advance. With the connivance of Joseph Bonaparte, Lieutenant of the Realm, made a secret convention with the victorious Allies, for which the Bonapartists never forgave him. Served the Bourbons after the Restoration, but ended his career by settling in Vienna and becoming tutor to Napoleon's son, the Duke of Reichstadt. **55, 63, 66–7, 75, 77–80, 82, 87, 91, 105, 186**

Masséna, André, Duc de Rivoli (1756–1817) : son of a small wine merchant in Nice, began his career as a cabin-boy. A general by 1793, won a series of battles against the Austrians and Sardinians ending with the great victory of Rivoli (1797). Napoleon thereupon named him '*enfant chéri de la victoire*'. Commanded successfully in Switzerland, defeated the Russians and held Genoa for Napoleon until the successful Battle of Marengo. In 1804, when Napoleon's Empire was established, became one of the first Marshals. Held Italy against the Austrians, saved the day at the Battle of Aspern-Essling and commanded the right wing at Napoleon's victory of Wagram. Then created Prince of Essling as well as Duc de Rivoli. His fall from grace was in Spain where despite superior forces he was outgeneralled by Wellington. Losing Napoleon's favour, became Governor of Marseilles where he sat on the fence during the Hundred Days. Refused to serve on the court martial which condemned Ney to death, even though Ney's insubordination had been one of the heaviest crosses he had to bear in the Peninsula. **19–20, 22–24, 26–27, 29, 31–2, 35, 38–9, 42–5, 47–9, 51, 53, 55, 63, 79, 81, 87, 96, 106, 187, 210–11**

Mortier, Edouard Adolphe, Duc de Trévise (1768–1835) : became a general in 1799, commanding a division under Masséna at the Battle of Zurich, and was created a Marshal in 1804. Fought in the Friedland campaign and was Governor of Silesia. Went to Spain in 1808 and won two victories against the Spaniards. Fighting well in the final rearguard action of 1814, was accepted by Louis XVIII, deserted to Napoleon in the Hundred Days, but fell ill before Waterloo. Was forgiven in 1819 and admitted to the Chamber of Peers. After the fall of the Bourbons in 1830 became French Ambassador to Russia. In 1835 accompanied Louis Philippe to a military review and was killed by a bomb aimed at the King. **49**

Ney, Michel, Duc d'Elchingen and Prince de Moskova (1769–1815) : father was a cooper by trade and mother was a German. Called by Napoleon 'the bravest of the brave' but, as Masséna discovered, was not a placid subordinate. At once a dashing cavalry officer and an inspired infantry leader, was also renowned as a trainer of troops. Took a notable part in the battles of Hohenlinden, Ulm, Jena, Eylau and Friedland and was among the first to be created a Marshal. After his quarrel with Masséna in the Peninsula and subsequent dismissal from Spain, Napoleon gave him the 3rd Corps in the advance on Moscow in 1812. Commanded the victorious centre at the Battle of Borodino and was thereafter the hero of the retreat from Moscow. In April 1814 was one of the army leaders who told Napoleon he must go, and Louis XVIII recognised this by making him a peer and giving him the Governorship of Besançon. Felt out of place at the Bourbon court, however, and the courtiers snubbed his wife. It seems that when Napoleon landed from Elba, Ney seriously intended to bring him to Paris as a prisoner, but on impulse changed sides. It was not till three days before Waterloo that Napoleon gave him a command, so that his conduct of the French troops at the Battle of Quatre Bras was of necessity an improvisation. At Waterloo made four cavalry charges against the unbreakable British squares and then dismounted to lead the Imperial Guard in its last unavailing attack. His morale collapsed: made a defeatist speech in the Chamber of Peers and then fled from Paris. Arrested in August 1815, tried by the House of Peers and executed on 7 December in the Luxembourg garden. Louis XVIII would have preferred to spare him and Wellington, who might have been able to do so, refused to intervene. **19, 38-9, 43-5, 186, 199, 214**

Philippon, Armand, Baron (1761-1836): the hero of Badajos. Fought in Napoleon's 'Grande Armée' from 1805-07 and was present at Austerlitz. Defended Badajos brilliantly first against Beresford and then in Wellington's final assault. Surrendered in a church, was sent to England as a prisoner, but contrived to escape almost immediately and to rejoin Napoleon's armies. Louis XVIII made him a Chevalier of St. Louis. **62, 90, 95**

Reynier, Jean-Louis, Comte de (1771-1814): took part in the Egyptian expedition. Became Minister of War when Murat was given the kingdom of Naples and then went to Spain where he became a corps commander under Masséna. **47**

Soult, Nicholas Jean, Duc de Dalmatie (1769-1851): his father, who was a notary in the Tarn, intended him for the legal profession, but he enlisted as a private in the army of Louis XVI. Rose rapidly from the ranks and established his military reputation under Masséna at the Battle of Zurich in 1799. Made a Marshal in 1804, commanded a Corps at Ulm and led the attack which brought victory at Austerlitz. The rest of his military career is included in the story of the Peninsular War. Was Napoleon's Chief of Staff at Waterloo. Subsequently, as a politician, turned his coat with remarkable facility as régime succeeded régime in France. **18-19, 48, 59, 63, 67, 89-91, 95-7, 105, 127-8, 132, 135, 142, 145-7, 150-5, 157, 161, 163, 166, 169, 171-5, 178, 182, 186-7**

Suchet, Louis Gabriel, Duc d'Albufera da Valencia (1770-1826): son of a silk manufacturer at Lyons, distinguished himself in the Swiss and Italian campaigns and became Masséna's second in command, contributing much to Napoleon's crossing of the Alps in 1800 and the subsequent Battle of Marengo. Fought at Austerlitz, at Jena and in Poland. Given command of the French Army in Aragon, routed the Spanish armies of Blake and O'Donnell and governed Aragon without set-back for two years. Promoted to be a Marshal. In 1812 captured Valencia and defended eastern Spain successfully against both the Spaniards and the British troops brought there from Sicily. When Wellington advanced to the Pyrenees, Suchet's unbeaten army on his right flank was a constant anxiety. By the time Suchet joined Soult near Toulouse in 1814, it was too late to stem the advancing British tide. Louis XVIII gave him a peerage in 1814, but deprived him of it after he had rallied to Napoleon during the Hundred Days. **75-6, 78-9, 91, 95, 128, 130, 142, 146, 155, 157, 165-6, 186**

Thouvenot, Pierre, Baron (died 1817): having served in the royal army before the Revolution, became chief of staff to Dumouriez at the outset of the revolutionary war and was promoted general in 1802. Appointed to the French army in Spain, he was quartered first at Bayonne and then given command at St. Sebastian. Served in Soult's Army of the Pyrenees and was made Governor of Bayonne at the end of 1813, defending the fortress in the British siege and being responsible for the calamitous sortie which took place after the war had ended. Charles Colville negotiated with him the final surrender of Bayonne. Decorated with both the Legion of Honour and the Bourbon Order of St. Louis. **175, 177-9**

SPANISH SOLDIERS AND GUERILLA LEADERS

Ballesteros, General Francisco: one of the Marques de la Romana's lieutenants, harassed the French by using the Royal Navy for constant descents on the coast, first in the north and then near Algeciras. Disobeyed orders for a flank attack on the French army of Andalusia in 1812 and was subsequently dismissed by the Spanish Government. **75-6**

Blake, General Joaquin (1739-1827): an Andalusian of Irish descent. Commanded the Spanish army in Galicia where Bessières defeated him in 1808. Lost further battles with Marshals Lefebvre and Victor. Suchet beat him at Saragossa and Sagunto and finally captured both Blake and his army at Valencia. **75-6**

España, General Carlos de (1775-1839): a Frenchman, whose royalist family lived at Foix. Emigrated to England to avoid the guillotine, but then sought permission to join the Spanish army. Fought the French with vigour and success, except at the Battle of Salamanca where he failed to guard a vital bridge and thus allowed the French army to escape. Louis XVIII invited him to return to France, but he replied that all his French blood had been shed by his former compatriots while he was fighting for Spain. After the war was Captain-General of both Navarre and Aragon. Became Governor of Catalonia, acting ruthlessly for the extreme monarchists in support of Ferdinand VII and thus finding himself opposed by the liberal Mina, his former guerilla ally. **76, 145, 158, 163, 167**

Freyre, General Manuel (1765-1834): fought at Salamanca. In 1813, with Longa, defeated the French at San Marcial in the Pyrenees when Soult attempted a diversionary attack to save San Sebastian. In April 1814 made an unsuccessful attack on the French centre at Toulouse and suffered heavy casualties. **152**

Giron, Pedro Augustin, Duque de Ahumada (1788-1842): in 1811 marched at the head of his troops into battle at Arroyo Molinos and defeated the French. Commanded an army of Galicians in the Vitoria campaign, and afterwards in the Pyrenees. **152**

Longa, Colonel Francisco (1770-1831): one of the most dashing and successful of the guerilla chieftains. Had only a hundred men in 1809, but his success in ambushing convoys and surprising enemy detachments brought him both fame and reinforcements. At Vitoria served under Sir Thomas Graham and cut the main French line of retreat. With Freyre distinguished himself by defeating the French at San Marcial in the Pyrenees. **51, 128, 147, 152, 234**

Mina, General Francisco Espoz y (1781-1836): a Navarrese of radical opinions who began guerilla operations against the French in 1808, fought over a hundred actions and was repeatedly wounded. Held thousands of French troops immobilised in the mountains and was never surprised or captured. In 1813 and 1814 he was under Wellington's command and made a notable contribution to success in the Pyrenees. After the war King Ferdinand exiled him because of his liberal views, but in England he was hailed as a hero and Wordsworth sang his praises in a sonnet. On Ferdinand's death returned to Spain and led an army against the Carlist rebels. **51, 128, 130, 152, 234**

Morillo, General Pablo, Conde de Cartagena (1778-1837): began his career in the ranks as a marine, fighting in the battles of Cape St. Vincent and Trafalgar against the British. Changed sides when the Spaniards began their war of liberation and was commissioned for his conspicuous bravery at the Spanish victory of Baylen (1808). Led guerilla bands first in Murcia and then in Galicia, before joining in the Battle of Vitoria where his men distinguished themselves on the right of the line. After the war played a notable part in the Spanish campaigns in South America, but so wavered between the Absolutist and Constitutionalist factions in Spain that neither party trusted him. **152–3, 158**

O'Donnell, Enrique José, Conde de la Bispal (1769–1834) : after early successes in Gerona, which earned him wide praise, showed little military prowess. Appointed a member of the Spanish Council of Regency, he was accused of excessive fraternal intervention on behalf of his disgraced brother, José, who had been ambushed and overwhelmingly defeated at Castella. **23, 33, 163**

La Romana, Pedro Caroy Sureda, Marques de (1761–1811) : Wellington thought him the best of the Spanish generals and liked him as a man. He and his army of 9,000 men, which had been occupying Denmark for Napoleon, were spirited away by the Royal Navy and transported to Spain. In Galicia, with the assistance of irregular guerilla bands, proved a match for Marshal Ney, and subsequently lent Wellington 7,000 men to strengthen the garrison in the lines of Torres Vadras. He died, much lamented, in Wellington's presence. **24, 34, 37**

OTHERS MENTIONED

Angoulême, Louis Antoine, Duc de (1775–1844) : elder son of the Comte d'Artois, afterwards Charles X of France. The last Dauphin. **152, 164, 173, 181**

Angoulême, Marie Therèse, Duchesse de (1778–1851) : daughter of Louis XVI and Marie Antoinette, and the only one of their three children to survive childhood. **164, 176, 187**

Artois, Charles Philippe, Comte de (1757–1836) : youngest brother of Louis XVI. Reigned as Charles X 1824–30. **176**

Bathurst, Henry, 3rd Earl (1762–1834) : Foreign Secretary in 1809 and thereafter Secretary for War and the Colonies. Government spokesman on military affairs throughout most of the Peninsular War. **125, 157**

Berri, Charles Ferdinand, Duc de (1778–1820) : younger brother of Angoulême. His marriage, while exiled in England, to one Anna Brown was hushed up and annulled. A more suitable wife was found and she produced a son, the Comte de Chambord, last of the senior line of the Bourbons. Berri was assassinated at the Opéra in Paris. **172, 207, 223**

Blücher, Gerhard Leberecht, Count, Prince of Wahlstadt (1742–1819) : gallant, stalwart but largely unsuccessful Prussian general, whose arrival at the end of the day clinched Wellington's victory at Waterloo. **162, 183, 193, 196, 208, 212, 215**

Brougham, Henry, 1st Lord (1778–1868) : Attorney-General to the Princess of Wales (Queen Caroline) whom he defended at her trial by the House of Lords in 1820. Lord Chancellor 1830–34. **232**

Bunbury, Sir Henry, 7th Bt. (1778–1860) : Under Secretary of State for War 1809–16. **162**

Burdett, Sir Francis (1770–1844) : Radical politician; M.P. for Westminster; advocate of parliamentary reform and opponent of the war against France. Married

Sophia, daughter of Thomas Coutts. Ended his political career as a Conservative M.P. **100, 132**

Cardigan, James Brudenell, 7th Earl of (1797–1868) : ill-tempered Colonel of the 11th Hussars. Led the Charge of the Light Brigade in 1854. **222, 228**

Caroline of Brunswick, Queen (1768–1821) : daughter of George III's sister, Princess Augusta, and thus first cousin of George IV whom she was forced to marry in 1795. Her only child, Princess Charlotte, heiress to the British throne, died in childbirth in 1817. **224–5**

Elphinstone, Hon. Mountstuart (1779–1859) : Governor of Bombay 1819–27. **222, 227, 234**

Fouché, Joseph, Duc d'Otranto (1759–1820) : Prefect of Police and Minister of the Interior under Napoleon, against whom he conspired when he saw his power begin to wane. **209**

Hunt, James Leigh (1784–1859): poet and author. Friend of Byron, Keats and Shelley. An extreme radical in his early years and imprisoned for a seditious attack on the Prince Regent. **232**

Lowe, Sir Hudson (1769–1844) : Governor of St. Helena and gaoler of Napoleon from 1815 to 1821. Generally condemned for being harsh and unimaginitive in handling his prisoner, though Napoleon was looked upon in 1815, with more than a little justice, as the great disturber of peace and a continuing menace. Subsequently appointed a lieutenant-general and Governor of Antigua. **213, 226–7**

Maitland, Sir Frederick Lewis (1777–1839) : Commander of H.M.S. *Bellerophon* to whom Napoleon surrendered in July 1815. Later Commander-in-Chief in the East Indies and China. **213**

Orange, Prince of (1792–1849) : William, elder son of King William I of the Netherlands. Fought in the Peninsula and gallantly at Waterloo. Succeeded as William II on the abdication of his father in 1840 and transformed the government into a constitutional monarchy. **109, 136, 155**

Orange, Prince Frederick of (1794–1881) : brother of the Prince of Orange. Despite his youth, nominal commander of the Dutch and Belgian troops stationed at Hal, alongside Charles Colville's 4th Division, to hold Wellington's right wing in his Waterloo campaign. **194, 199, 201**

Perceval, Right Hon. Spencer (1762–1812) : younger son of the Earl of Egmont. Chancellor of the Exchequer 1807; Prime Minister 1809; assassinated in the Lobby of the House of Commons. **100**

Provence, Louis Stanislas Xavier, Comte de (1755–1824) : brother of Louis XVI. Reigned as Louis XVIII from 1814 to 1824. **173**

Rowley, Sir Josias, Bt. (1765–1842): nephew and grandson of distinguished admirals. John, Lord Colville's predecessor in command of the Irish naval station and subsequently Commander-in-Chief, Mediterranean. **226**

Whitbread, Samuel (1758–1815) : Radical M.P. for Bedford. Introduced reforms of the Poor Law, but was widely disliked for his anti-war policy which split the Whig Opposition. Championed Caroline, Princess of Wales; rebuilt Drury Lane; and committed suicide in 1815. **100, 232**

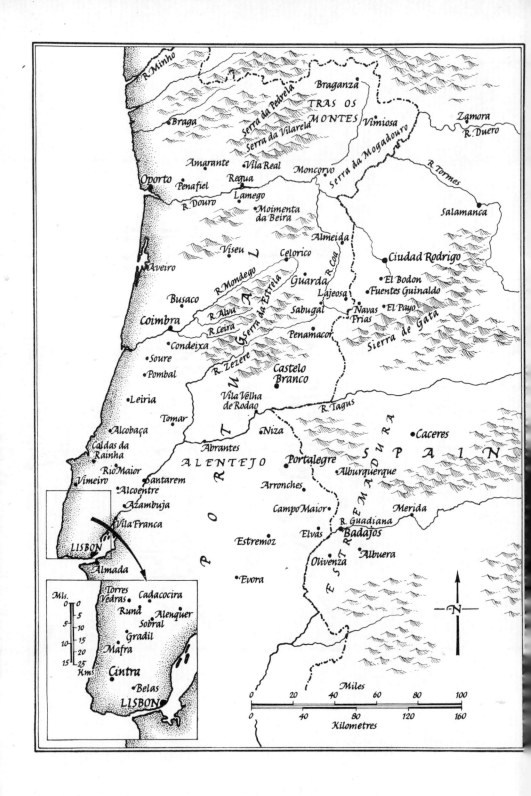